D0162731

Censored

Censored

DISTRACTION AND DIVERSION INSIDE CHINA'S GREAT FIREWALL

Margaret E. Roberts

PRINCETON UNIVERSITY PRESS

PRINCETON AND OXFORD

Published by Princeton University Press,
41 William Street, Princeton, New Jersey 08540

In the United Kingdom: Princeton University Press,
6 Oxford Street, Woodstock, Oxfordshire, OX20 1TR

press.princeton.edu

ISBN 978-0-691-17886-8

Library of Congress Control Number 2017962808

British Library Cataloging-in-Publication Data is available

This book has been composed in Minion Pro

Printed on acid-free paper ∞

Typeset by Nova Techset Pvt Ltd, Bangalore, India
Printed in the United States of America

10 9 8 7 6 5 4 3 2 1

For my parents,
Don and Barbara Roberts

CONTENTS

ACKNOWLEDGMENTS

Writing a book is not something done in solitude; rather, it is reliant on the insights, conversations, support, and feedback of an entire community. I am indebted to many for their help throughout this process. The origins of this book are in my conversations with Gary King and Jennifer Pan, with whom I originally began working on censorship and who encouraged me to pursue the idea beyond what is censored to how censorship impacts people. Their ideas and feedback are embedded in this work, and I am thankful to them for being wonderful mentors, collaborators, and friends. Similarly influential was Brandon Stewart, whose work appears within this manuscript, and who through a long friendship and collaboration has strongly impacted how I think both about data analysis and social science.

This book grew out of my dissertation that began at Harvard. I owe a great debt to my many colleagues in graduate school whose ideas, criticisms, and friendship enriched my time at Harvard and vastly improved my work. Not only Brandon and Jen, but also the rest of my reading group—Shelby Grossman, Chiara Superti, Amanda Pinkston, and Vanessa Williamson— read many versions of my work and provided invaluable feedback. My dissertation committee—Gary King, Jeff Frieden, Elizabeth Perry, and Dustin Tingley—provided me with incredible feedback and support throughout my time at Harvard. They provided outstanding examples of scholars and teachers, and I learned a tremendous amount from them.

When I moved to University of California, San Diego, I was immediately welcomed into a warm community of scholars who took me under their wing. I could not be more indebted to

Susan Shirk and Lei Guang and the 21st Century China Center for providing feedback, mentorship, and funding while I was finishing the manuscript. My other colleagues in Political Science, School of Global Policy and Strategy, and at the San Diego Supercomputer, in particular Claire Adida, Jude Blanchette, Jesse Driscoll, Amarnath Gupta, James Fowler, Stephan Haggard, Seth Hill, Ruixue Jia, David Lake, Kai Lin, Megumi Naoi, Barry Naughton, Simeon Nichter, Sam Popkin, Christina Schneider, Branislav Slantechev, Victor Shih, David Wiens, and Yiqing Xu, were generous with their time and provided me invaluable feedback on my work. Thanks to Justin Grimmer, Tim Groeling, Xiao Qiang, and Jeremy Wallace for traveling to San Diego and providing detailed feedback on the manuscript for my book conference. Thanks to Will Hobbs who worked with me on censorship and who helped me think more deeply about how sudden information changes can impact censorship outcomes.

I offer thanks to those people who supported me during my fieldwork in China. In particular, Kai Lukoff and Maoliang Ye provided incredible support and valuable conversations during my time in Beijing. A special thanks to Tianguang Meng for his tremendous insights and support. Peter Volberding and Jeff Javed were the best fieldwork roommates anyone could ask for. Thanks to Frances Chen, Yichen Guan, Yingjie Fan, Amy Jiang, Adam Jin, Heather Liu, Junjie Liu, Fei Meng, Hongmiao Wang, and LuShuang Xu for their assistance at different points in the process. Thanks also to those who helped me who prefer to remain anonymous.

Many others provided valuable feedback throughout the process. Other than those I have already listed, Alexei Abrahams, Pablo Barbará, Chris Cairns, Any Catalinac, Joan Cho, Jeff Colgan, Greg Distelhorst, Ruben Enikolopov, Roya Ensafi, Nick Feamster, Scott Gehlbach, Anita Gohdes, Judy Goldstein, Sheena Greitens, Andy Hall, Jingkai He, Nancy

Hearst, Yue Hou, Haifeng Huang, Kyle Jaros, Ashley Jester, Iain Johnston, Aaron Kaufman, Jeehye Kim, Patrick Lam, Peter Lorentzen, Chris Lucas, Andrew MacDonald, Dan Mattingly, Gwyneth McClendon, Blake Miller, James Ashley Morrison, Rich Nielsen, Maria Petrova, Maggie Peters, Jakub Redlicki, Jake Shapiro, Daniel Smith, Jim Snyder, Arthur Spirling, David Steinberg, Zachary Steinert-Threlkeld, Daniel Treisman, Alex Storer, Brian Tsay, Sam Tsoi, Disy Trinh, Rory Truex, Josh Tucker, Felicity Vabulas, Jessica Weiss, Vanessa Williamson, Yuhua Wang, Jason Wu, and Yin Yuan. For those who I have forgotten to list, it is not out of lack of appreciation but rather out of my own forgetfulness.

This book would not have been possible without the financial support of generous research institutions. I thank 21st Century China Center, the Carnegie Corporation of New York, the Policy Design and Evaluation Lab, National Science Foundation (grant 1500086), DARPA (contract W31P4Q-13-C-0055/983-3), Hellman Fellows Fund, Institute for Quantitative Social Science, and the Weatherhead Center for International Affairs for financial support. I thank the Ashford family for their generous funding and personal support throughout my time at Harvard through the Ashford Fellowship.

Thanks to Eric Crahan and those at Princeton University Press for their support throughout the process. The book was much improved by anonymous reviewers who read this manuscript and provided feedback. Thanks also to Madeleine Adams for reading and improving the manuscript.

A final thanks to my wonderful family for entertaining and improving my ideas and reminding me to take breaks. First and foremost, thanks to my husband David for constantly challenging me to communicate my ideas more clearly, providing me unconditional love and support, and for being an outstanding example of a scholar. This book would not have been possible without him. Thanks to my siblings Emily, Heather, and Allen for reading the book many times, entertaining me with food, jokes, and playlists, and reminding me to speak to a broader audience. Thanks to my first teachers and mentors, my parents Don and Barbara, for three decades and counting of thought-provoking conversation. I have always tried to emulate their thirst for knowledge and commitment to truth. I dedicate this book to them.

Censored

CHAPTER ONE

Introduction

China has four million websites, with nearly 700 million
Internet users, 1.2 billion mobile phone users, 600 million
WeChat and Weibo users, and generates 30 billion pieces
of information every day. It is not possible to apply
censorship to this enormous amount of data. Thus
censorship is not the correct word choice. But no
censorship does not mean no management.

— Lu Wei, Former Director, State Internet Information
Office, China, December 2015[1]

1.1 THE PUZZLE OF POROUS CENSORSHIP

As more people around the world gain access to the Internet,
government censorship seems an increasingly futile exercise.
Traditional conceptions of censorship that could completely
control information, such as watertight bans on access,
prepublication review, or government-enforced prohibitions on
content, seem silly when you consider that every second millions
of Internet users around the world are sending one another
instant messages, participating in online forums, and tweeting
to hundreds of thousands of followers. Even the world's most
famous censors recognize this reality. As the former "gatekeeper
of the Chinese Internet" Lu Wei stresses in the epigraph to this
chapter, the thirty billion pieces of information generated each
day by Chinese citizens quite simply cannot be censored.

[1] "美记者质疑中国 "网络审查" 鲁炜:内容审查用词不当" December 9,
2015. Available at: http://news.china.com/domestic/945/20151209/20903585.html.

Yet recognizing the impossibility of complete control of online discourse has not kept authoritarian regimes from spending billions of dollars trying. On the face of it, authoritarian efforts of information control seem halfhearted. Even censorship in one of the most sophisticated censorship regimes in the world—China—could be seen as faltering attempts at "information management." For the most part, these efforts at censorship are porous—frequently circumvented by savvy Internet users, accidentally evaded by citizens wasting time on the web, and rarely enforced with punishment.[2]

Indeed, most censorship methods implemented by the Chinese government act not as a ban but as a *tax* on information, forcing users to pay money or spend more time if they want to access the censored material. For example, when the government "kicked out" Google from China in 2010, it did so simply by throttling the search engine so it loaded only 75 percent of the time.[3] If you wanted to use Google, you just had to be a bit more patient. The Great Firewall, China's most notorious censorship invention that blocks a variety of foreign websites from Chinese users, can be circumvented by savvy Internet users by downloading a Virtual Private Network (VPN). Social media users in China circumvent keyword censoring of social media posts by substituting similar words that go undetected for words that the government blocks, making content easy to find if you spend more time searching.[4] Newspapers are often instructed by

[2] Yang (2009a, pg. 2) describes many of the ways in which Chinese netizens circumvent Internet control and calls government control over the Internet "only partly effective." Xiao (2011) similarly emphasizes how Internet controls in China are easily evaded.

[3] Millward, Steven, "Google+ Not Actually Blocked in China, Just Being Slowly Throttled," *Tech in Asia*, June 30, 2011. Available at: https://www.techinasia.com/google-plus-china.

[4] Branigan, Tania, "How China's internet generation broke the silence," *Guardian*, March 24, 2010. Available at: https://www.theguardian.com/world/2010/mar/24/china-internet-generation-censorship; Hiruncharoenvate, Lin and Gilbert (2015).

censors to put stories on the back pages of the newspaper, where access is just a few more flips of the page away.[5]

Porous censorship is not unique to China or even to the modern time period. Instead of shutting off the whole Internet, Iran has been known to simply throttle it and make it slower during elections.[6] The Russian government uses armies of online bots and commentators to flood opposition hashtags and make it more difficult, but not impossible, for people to find information on protests or opposition leaders.[7] Even before the Internet, in the late nineteenth century, British censors banned translations of French literature they considered obscene, but allowed untranslated versions to circulate freely, allowing unlimited access to those willing to expend the effort to read them in French.[8] In East Germany during the cold war, the government decided against enforcing restrictions on satellite dishes that enabled citizens to watch West German television, effectively allowing East Germans who were interested enough to find a way to buy a satellite dish to have access to it.[9]

Why do governments attempt to control information when these controls are easily circumvented? Conventional wisdom posits that these porous censorship strategies are futile for governments as citizens learn quickly to circumvent censorship that is not complete or enforced. Many have stressed that information, which is often called "non-excludable" because it is

---

[5] "Ministry of Truth: Personal Wealth, Income Gap," *China Digital Times*, February 6, 2013. Available at: https://chinadigitaltimes.net/2013/02/ministry-of-truth-personal-wealth-income-gap/.

[6] See Aryan, Aryan and Halderman (2013, pg. 5) and Esfandiari, Golnaz "Iran Admits Throttling Internet to 'Preserve Calm' During Election," *Radio Free Europe*, June 26, 2013. Available at: http://www.rferl.org/a/iran-Internet-disruptions-election/25028696.html.

[7] Goncharov, Maxim, "The Dark Side of Social Media," *TrendLabs Security Intelligence Blog*, December 7, 2011. Available at: http://blog.trendmicro.com/trendlabs-security-intelligence/the-dark-side-of-social-media/.

[8] Reynolds (2014, pg. 188).

[9] Kern and Hainmueller (2009, pg. 394–395).

easily shared, is difficult to control once it has become known to a portion of the public, as it can spread quickly.[10] "Information wants to be free," originally coined by Stewart Brand, captures the idea that information technology makes information easy to copy and thus difficult to control.[11] More puzzling is that many governments have the capacity to enforce censorship more forcefully, but choose not to do so. Periodic VPN crackdowns indicate that China could make the Firewall less permeable, but much of the time the government chooses not to.[12] The government could implement draconian punishments for those who evade censorship, creating strong disincentives for circumvention, but most circumvention is not even illegal. Using censorship that taxes, rather than prohibits, information in China—and in other countries around the world—seems to be a design choice, not an operational flaw—but why?

1.2 DISTRACTION AND DIVERSION

In this book, I shed light on the puzzle of porous censorship by showing that even easily circumventable censorship has an important impact on information access for the typical person in most circumstances, and, for this very reason, is strategically useful for authoritarian regimes. Many censorship methods require citizens to spend more time or money accessing

---

[10] Taubman (1998, pg. 266) stresses that the decentralized nature of the Internet means no censorship methods are foolproof. Yang (2009b, pg. 30) contends that online activism is powerful because it can be more easily multiplied. Esarey and Xiao (2011) show that digital media has more critical content than newspapers in China.

[11] Barlow, John Perry, "The Economy of Ideas," *Wired*, March 1, 1994. Available at: https://www.wired.com/1994/03/economy-ideas/.

[12] "China Cracks Down on VPNs During Political Meetings," *Wall Street Journal*, http://blogs.wsj.com/chinarealtime/2016/03/10/china-cracks-down-on-vpns-during-political-meetings/.

information that the government would like to slow down. Only a minority of citizens who are interested enough in the information and have the education and resources to pay the costs of evasion are motivated and equipped enough to circumvent censorship. For the majority of citizens, who are less interested in politics and are not willing to spend significant time becoming informed,[13] small costs of access and government distractions can divert citizens to information that is less dangerous to the regime. Even though it is possible to access most information, as normal citizens get lost in the cacophony of information available to them, their consumption of information is highly influenced by the costs of obtaining it. I argue that there are massively different implications for the spread of political information of having certain information completely free and easy to obtain as compared to being available but slightly more difficult to access.

Part of the inconsistency between conventional wisdom about censorship and the reality of censorship results from the lack of conceptual clarity about the mechanisms by which censorship affects the public's consumption of information. We lack a theory of censorship. I provide a typology of the three ways in which censorship can affect individuals. What most people think of when they think of censorship is *fear*—threats of punishment, such as losing a job, prison, or worse—which may deter citizens from spreading or accessing information. Fear works by prohibiting particular information and through this inducing self-censorship. But the threat of punishment must be observable to be credible—those who are not aware

---

[13] Many scholars in political communication have shown that most people are not willing to spend time informing themselves about politics. For example, Sniderman, Tetlock and Brody (1991) show that voters rely on heuristics to make political judgements, Popkin (1994) explores how voters use information shortcuts to make choices, Conover and Feldman (1984) develop a theory of how people have ideology under low information, and Hamilton (2004, pg. 11) explains how media consumers can be rationally ignorant.

of punishment cannot be deterred by it. Although fear is a more complete form of censorship because it can be enforced, fear is problematic for authoritarian regimes because it can cause backlash, draw attention to censored information, and create information-gathering problems for governments. Fear is more difficult to use in the digital age because prohibitions on information are difficult for governments to enforce when information is easily copied.

The other two less well-known censorship mechanisms I introduce—*friction* and *flooding*—have proven themselves more useful in the age of the Internet. Friction—increasing the costs, either in time or money, of access or spread of information—diverts citizens' attention by imposing barriers to information access. A slow webpage, a book removed from a library, reordered search results, or a blocked website can all be used to increase the costs of access to information. Friction is often circumventable—it can be evaded simply by sustaining these costs. However, it does not have to be observable in order to work and therefore can more easily be explained away or go unnoticed. Friction's counterpart, *flooding*, is information coordinated as distraction, propaganda, or confusion, such as astroturfing, online propaganda, or government-mandated newspaper articles. Flooding competes with information that authoritarian governments would like to hide by diluting it and distracting from it. As with the friction mechanism, while flooding can be discounted or avoided, flooding requires the consumer to take time and effort to separate out good information from bad information.

I offer a wide range of empirical evidence—from online experiments to nationally representative surveys, datasets of millions of geo-located social media posts, and leaked propaganda archives—to show that friction and flooding effectively divert and distract most people away from censored information. Even though a minority of people will pay the costs to circumvent censorship, friction and flooding are useful to governments because they separate those who are willing to pay the cost of evasion from those who are not, enabling the government to target repression toward the most influential media producers while avoiding widespread repressive policies. I focus my empirical evidence on the citizen production and consumption of information on the Chinese Internet. China is a nearly ideal case for testing how each mechanism of censorship affects citizens' consumption of information and political behavior because the Chinese government implements a wide variety of censorship tactics, which function through each of the three censorship mechanisms. Furthermore, China's censorship system has become the model for many authoritarian regimes: evidence exists that others are trying to emulate it.[14] A better understanding of how the Chinese censorship system works will allow us to predict the future impacts of information control across a wide range of authoritarian regimes.

Censorship is difficult to study empirically because it is often intended to go undetected. Recently, entire subfields in computer science have emerged dedicated to detecting censorship because governments are not typically forthcoming with their tactics.[15] In this book, I move beyond what is censored to take up the challenging task of measuring individuals' reactions to censorship *while* they are being subjected to it. Using large social media datasets, measures of the spread of online information, online experiments, and surveys, I answer the questions: How do individuals react when observing censorship? How does Internet users' behavior change when particular pieces of information are more difficult to access? Are Internet users who come across distracting online propaganda likely to spread

[14] See Diamond (2015, pg. 151), and Soldatov, Andrei and Irna Borogan, "Putin brings China's Great Firewall to Russia in cybersecurity pact," *Guardian*, November 29, 2016, https://www.theguardian.com/world/2016/nov/29/putin-china-internet-great-firewall-russia-cybersecurity-pact. As a result, scholars have advocated for more research on the Chinese censorship system; see Shorey and Howard (2016).

[15] For an overview of the challenges measuring censorship see Burnett and Feamster (2013).

and share it? The evidence I present shows that although many people are resistant to censorship when they notice and observe it, they are very affected by it when they are inconvenienced by it, do not notice it, or can explain it away.

My findings of how censorship influences individuals may explain why we see so many regimes using porous censorship strategies even though these methods are easy to thwart. Although many would see the fact that a minority of capable citizens can route around censorship as detrimental to the regime's censorship efforts, I argue that circumventible censorship can be useful to authoritarian regimes precisely because it has different effects on different segments of the population. Porous censorship drives a wedge between the elite and the masses. The savvy members of the elite easily circumvent censorship, discount propaganda, read blocked information, and enter into banned social networks. By contrast, friction and flooding prey on the rest of the public's short attention spans, busy schedules, and general lack of interest in politics, nudging them toward an information environment that is disconnected from their more well-educated, well-to-do, and politically sophisticated counterparts. By separating the elite from the masses, the government prevents coordination of the core and the periphery, known to be an essential component in successful collective action.[16] Although a portion of savvy and politically concerned citizens may be willing to pay the costs imposed by friction and flooding, less interested individuals often are not, making wider discontent among the broader population significantly less likely and reducing the accountability of political entities.

The strategy of porous censorship allows the government to avoid widespread use of observable repression, which is well

---

[16] Barberá et al. (2015) show that the periphery is critical to the success of protests, Steinert-Threlkeld (2017) shows that the periphery can even instigate successful protests, and Chenoweth and Stephan (2011, pg. 39–40) show that total numbers and recruitment are a strong predictor of successful protest movements.

known to spark popular backlash.[17] Autocrats face significant trade-offs when making citizens fearful of speaking out. Highly constraining forms of censorship that operate through deterrence must be observable to their targets; otherwise deterrence cannot work. As I will show using social media data, surveys, and online experiments, when censorship is observable, political entities call attention to the information they would like to make off-limits. The observation of censorship intended to create deterrence can instead create opportunities for push-back, signal government weakness, and create increased interest in the off-limits topic. Repression that deters citizens from speaking out also creates information and surveillance problems for the government, as governments often rely on input from the media and population to identify local corruption and on information in the public sphere to identify new pockets of dissent.[18]

Incomplete censorship, by contrast, is more easily masked by political entities, giving the government the cover of plausible deniability.[19] Flooding can front as concerned citizens who are voluntarily writing pro-government content online or are spontaneously gathering in a pro-government parade, and friction can front as technological errors or algorithmic quirks, which ordinary citizens may not be aware of or may explain away. If a link on the Internet redirects to an error page, it is difficult to tell whether the page is down or the government has blocked it. If a book is missing from a library shelf, is it lost, not ordered, or removed by the government? If a social media post does

---

[17] Dickson (2016, pg. 7).

[18] Egorov, Guriev and Sonin (2009); Liebman (2005); Lorentzen (2014); Shirk (2011, pg. 19); Stockmann (2012, pg. 140); Qin, Strömberg and Wu (2017).

[19] Stockmann (2012) makes a similar argument about the traditional media in China, arguing that the commercialization of the media provides cover for government propaganda. The concept of plausible deniability has also been used widely in the literature on repression, for example, Conrad and Moore (2010, pg. 461) argue that plausible deniability of torture allows the state to shift the blame.

not appear in a news feed, is it because the algorithm predicts you might not be interested in it, or because of government manipulation?[20] Because information is widespread and has many substitutes, small impediments to reading information and even silly distractions can significantly affect users' consumption of political information.

The strategy of porous censorship does, however, have an Achilles' heel. Although for most citizens most of the time, small impediments to accessing information and government-encouraged distractions can divert them to more benign information, there are cases when the typical citizen will take the time to seek out restricted information and evade censorship. I show that in periods of crisis, such as the 2015 Tianjin explosion, citizens are more likely to spend time seeking out methods of accessing restricted information. Similarly, when censorship is imposed suddenly and disrupts habits, such as the case of the Instagram block during the 2014 Hong Kong protests, citizens are more likely to find ways to continue consuming information and entertainment to which they are accustomed.[21] Thus, the strategy of porous censorship can be counterproductive and dangerous to the regime when it uses this censorship too decisively during times it needs censorship most. If information were to disrupt the Chinese political system, it would be during a period when the majority of people were willing to pay the price imposed by censorship to collectively inform themselves.

1.3 IMPLICATIONS AND CHALLENGES TO CONVENTIONAL WISDOM

The findings I present in this book challenge many conventional notions of censorship and have implications for research

---

[20] See Knockel, Ruan and Crete-Nishihata (2017) for an example of how censorship is used surreptitiously in the Chinese social media platform WeChat.

[21] Hobbs and Roberts (2016).

in digital politics, the politics of repression, and political communication.

Censorship Is More Than Fear

First, this book speaks to the strategies that modern autocracies use to prevent large-scale dissent. Many scholars have puzzled over the resilience of some authoritarian regimes.[22] Some argue that the resilience of autocracies is due in part to successful repression; that autocrats have survived by forcefully extinguishing opposition groups.[23] Others have maintained that autocrats are successful in part by creating institutions that are better able to share power with the opposition and respond to citizens' concerns.[24] Still others have credited authoritarian resilience to brainwashing or enforced symbolism, through cult-like nationalism, religion, or ideology.[25]

In this book I demonstrate that autocrats have methods outside of direct repression, accommodation, or brainwashing to maintain power, even in the modern era. Autocrats have a large toolbox available to them to nudge citizens away from activist circles, dangerous information, and focal points that could facilitate coordination.[26] These methods are not forceful, do not accommodate, and are often not meant to directly persuade. Instead, they create small inconveniences that reroute users

[22] Nathan (2003); Anderson (2006); Gilley (2003).

[23] Davenport (2007, pg. 7) describes the "Law of Coercive Responsiveness," that autocrats respond to opposition movements with force. Brownlee (2007, pg. 33) argues that autocrats have been able to repress opposition groups to consolidate power.

[24] Wintrobe (1990, pg. 851) and Wintrobe (1998) stresses the patronage and public services dictators can provide as a substitute for repression. Dickson (2016); He and Warren (2011); and Lorentzen (2013) elaborate on how the Chinese government creates channels to respond to citizens' concerns. Magaloni (2008); Bueno De Mesquita et al. (2003); and Boix and Svolik (2013) describe how dictators create power-sharing institutions to prevent overthrow by other elite.

[25] See Wedeen (1999).

[26] Note that this is the same "nudge" logic with a darker take as that used in the behavioral economics literature; see Thaler and Sunstein (2009).

to information and social networks that are more palatable to the regime, decreasing the mobilization capacity for opposition, often without citizens being aware of it. Although less forceful than repression or brainwashing, these methods are surprisingly effective in changing the behavior of the vast majority of citizens who are too busy to engage deeply in politics.

Censorship Is Customized

Second, this book speaks to a long-standing question of whether and how governments can control social media in the information age. Many scholars believed that the Internet, which expanded the number of citizens involved in public discourse, would force governments to become more accountable to citizens because of the speed with which large numbers of citizens could participate in everyday public debate.[27] Yet the failure of the Internet to create the expected accountability in some authoritarian regimes led other scholars to argue that this new technology in fact played into the hands of the autocrats.[28] Some of these writers hypothesized that the Internet had not reached its political potential because of extreme self-censorship and fear.[29] Others discerned that the Internet created opportunities for authorities to use sophisticated hidden technologies that could manipulate citizens without their consent or being aware of it.[30]

The findings in this book cut a middle path between these arguments by showing that Internet censorship has very different impacts on different types of individuals, which allows

[27] Ferdinand (2000, pg. 5), Lynch (2011), Bellin (2012, pg. 138), Diamond (2010, pg. 70).
[28] Morozov (2011), MacKinnon (2012), Kalathil and Boas (2010), Rød and Weidmann (2015), Steele and Stein (2002).
[29] Kalathil and Boas (2010, pg. 26), Wacker (2003, pg. 88).
[30] MacKinnon (2012, pg. 6), Morozov (2011, pg. 97).

governments to use these differential effects strategically to maximize censorship's impact while minimizing its costs. The findings in this book suggest that the low probability of the government following through on punishment for millions of Internet users who engage daily in off-limits discussion has diminished the government's ability to enforce self-censorship on those engaged in public discourse. Self-censorship, by itself, does not "purify" the Internet in many authoritarian regimes as some have suggested, and online criticism of autocrats is commonplace.[31] For the majority of citizens, this book provides evidence that political entities have a wide range of effective tools available to them to interfere with the Internet without citizens being aware of it or motivated enough to circumvent it.[32] However, these tools work not because they are sophisticated enough to prevent access to information, but precisely because they have holes: they can affect the majority of the public's information-seeking behavior simply by inconveniencing them, without interfering so much to cause widespread public backlash. Small costs of access, not draconian punishments or sophisticated manipulation, can have huge effects on the behavior of the majority.

Because censorship affects different segments of the population differently, its impact is more than simply hidden manipulation and instead is a story of customized repression. The fact that the majority are affected by diversion and distractions allows regimes the flexibility to selectively target punishment for speech toward journalists, activists, and other high-profile elites. Because friction and flooding are not effective for highly capable and motivated individuals, autocrats use targeted

---

[31] Zhang, Yuxin, "China: Self-Censorship Displaces Western Threats," *Diplomat*, March 3, 2015. http://thediplomat.com/2015/03/china-self-censorship-displaces-western-threats/.

[32] This finding provides support for some of the arguments in MacKinnon (2012) and Morozov (2011).

fear to contain the spread of information at elite levels.[33] Just as the Internet has enabled more micro-targeting of information and advertising toward particular individuals, the evidence I present suggests that censorship as well is becoming increasingly customized to individual behavior and capabilities.

Despite the cunning of the Chinese censorship system, I highlight the ways in which the censorship system can be undermined in particular periods. I show that the regime is more constrained in making censorship porous during crises when individuals are motivated to seek out information. The more that citizens are willing to overcome friction, the less able the government is to use censorship methods other than fear. This puts the government in a difficult situation, as direct repression will frequently cause backlash. Although the government will try to ramp up all forms of censorship during periods of crisis, these are also the periods that are most likely to force government accountability and concessions.

More Media Does Not Always Lead to Better Information

I caution against a rosy economic model of information where more producers of information will always lead to better information outcomes. Some scholars have posited that as the number of producers of information and media outlets increases, the government's influence over the media will decrease because governments will have a more difficult time forcing media to keep silent.[34] One implication is that the digital age, where there are many more producers of information, will lead to a less biased news media.[35]

---

[33] This finding is more in line with arguments made in studies that emphasize the impact of fear in controlling the spread of information. Kalathil and Boas (2010); Wacker (2003).

[34] See Besley and Prat (2006, pg. 4), Gentzkow, Glaeser and Goldin (2006, pg. 189).

[35] Edmond (2013, pg. 1441).

However, these models only consider coercion of media and media capture as methods of censorship and do not consider the impacts that governments have on the *distribution* of information. The results in this book show that even if media that contains better information exists, if government can create frictions on the distribution of information through censorship, then this media will not reach most of the public.[36] Governments that have direct control over information distribution can use friction to de-prioritize media that they find to be objectionable. Even if articles on the Internet contain good information, if they are buried in a search engine by government censorship, very few people will access it.

Moreover, even if governments do not directly control the distribution of information, they can use the fact that anyone can enter into the Internet discourse to flood the information environment with their own version of events. By hiring paid commentators or distributing online propaganda, governments can crowd out information that they find objectionable, undermine the credibility of competing media, and distract citizens from events that reflect badly on them. Counterintuitively, the ability for anyone to produce media can result in the production of less reliable information because some governments and entities will have incentives and resources to produce and spread unreliable information en masse.

A Broader Definition of Censorship Has Implications for Democracies

Last, because this book is about censorship that does not always function through fear, it has broader implications for censorship outside of authoritarian systems. Democracies generally have

---

[36] Edmond (2013, pg. 1442) allows for the possibility that governments can invest in "large-scale fixed investments for information control" online that may allow them to control the Internet despite the decentralized nature of the Internet.

laws that prevent them from directly repressing free speech—
they cannot use fear-based methods of censorship. However,
democratic governments have vast powers to affect the costs
of access to information by producing legislation that regulates
information such as the availability of data, the transparency
of the government, and the functioning of the Internet. The
findings in this book suggest that even small impediments to
access imposed by any regime can have significant political effects, and therefore that manipulation of information in democracies can also have a widespread impact on the public's political
knowledge.

As I will discuss in the conclusion, recent events in democracies highlight the importance of a broader definition of censorship. Evidence that taxes on the accessibility of information
can have large political impacts[37] suggests that society should
be concerned with the extent that a few Internet companies and
Internet service providers have primary control over the speed
and convenience with which information can be accessed. If
too few individuals, companies, or politicians wield significant
power to make certain political information easy to access while
making other information more difficult (for example through
fast lanes on the Internet or reordering search results) in an
effort to advance their own interests, this could have political
impacts in democracies similar to the impacts of search filtering
and firewalls in autocracies. Similarly, as traditional media have
been decimated by competition from the Internet, small costs
of access to data imposed by federal or local government may
have an impact on content reported to the public in the traditional press. The broader definition of censorship I provide in
this book emphasizes the importance of institutionalizing and

---

[37] Byrnes, Nanette, "How the Bot-y Politic Influenced This Election," November
8, 2016. Available at: *MIT Technology Review* https://www.technologyreview.com/
s/602817/how-the-bot-y-politic-influenced-this-election/. Epstein and Robertson
(2015), Bond et al. (2012).

facilitating government transparency and competition between information distributors as well as producers in democracies so that what information is provided, at what speed and when, to the press and public is not completely the result of political motivations and strategy.

Citizens in democracies recently have been shown to be susceptible to flooding as well. Distractions and misinformation spread online by cheap Internet commentators or automated bots increase the burden on the public to separate the signal from the noise, and many confuse good and bad information.[38] Denial of service attacks that flood the websites of media, Internet companies, nongovernmental organizations, and government with too much traffic so that they become unavailable have the power to silence information channels selectively.[39] As soon as these strategies are used for political purposes, they become political censorship. Although much censorship research has focused on the Internet in autocracies, more research needs to be done to study how censorship extends to democratic environments on the Internet as these undoubtedly have important political impacts.

1.4 THE PLAN OF THE BOOK

I proceed by offering a theory of the strategic interplay between government censorship and citizens' consumption and production of information. First, I describe the incentives of the government—why it would choose to censor and the costs it might incur from censorship. Next, I develop a model of how both citizens and the media interact with information.

[38] Nyhan and Reifler (2010), Ratkiewicz et al. (2011, pg. 301–302).

[39] Woolf, Nicky, "DoS attack that disrupted internet was largest of its kind in history, experts say," *Guardian*, October 26, 2016. Available at: https://www.theguardian.com/technology/2016/oct/26/ddos-attack-dyn-mirai-botnet.

Using this model, I elucidate the three main ways in which censorship can influence the media and the public—fear, friction, and flooding. I then provide examples of each of these mechanisms in various communication media, and describe when each will have more or less impact on the spread of information. Fear, which is censorship based on deterrence, is by nature very constraining but must be observable in order to have an impact. Fear has to be credible in order to create deterrence; otherwise, it may instead draw attention to authoritarian weakness or create backlash. Therefore, it is discreetly targeted toward the most capable and motivated individuals. Friction, which imposes small taxes on information access, and flooding, which creates distractions, by contrast, do not need to be obviously driven by political entities to have an impact on information consumption and dissemination. Friction and flooding are more porous but less observable to the public than censorship using fear, and therefore are more effective with an impatient or uninterested public.

Chapter 3 provides an overview of the modern history of censorship in China and outlines the institutional structure and methods of censorship in China today. It describes how the Chinese censorship system has evolved from a model that was designed to micromanage every citizen's consumption and production of information to one that relies on porous censorship. It provides an overview of the main methods by which the Chinese government censors the Internet and the bureaucratic system that implements this censorship. Practically, it describes why China provides a good empirical test for the impact of porous censorship.

Chapter 4 explores how citizens react when they observe censorship online in China. Although many scholars have suggested that fear and self-censorship are the main forms of control of the Chinese Internet, I show that typical Internet users do not act afraid after experiencing online censorship and instead are angered by observing it. Using a matched pair study of users who forward the same social media post, but where one experiences censorship and the other does not, I study how experience with censorship affects the writings of Internet users. I find that, all else being equal, those who have experienced censorship persist in writing about the censored topic and are more likely to complain about censorship, even as they become increasingly targeted with censorship. I then survey Internet users about how they would feel if they experienced censorship. I find that Internet users, particularly those who report having experienced censorship, are much more likely to report being unfazed or angry about censorship than fearful or worried. Last, using online experiments, I randomly assign users in a lab experiment to come across a censored webpage. I find that the observation of censorship creates more, not less, interest in the censored topic and also decreases support for government censorship policies. I explore how the Chinese government, likely aware that experience with censorship can undermine its reputation, adopts a two-pronged censorship strategy targeting high-profile users with fear-based censorship while attempting to make online censorship efforts less observable to the public.

Chapter 5 demonstrates that small, less observable frictions on information have a powerful influence on the online behavior of Chinese citizens. First, I analyze the spread of information about 120 self-immolation events in Tibet through social media in China. I find that the best predictor of the number of social media posts that accompany a self-immolation event is whether the event occurs on the weekend, when the censors are slower to censor, suggesting that the speed of censorship has important implications for the spread of information in China. Next, I estimate the effect of the Great Firewall on the behavior of citizens in China. Using surveys and direct measures of those evading censorship through data from the social media platform Twitter, I find that those who evade the Firewall are technologically savvy, well-educated, high-income Internet users in China who have high levels of political efficacy. I find that the Firewall pulls this political elite away from their potential followers. I show that newly blocked websites have precipitous declines in usage directly following their block, showing how small impediments to access have an immediate impact on traffic from typical Chinese users. But I find that friction has an Achilles' heel, and is more commonly circumvented during crises and moments of sudden implementation.[40]

In chapter 6, I demonstrate that flooding in both online and traditional news media in China coordinates messages to distract the public from sensitive events. Using plagiarism detection software and leaked archives from the Chinese government to identify instances of flooding both online and in traditional news media, I show that the government uses propaganda to distract with coverage of the mundane details of Party meetings or with encouraging quotes and positive thoughts directed at the public.[41] Using estimates of search results for reposting of propaganda articles around the web, I show that for the most part this strategy is effective—highly coordinated propaganda used by the Chinese government is more likely than articles that are less coordinated to be re-shared in both the domestic and international social media spheres.

Chapter 7 concludes with a discussion of the implications of my findings for politics in both democracies and autocracies as information technology and social media become more central components of political communication. I lay out specific directions for future research in the area of censorship and discuss censorship's potential for long-term political impacts on domestic and international politics.

---

[40] This draws on work with William Hobbs; see Hobbs and Roberts (2016).

[41] This draws on work with Brandon Stewart, Jennifer Pan, and Gary King; see Roberts and Stewart (2016); King, Pan and Roberts (2017).

CHAPTER TWO

A Theory of Censorship

2.1 WHY DO GOVERNMENTS CENSOR?

Just as political entities have incentives to promote particular types of information to their constituents,[1] they also have reasons to control, slow down, or prevent citizens from consuming other types of information. Governments are entrusted by the public to carry out particular responsibilities—to act in the public's interest, or at least in accordance with a selection of the public's demands.[2] Information is dangerous to political entities as they require support from at least some part of the citizenry, and information that reveals that they are not fulfilling their role can negatively affect their survival. In democracies, negative information can result in fewer votes, fewer political contributions, or even the forced resignation of politicians.[3] In autocracies, information can persuade citizens to discontinue their support for the regime, undermine regime policies in everyday life, or persuade citizens to go out and protest.[4] For political parties and interest groups, damaging information can

---

[1] Mayhew (1974) and Bernays (1923) describe how political parties and corporations advertise to their constituents and consumers.

[2] Even in autocracies, leaders have to work in some of the public's interest. Shirk (1993, pg. 107) describes how constituent preferences are aggregated in authoritarian regimes; Bueno De Mesquita et al. (2003, pg. 8) develops the idea of the selectorate within autocracies.

[3] Enikolopov, Petrova and Zhuravskaya (2011).

[4] Much of the literature on collective action explores this. For example, Tilly (1978, pg. 8) talks about the importance of beliefs in mobilization; O'Brien and Li (2006, pg. 38–39) explore how perceptions and information about state policy can generate rightful resistance in rural China.

galvanize citizens to discontinue political and financial contributions to a particular cause.[5]

Outside of accountability, information can also be dangerous to political entities insofar as information can act as a tool to facilitate coordination and protests that can threaten political entities' survival. At the most basic level, information can facilitate the logistics of collective action by communicating where and when protests will take place.[6] Information can also indicate shared discontent among citizens that may embolden individuals to take action against the regime.[7] Because large-scale protest can threaten a regime's survival, slowing the spread of these "signals of discontent" and logistical planning of protests can prevent or slow large-scale unrest.

In their ideal world, political entities would like no one to know dangerous political information that could reveal their lack of accountability to the public, decrease their political support or financial standing, or facilitate collective action to overthrow them. Conveniently, they have many tools to slow the spread of information. First, political entities often know more about their own performance than the public does.[8] They can selectively reveal or hide information to avoid accountability for their own financial and political gain.[9] Second, governments and other similarly powerful organizations have significant power over the infrastructure of the flow of information—from telecommunications to laws that govern speech—which allows

---

[5] Friedman (1999, pg. 24) describes how the media and information affects consumer boycott success; Popkin (1994, pg. 27) shows how information and the media influences how voters think about elections and the government.

[6] Little (2016) argues that information can hold autocrats accountable either by spreading negative information or by facilitating collective action. Enikolopov, Makarin and Petrova (2016) show that social media primarily played a coordination role in protests in Russia. See also González-Bailón et al. (2011).

[7] Lohmann (1994, pg. 42), Kuran (1989, pg. 42), Chwe (2001, pg. 7), Lewis (2008, pg. 52).

[8] Stiglitz (2002, pg. 461).

[9] Rose-Ackerman (1978).

them to control what and how information is shared between citizens. By changing laws, infrastructure, or incentives for media, governments can wield influence over the information that the public consumes, taking pre-emptive action against dissent.[10]

However, even though governments have interest in and power over constraining speech, there are costs associated with reducing transparency and implementing censorship. These trade-offs between the benefits and costs of repression and censorship are often referred to as "the dictator's dilemma."[11] One form of the dictator's dilemma is when the government would like to enforce constraints on public speech but repression could backfire against the government.[12] If the population indeed wants to hold an authority accountable, then the observation of censorship itself may be enough to undermine the political entity. Censorship could be seen as a signal that the political entity has something to hide and is not in fact acting as an agent for citizens. This could incentivize citizens to seek out information that the authority is trying to conceal. Francisco (2005), among others, has found that consistent repression can backfire against the regime by creating a more violent opposition or signaling opportunities for discontent.[13]

Another form of the "dictator's dilemma" is that even if the dictator would like to censor, by censoring the autocrat has more difficulty collecting precious information about the public's view of the government. Fear of punishment scares the public into silence and this creates long-term information collection problems for governments, which have interests in identifying and solving problems of governance that could undermine their

---

[10] Ritter and Conrad (2016, pg. 85), Guriev and Treisman (2015, pg. 6).

[11] See Wintrobe (1998, pg. 20), Francisco (2005); in China see Dickson (2016).

[12] Francisco (2005, pg. 58–59).

[13] For other work on backfire against repression, see Lichbach (1987), O'Brien and Deng (2015).

legitimacy. As Wintrobe (1998, pg. 20) puts it, dictators cannot know "whether the population genuinely worships them or worships them because they command such worship." Political entities in general, and autocracies in particular, have few methods to gather information about how citizens feel about their performance.[14] Significantly contracting the horizontal flow of information between citizens may harm the vertical flow of information from citizens to the government, potentially obscuring fixable political problems and preventing the government from addressing them before they become too significant to overcome.[15] Greater transparency facilitates central government monitoring of local officials, ensuring that localities are carrying out central directives and not mistreating citizens.[16] Allowing citizens to express grievances online also allows governments to predict and prevent the organization of protests.[17] If citizens and officials are too scared to report problems, the government may face unexpected widespread public dissatisfaction that could lead to revolution.[18]

What should perhaps be considered a third "dictator's dilemma" is that censorship can have economic consequences that are costly for authoritarian governments that retain legitimacy from economic growth. Communications technologies facilitate markets, create greater efficiencies, lead to innovation, and attract foreign direct investment.[19] Censorship is expensive—government enforcement or oversight of the media can be a drag on firms and requires government infrastructure. For example, governments that require social media companies to hire censors impose extra burdens on the development of

---

[14] Charron and Lapuente (2011, pg. 399); Egorov, Guriev and Sonin (2009); Liebman (2005); Lorentzen (2014); Stockmann (2012, pg. 140).

[15] Lorentzen (2015).

[16] Shirk (2011, pg. 19).

[17] Distelhorst and Hou (2017).

[18] Kuran (1997, Chapter 4); Chen and Xu (2017b).

[19] Shirk (2011, pg. 1), Choi (2003).

these firms.[20] Economic stagnation and crises can contribute to the instability of governments.[21] Censorship can exacerbate crises by slowing the spread of information that protects citizens.[22] When censorship contributes to crises and economic stagnation, it can have disastrous long-term political costs for governments.

This book focuses on the ways in which governments balance the overwhelming incentive to keep certain information away from the public against these significant costs of suppressing information. Although the strategies that governments use to suppress information vary by time period and target, I find that increasingly in a digital age political entities balance these competing incentives by making information they would rather the public not know more difficult to find without creating direct punishments for spreading or accessing it. By "taxing" particular types of information while still allowing access to this information, authorities slow information's spread while avoiding many of the costs of repression. I provide evidence of this by showing that small costs of access to information are enough to prevent the majority of people who are not very interested in politics from accessing it. Even though these forms

---

[20] The American Chamber of Commerce's recent survey of U.S. firms operating in China shows that 71% of firms report that censorship hurts their business. "2016 China Business Climate Survey Report." The American Chamber of Commerce in the People's Republic of China (2016). https://www.amchamchina.org/policy-advocacy/business-climate-survey/2016-business-climate-survey. Domestic firms are hurt by censorship also. See Tate, Ryan, "Costs of Censorship Haunt 'Chinese Twitter' IPO," *Wired*, April 17, 2014. https://www.wired.com/2014/04/weibo-ipo-cost-of-oppression/ and Beech, Hannah, "China's Great Firewall is Harming Innovation, Scholars Say," *Time*, June 2, 2016. http://time.com/4354665/china-great-firewall-innovation-online-censorship/.

[21] O'Donnell (1973); Gasiorowski (1995).

[22] Alexievich (2006, pg. 211–212); see also "Information Control and Self-Censorship in the PRC and the Spread of SARS," Congressional-Executive Commission on China White Paper, https://www.cecc.gov/publications/issue-papers/information-control-and-self-censorship-in-the-prc-and-the-spread-of-sars.

of censorship are porous and sometimes are not even considered to be censorship, they can prevent political authorities from being held accountable and, because they do not seem repressive, are also less likely to create a backlash. These techniques enable governments to selectively target their most powerful, repressive tools of censorship toward influential individuals and media, rather than typical citizens, and create the perception of free flow of information while still retaining effective control.

In order to understand how censorship affects the spread of information and the strategic interaction between citizens, the media, and the government, we first have to describe the incentives and costs citizens and media encounter when consuming and sharing information. In this chapter, I review our current understanding of how typical citizens consume information and propose a framework for thinking about how the media, individuals, and political groups collect, synthesize, and spread information. Then, I present a working definition of censorship. Based on how information is shared and what censorship is, I describe three mechanisms—*fear, friction,* and *flooding*—through which censorship impedes expression of and access to information and the strategic interaction between citizens and governments in the context of each mechanism. Throughout this discussion, I explain how these mechanisms are strategically used by governments to maximize the impact while reducing the costs of censorship.

2.2 CITIZENS ARE RATIONALLY IGNORANT

In order to understand how censorship works to influence the spread of information and the accountability of political entities, we must first have a basic model of how people consume information. By describing how individuals go about deciding what information to consume, we can then pinpoint how censorship methods will influence the likelihood that they read, watch, or listen to a given piece of information. Through decades of research, political scientists have already laid the empirical and theoretical groundwork for understanding citizens' consumption of information in both democratic and autocratic environments. I draw on their expertise here to provide a basic framework of when and why citizens consume political information and draw out how this might vary across contexts.

The public's basic problem is they have far more information than they could possibly consume in the time that they have—they are overwhelmed with available information and have only limited attention to focus on particular pieces of information.[23] How do consumers of information make the decision of what articles to read and what programs to watch from what sources, if they do not have time to consume everything? Citizens rely on the expected costs and benefits of the information to make this decision.[24] Downs (1957) describes useful information as that which aids citizens in consumption, production, or political participation. For example, information is useful if people can use it to make decisions about what car to buy, how to do their jobs better, or who will best represent them. Information in these cases is more likely to be useful the more likely it is to be true, and therefore citizens consume information from sources they trust and from sources that they believe share their views.

Consumers also benefit from the entertainment value of information.[25] They enjoy sharing and hearing information from friends in social situations or in gossip. Those who look for information that they enjoy might select sources that focus on the drama of the events.[26] By the same logic, consumers avoid or resist information that creates cognitive dissonance, or conflicts

---

[23] Sniderman, Tetlock and Brody (1991); Conover and Feldman (1984); Popkin (1994); Hamilton (2004).

[24] Lupia and McCubbins (1998, pg. 25–26), Hamilton (2004, pg. 8).

[25] Downs (1957, pg. 214–216).

[26] Prior (2005, pg. 577), Baum (2002, pg. 91).

with their long-held beliefs or experiences.[27] Such information makes consumers uncomfortable, and therefore they derive less benefit from consuming it than information that accords with their current beliefs.

Even though they would like to consume information that benefits them, consumers have difficulty evaluating what information is useful or entertaining. In the best case, information is an *experience good*, where citizens know the value of information only after they consume it.[28] For example, a person can verify that a telephone number on a website indeed reached their representative or can verify that consuming a piece of information was entertaining after reading it, but cannot tell before. But in many cases, information is worse—a *credence good*—where even after consuming information, citizens do not know its veracity.[29] For example, after reading a rumor about a politician we may still not know whether the information is true. Therefore, people often decide to consume information if they receive signals that it may be important or if it is from sources that they trust. If everyone is talking about an article or news program, a citizen might be more likely to read or watch it. The placement of a news article within a publication or the decision of a news organization to include a story may signal to a citizen that the story is valuable. Citizens therefore rely extensively on the media and on political elites to set the agenda for the information that they consume and to provide them with trustworthy information.[30]

---

[27] See Festinger (1957, pg. 30) on cognitive dissonance and avoidance of information; see Nyhan and Reifler (2010, pg. 307) on the potential for corrections to backfire and increase misperceptions.

[28] Hamilton (2004, pg. 9).

[29] See Darby and Karni (1973, pg. 68–69) for a discussion of credence qualities of goods.

[30] McCombs and Shaw (1972); Zaller (1992, pg. 48) discusses how accessibility of information influences public opinion; Iyengar (1990, pg. 4) discusses how accessibility is influenced by the media.

Consumers of information are likely to seek out information if its benefits outweigh its costs of access. Consumers of information are influenced by the monetary cost of information and the amount of time they have to spend consuming it. Some information is almost inescapable, such as information blared on a megaphone or billboards on the street; this information is difficult for citizens to avoid consuming, regardless of its benefits. However, for information that takes energy to seek out and consume, changes in the cost of information influence consumption. The amount a consumer is willing to pay in terms of time and money depends on the benefits they can expect to get from the information. A trading company might be willing to pay for a subscription to a high-cost periodical about markets, whereas an individual trading small amounts of money in the stock market may not. A person affected by an oil spill may check out a library book or spend time searching on the Internet about the potential health consequences, whereas a citizen far away from the spill may not.

Some citizens naturally benefit more from spending time informing themselves than others. What communication scholars have called the "political elite"—a small subsection of people who are well educated, are interested in politics, and have political connections—spend more time thinking about and informing themselves about politics because doing so is consistent with their own self-interest.[31] However, even these individuals who may have monetary interest in or impact on politics because of their jobs, connections, or investments are not able to read *all* information and have to select information to read. Although they might spend more time overall consuming information, elites are also affected by the expected benefits and costs of

---

[31] Zaller (1992, pg. 6) defines the political elite as those who "devote themselves full time to some aspect of politics or political affairs"; Converse (1964) shows that elites think about and interact with political information differently than the mass public.

information and consume information with a higher expected benefit and lower expected cost.

Outside of the elite, most people have very few substantial incentives to be informed about politics.[32] Since citizens have a low probability of being pivotal in political situations like voting or protest, the utility of being informed to make better decisions on how to participate is also low. Citizens are for the most part *rationally ignorant* and spend little time investing in information about politics because doing so is unlikely to benefit them. In general, scholars have found that typical consumers of information are very poorly informed and consume little political information.[33] Zaller (1992, pg. 18) describes consumption of political information as having a low mean with a high variance. At best, typical citizens are motivated to be informed about the happenings inside their own society so that when information appears that pertains to their well-being,[34] they can react in a way that maximizes their utility. Whether because of too little time, belief that they have little control over their political situation, or distractions from entertainment, there is substantial evidence that most citizens in even developed democracies are not at all informed about their political situation and have very little intention to spend the effort to inform themselves.[35]

In autocracies, scholars have speculated that citizens spend even less time consuming political information because they have few opportunities to participate outside of state-organized political organizations, few incentives to seek alternative viewpoints, and reasons to avoid cognitive and moral

---

[32] Hamilton (2004, pg. 11).

[33] Downs (1957, pg. 259), Angus et al. (1960, pg. 180–181), Converse (1964, pg. 34), Graber (1988, pg. 105).

[34] RePass (1971, pg. 391), Krosnick (1990, pg. 66–67)

[35] See also Delli Carpini and Keeter (1996, pg. 62–105), Caplan (2007, pg. 94–113), Lewis-Beck (2008, pg. 161–180).

dissonance.[36] Those living in autocratic environments also typically are exposed to fewer alternative viewpoints.[37] When citizens in autocracies are exposed to political information, there is substantial evidence that they are likely to accept the views expressed in the mainstream media.[38] Even if they do not agree with the information, if citizens feel that they cannot publicly oppose the government, many will seek out information that confirms the government viewpoint to avoid hearing negative information about politics that are difficult to change. Of course, there may be periods when citizens are more likely to seek out political information. Evidence suggests that when there is greater uncertainty about the political situation, such as during crises or government transition, citizens in autocracies are more likely to seek out information and may be more affected by media.[39]

Using this evidence, the theory in this book is based on a model that citizens, both in democracies and to a greater extent in autocracies, are typically willing to pay only small costs to inform themselves of their political situation. For the most part, citizens consume information that is easy to access, confirms their beliefs, and is from sources that they have reasons to trust. Citizens have a highly *elastic* demand for political information: small increases in the cost of political information will strongly decrease the probability that a citizen consumes it. Citizens will spend time and money searching for and understanding political information only if they receive signals that knowing

---

[36] See Festinger (1957, pg. 30) for a discussion of cognitive dissonance; relatedly Frey (1986) discusses selective exposure to information. Kuran (1998, pg. 158–161) discusses how moral dissonance can lead to rationalization.

[37] Stockmann (2012, pg. 41) finds that Chinese people seek information that is consistent with their beliefs. Stockmann (2012, Chapter 8) finds that Chinese citizens will select Chinese newspapers to read that they find more reputable, but will not invest substantial time in seeking out Western sources that are less readily available.

[38] Geddes and Zaller (1989, pg. 327–341).

[39] This comes from the theory of *media dependency*—that crises force citizens to rely on mass media, see; Ball-Rokeach and DeFleur (1976); Loveless (2008).

that information will be immediately pertinent to their own lives, if they happen upon it as a by-product of information they are consuming for other reasons,[40] or when they are in a crisis situation that creates incentives to gather and search to information.

2.3 TRADITIONAL MEDIA CARE ABOUT STORY COSTS

If citizens rely on low-cost information from sources that they trust, undoubtedly the traditional media plays a large role in what citizens consume. But how do free and commercialized media decide what to cover, when they are not politically constrained?[41] There are infinitely many possible stories the media could cover on any given day. How do the media decide what information to collect, present, and write up for their readers?

Like citizens, the media face a cost-benefit trade-off in the stories that they cover. The financial benefit to the media from reporting on a story is based primarily on how many readers they can attract to their publication. The more subscriptions, clicks, or views a media outlet receives, the more money it can receive from advertisers.[42] As such, traditional media will typically create stories that pander to a particular group of tastes or a particular type of person.[43] Among their target

---

[40] For example, their own entertainment; see Baum (2003).

[41] Although the media is not free in many countries around the world, in this section I focus on the media's incentives when it is free and commercialized and turn to government constraints on the media later in the chapter.

[42] Hamilton (2011, pg. 277–288) outlines five incentives of media—advertising, subscription, persuasion, nonprofit, and expression. Here we consider the first two, though later in the chapter the other three are discussed.

[43] Mullainathan and Shleifer (2005); Gentzkow and Shapiro (2006) describe how audience preferences affect the content of news.

audience, media stories will direct content to their marginal consumer, rather than necessarily their loyal base, in order to attract the greatest numbers of people. Commercialized media will also be particularly interested in attracting consumers that advertisers would like to target, those who are easily swayed by advertisements or who purchase goods for their households.[44]

Because citizens' trust will be important in attracting an audience to news stories, the media will be very concerned with their own credibility. A media outlet that is seen as providing false information or missing important stories in its purview will be less frequented than one that is thought to be more reliable.[45] Traditional media, therefore, would like to develop a track record for stories that the public, and in particular the marginal consumer, believes are important and of interest.

However, media face the same trade-offs consumers do in that there are costs associated with writing stories. Some stories, particularly those that involve investigation, may involve months of document review, travel, and interviews. Other stories could involve very low costs, such as reporting what a politician stated in a press release, the outcome of a baseball game, or even reprinting a story another media outlet

---

[44] See Hamilton (2004) for a detailed discussion of media bias that arises from the market. Of course, the media may also be motivated by what they see as their journalistic contribution or their philanthropic contribution, even if the mass public may not be most interested in these types of stories; see Zaller (1999); Hamilton (2011). High-quality stories that challenge the status quo might win awards or improve the journalist's reputation in the eyes of other journalist professionals. Though even with journalists' personal preferences for impact, successful journalists also must attract large audiences, and therefore to a certain extent journalists are subject to mass preferences and cannot solely follow their own definition of impact; see Zaller (1999).

[45] Whereas untrustworthy sources are avoided by much of the public, "objective" reporting is not always valued by the marginal consumer and will not always be in the interest of the news outlet, as consumers may value a particular perspective. An outlet's slant can provide branding that distinguishes one news outlet from another; see Hamilton (2004, Chapter 2).

produced. If these two types of stories are of equal interest to the audience, the media outlet will typically report the low-cost story rather than that with high fixed costs because the expected net benefit of low-cost stories is larger.[46]

At times, the costs and benefits of a story will be uncertain, which will affect the probability that the media will pursue it. The media might easily assess their audiences' interest in the outcome of, say, a baseball game, but journalists cannot always tell immediately which stories will be useful to spend time and money investigating before the information has actually been extracted and analyzed. Investigative journalism, like research, has many dead ends and is a "precarious profession."[47] Media must rely on signals of importance and projected costs to know what stories to pursue. If information is too difficult to access, an investigative story will not be successful no matter how potentially interesting it is. Risk-averse media will be more likely to pursue stories that have a higher certainty of success. To reduce costs, the media frequently rely on data collection and analysis by third parties, such as the government. In these cases, a story's success will depend on the degree of transparency of these parties. Data availability will affect the media's costs of production of a story and eventually citizens' cost of access to the story.[48]

2.4 CITIZENS EXCHANGE LOW-COST INFORMATION THROUGH SOCIAL MEDIA

Increasingly, as information has become more accessible to the public directly through the Internet and the traditional media

---

[46] For more discussion of how marginal costs influence the content of reporting, see Hamilton (2011), Petrova (2012), Besley and Prat (2006), Gentzkow, Glaeser and Goldin (2006).

[47] Mollenhoff (1981, pg. 4).

[48] Hamilton (2005, Chapter 2).

have lost resources from online competition, information has bypassed the media completely, and information can flow directly between individuals. Social media may present unfolding events and accounts of individuals, such as real-time accounts of earthquakes or protests, directly to the public, without the filter of the traditional media.[49] Sometimes those who are more interested in politics or more informed than the average individual will take it upon themselves to gather information directly, synthesize stories, and distribute them to the public through social media, even though they are not members of the traditional media. Other times, the wider public themselves share information and accounts with one another without aggregation or filter.[50] In these cases, information and stories become known and widely shared without passing through the media.

However, despite the power of social media to share direct accounts of events, most information shared on social media is still stories produced by the traditional media, and therefore traditional media continue to have a powerful influence over what consumers read and share, even in an online environment.[51] The information that passes directly between individuals is also more likely to be low cost and most accessible, such as opinion or entertainment, because the public has relatively little time and few tools to gather and synthesize information.[52] As a result, it sometimes can be lower-quality information—or even false information—since the public is not invested in its own credibility or reputation, like the media.[53] Even so, this pathway for information to bypass the media cannot be discounted and

---

[49] Shirky (2008).

[50] Tufekci and Wilson (2012).

[51] Mitchell et al., "The Modern News Consumer," *Pew Research*, http://www.journalism.org/2016/07/07/pathways-to-news/.

[52] Carpenter (2008, pg. 539).

[53] See Del Vicario et al. (2016) for a discussion of the spread of online misinformation.

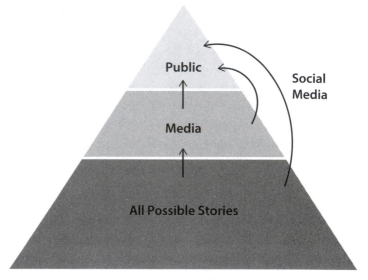

Figure 2.1: Pyramid that represents the collection and distribution of information.

is dangerous for authoritarian governments.[54] Whereas before information could be controlled simply by controlling the media, with social media such control is much less straightforward.

Figure 2.1 presents a diagram that summarizes the collection and distribution of information in a pyramid. The bottom of the pyramid represents all potential stories, information disaggregated in data, events, individuals, and documents that could be synthesized, analyzed, and presented to the public. The bottom level of the pyramid is too large for any one person to consume given a limited attention span. The second tier of the pyramid represents the stories the media synthesize for the public. Which stories filter from the bottom to the second tier will depend on how costly they are for the media to synthesize and how lucrative the media expect them to be for their business model. The top of the pyramid are the stories

[54] Tufekci and Wilson (2012).

that are consumed by the public, a subset of those synthesized by the media. Each level of the pyramid is a subset of the level before, filtered by the public's demand for information, their trust in the media sources that present the stories, and the cost of access to information. Social media, which are represented in the diagram by an arrow from the bottom and middle tiers to the top tier of the pyramid, allow events to be presented without the filter of the media and provide another avenue for stories already produced by the media to be shared among individuals.

2.5 WHAT IS CENSORSHIP?

For the reasons discussed before, political groups may have an interest in affecting the flow of information between levels of the pyramid. Formally, I define censorship as the *restriction of the public expression of or public access to information by authority* when the information is thought to have the capacity to undermine the authority by making it accountable to the public.[55] Central to this definition are the actions that could be restricted by censorship. In this book, I consider two types of actions that are restricted by censorship: expression of information and access to information.[56]

Expression refers to the ability of a person or the media to share information unimpeded in the public sphere, whether through writing or public speech. People may be restricted from expressing themselves because they are prohibited by the law, or they are fearful to do so because they have been intimidated. They may also have had the tools of expression withheld from

---

[55] The skeleton of this definition is from Lasswell (1930).

[56] These actions come from the freedoms discussed in Ingram (2000, Chapter 1), which includes another form that we don't consider here: freedom of communication. I consider freedom of communication as subsumed by freedom of access and expression.

them; for example, they may not have access to the Internet or may purposely have been kept illiterate.[57] Infringements on media and individual expression can occur at any level of the information pyramid. Those with primary information may be unable to express their views in interviews to the media, preventing the flow of information from the bottom to the middle level. Or citizens and the media may be unable to print or share an already prepared story, preventing information from spreading from the middle to the top level of the pyramid.

Expression is different than access to information, which is the ability to consume information. Barriers imposed on access to information also can occur at any level of the pyramid. The media may be restricted from accessing certain types of data or particular people for interviews. Authorities may prevent the media and individuals from accessing data or analyses that they have collected and generated. Books may have been written, but may be difficult to access if they are banned from libraries or schools. Websites may exist, but they may be blocked by firewalls or removed from the indices of search engines.

Freedom of access to information is often as treated secondary to freedom of expression;[58] however, this is like arguing that the chicken is more important than the egg: access is necessary for expression, since the expression of information often relies on it first being accessed or collected. Similarly, expression is necessary for access—it is difficult to access unexpressed information. The two are inextricably linked, and both constrain the movement of information up the pyramid. However, as I will explain later, barriers to access are often less observable than restrictions on expression, and therefore can be more easily used by political entities when direct repression is too costly.

---

[57] Milner (2006); Weidmann et al. (2016).
[58] Ingram (2000, Chapter 1).

2.5.1 How Is Information Restricted?

Now that we have specified what is restricted, what do we mean by restriction itself? Unlike popular illustrations of censorship, like a journalist with tape over their mouth or a TV producer with a hand over the red button on live television, restriction does not need to be complete to be considered censorship. Restriction is imposing any type of cost on expression or access to information, be it large or small, as long as this restriction is conducted purposefully to decrease the accountability of the authority. Much of censorship is incomplete or porous. Censorship also does not necessarily have to involve laws or punishment. One of the most-cited examples of censorship in China is the Great Firewall, which is by no means complete censorship as it can easily be circumvented by a Virtual Private Network (VPN).[59] However, the costs of doing so are not insignificant, as finding a VPN takes time and often costs money. Censorship lies on a continuum of costliness; and, as I will demonstrate later, even small restrictions on freedom of access and expression can have significant impacts on the spread of information and may sometimes be more effective than more repressive forms of censorship because they are less likely to draw attention to government censorship efforts.

2.5.2 Who Is "Authority"?

Although the main focus of this book is on censorship conducted by governments, the government is not the only political entity that can censor. Most of the literature on censorship has referred to the government as the primary

---

[59] Using a VPN is not penalized in China at the time of writing; however, there has been some discussion of making them illegal; see "Chongqing regulations may penalize VPN users," *Global Times*, March 28, 2017. http://www.globaltimes.cn/content/1040014.shtml.

perpetrator, primarily because the government is often the entity with the most power to control freedom of expression and freedom of access to information and is the primary agent accountable to the public. By shaping laws, the government can make particular types of expression illegal, and because the government often has control of telecommunications infrastructure and government data, it can easily influence the costs of access to information. Facing elections or political opponents, governments purport to represent their constituents and rely on public opinion for the maintenance of their own power, and therefore have strong incentives to manipulate the spread of information.

However, there are other political entities that the public wishes to hold accountable and that have power over the costs of expression of and access to information. Many organized groups have sufficient resources to collect or discourage the collection of information.[60] For example, bureaucracies are often the primary source of data on their own performance, and, unless legally mandated, they sometimes opt not to collect this information, collect it in a way that obscures their performance, or simply make it unavailable to the public.[61] Interest groups, with a political objective and the money that underlies it, can effectively manipulate information. These groups collect data on the topic that they are concerned about and make this data either easily available or difficult to access for reporters, citizens, and the media. They can commission studies that often turn out to support their cause. These groups may have the power to lobby the government to ban particular types of research or publication of information.[62]

---

[60] Typically groups that have solved the "collective action problem," as in Olson (2009).

[61] Gormley and Balla (2013, Chapter 1).

[62] For more discussion of interest groups and censorship, see Petrova (2012), Sobbrio (2011), Alston, Libecap and Mueller (2010).

Companies can influence access to information and are at times held accountable to the public. In many cases, keeping information secret is imperative to the functioning of a company, be it for property rights protection or protection of the company's business plan from competitors. However, there are aspects of company activity where they are accountable to the public, for example, in the realm of product safety or environmental and labor regulation. Companies are also increasingly handling local public services, being hired to carry out foreign military operations, or taking on the role of government.[63] To the extent that companies nominally acting in the interest of the public conceal information in order to reduce their accountability to the public, their activity would be classified, under this definition, as censorship.[64]

2.6 THE MECHANISMS OF CENSORSHIP

I now turn to how government censorship affects which stories come to the attention of the media and the public. Instead of enumerating the many different ways in which governments censor across different media and technologies, I create a typology of censorship restrictions based on the *mechanism* through which censorship slows the flow of information.[65] The technology used to censor and the information medium that is targeted by censorship both change over time. However, the ways in which authorities limit the freedom of expression and access to information by changing the incentives of individuals and the

---

[63] Calland (2007), Avant (2005, pg. 60).

[64] See Soley (2002) for a more complete exploration of corporate censorship. Crabtree, Fariss, and Kern (2015) explore private censorship in Russia. Lam (2017) explores private censorship in Hong Kong.

[65] For an overview of online censorship technologies, see Deibert et al. (2008), Deibert et al. (2010), and Deibert et al. (2011), Freedom House's "Freedom the Net" project provide reports of censorship across time and countries.

media are general to all of these technologies, time periods, and media. By defining censorship by its mechanism, we understand it in its most general sense and can more easily understand its new incarnations in the future.

Each of the mechanisms of censorship I lay out below influences the cost-benefit calculation for the media and citizens to express or access information and therefore filters information between the levels of the pyramid. However, these mechanisms have different levels of observability to the public and thus vary in their probability of creating political backlash, economic costs, or information-gathering problems for the authority. By analyzing how each mechanism affects its target and the costs it has for its implementer, I elucidate the strategic interactions among governments, citizens, and the media.

The first way that censorship operates—fear—affects the flow of information by *deterring* the media or individuals from distributing, analyzing, collecting, or consuming certain types of information. Fear creates the awareness of consequences of facilitating the flow of information. It makes expression or access to information more costly because of its punitive consequences. It is explicitly consequential, but very observable, and therefore has a greater potential to backfire and create information-gathering problems for the authority.

Friction, the second type of censorship, acts like a tax on information by directly increasing the costs of distribution of and access to information, *diverting* the media and individuals away from censored information. If information is simply more costly to collect, analyze, or distribute, even if there are no punitive costs of accessing or distributing that information, individuals and the media will be less likely to come across it or distribute it. Individuals may not even be aware that the information is purposely made costly to access. Simply by becoming frustrated accessing it or by being entirely unaware that it can be accessed, the public will be less likely to pay attention to it. Friction is not explicitly consequential and is often less observable than fear and therefore is less likely to create direct backlash among citizens. However, friction is often more porous than fear and can be circumvented, particularly during periods of crisis or heightened political awareness.

Flooding, the last type of censorship, vastly decreases the costs of particular information in order to increase the relative costs of competing information. Flooding can influence the media by presenting them with cheap, prepackaged, easy-to-publish information. Or it can influence the public, which has too much information to consume in too little time, pushing particular types of information to the top of the pyramid in order to de-emphasize others. Flooding creates *distractions* that require individuals to spend more energy to sift through the available information. Flooding is even less observable than friction because it affects the costs of information indirectly. As a result, it has the least potential for backlash from citizens because even if citizens realize a particular piece of information is being promoted by the government, they may not be sure what it is meant to compete with or obscure. However, flooding is the most porous form of censorship as it does not interfere directly with the information it competes with.

Fear, friction, and flooding are exhaustive categories of censorship in that they can be used to describe all forms of censorship, but they are not necessarily mutually exclusive. Censorship can act through two or more mechanisms simultaneously. For example, the government putting an activist in jail could create both friction for journalists hoping to write about stories for which the activist is a source and fear that the government is serious about cracking down on stories related to those that the activist has knowledge about. Similarly, the removal of a genre of book from the library will create both friction for citizens at the library and flooding if the books are replaced by others that provide a distraction or interest citizens in political propaganda.

For the remainder of this chapter, I will discuss each of these mechanisms of information manipulation in turn. Using examples from different countries, a variety of political entities, and across time periods, I will develop an intuition of how each mechanism differs from the others and its various incarnations across time and space, including the current age of the Internet. I explain when and where these different mechanisms will be more or less successful at stopping the spread of information, suggesting when authorities will decide to use them for the purpose of censorship.

2.7 FEAR

Raif Badawi, a Saudi Arabian blogger, was arrested on June 17, 2012. Saudi police accused him of insulting Islam through the Internet, and of apostasy, or the abandonment of Islam. Badawi's primary crime was that he had created the website Liberal Saudi Network, which questioned aspects of Islam and sought freer discussion of politics in Saudi Arabia. On May 7, 2014, Badawi was sentenced to ten years in prison and one thousand lashes. On January 9, 2015, the first fifty lashes were administered, and they were scheduled to be repeated every Friday for twenty weeks.[66] Badawi was not new to this type of treatment by the Saudi regime. In 2008, he had been questioned for apostasy and subsequently released.[67]

Badawi's arrest and sentence is only one of many examples of the first way in which censorship operates: fear. Whereas Badawi

---

[66] "Saudi blogger Badawi 'flogged for Islam insult'," *BBC*, January 9, 2015. http://www.bbc.com/news/world-middle-east-30744693.

[67] "Saudi Arabia: Website Editor Facing Death Penalty," *Human Rights Watch*, December 22, 2012. https://www.hrw.org/news/2012/12/22/saudi-arabia-website-editor-facing-death-penalty.

was not deterred from writing, as others in his situation might have been, the punitive action and public floggings that resulted from his writing have one purpose—to illustrate the punishment that accompanies particular types of speech and deter others who may be considering similar types of activities. Censorship through fear functions by dissuasion—by prohibiting the expression of or access to information and articulating its punishment so that citizens are discouraged from doing so. Censorship through fear is based fundamentally on the *awareness* of the punishment that can be expected if the collection, production, or consumption of particular types of information is carried out.

2.7.1 Legal Deterrence

Perhaps the most observable way fear is produced is through censorship laws. Governments create laws that prohibit particular types of expression or consumption of information and then publicize these laws so that citizens and the media are aware of the punishment that will befall them if they commit the crimes associated with the laws. Many authoritarian governments have laws that prevent public speech on particular topics; for example, Saudi Arabia outlaws insulting Islam through the Internet. Russia recently outlawed spreading false information on the Internet and requires the author to prove the information's veracity rather than the government to disprove it.[68] Similarly, Iran has Internet censorship laws that prohibit information that is "immoral" or endangers national security.[69] The Chinese

[68] Stone, Jeff, "Russian Internet Censorship, Social Media Crackdown Makes It Easy for Putin to Stay Popular," *International Business Times*, August 6, 2014, http://www.ibtimes.com/russian-internet-censorship-social-media-crackdown-make-it-easy-putin-stay-popular-1651078.

[69] Fassihi, Farnaz, "Iran's Censors Tighten Grip," *Wall Street Journal*, March 16, 2012, http://www.wsj.com/articles/SB100014240527023037173045772 79381130395906.

government has a Law on Guarding State Secrets, which prevents the publication or spread of any "state secrets," the definition of which is sufficiently vague to cover the discussion of many different types of information.[70] In totalitarian societies, like North Korea, fear controls the lives of individuals who must be extremely careful not to even insinuate political narratives outside of the government line.[71]

Journalists and other traditional producers of media are subject to laws that could cost them their jobs or lead to their arrest. Reporters Without Borders estimates that 826 journalists around the world were formally arrested in 2013.[72] Governments can control media organizations and journalists by requiring them to obtain licenses or press cards or by controlling personnel appointments directly. Academics can be dismissed from their jobs when they interfere too much with politics,[73] and countries can reject visas of international journalists and academics who do not follow publication guidelines.[74] Governments may anticipate periods when elites and media might cause trouble, arresting them in anticipation of their speaking out.[75]

---

[70] "1989 Law on Guarding State Secrets" *Congressional-Executive Commission on China*, http://www.cecc.gov/resources/legal-provisions/1989-law-on-guarding-state-secrets-chinese-and-english-text; Xu, Beina and Eleanor Albert, "Media Censorship in China," *Council on Foreign Relations*, February 17, 2017, http://www.cfr.org/china/media-censorship-china/p11515.

[71] See Demick (2010, pg. 51–56) for an example derived from interviews with North Korean defectors.

[72] "71 Journalists Were Killed in 2013," *Reporters Without Borders*, January 25, 2016, https://rsf.org/en/news/71-journalists-were-killed-2013.

[73] Buckley, Chris, "Outspoken Chinese Professor Says He Was Dismissed," *New York Times*, October 19, 2013, http://www.nytimes.com/2013/10/20/world/asia/xia-yeliang-an-outspoken-chinese-professor-says-he-has-been-dismissed.html?_r=0.

[74] "Spiked in China? A ChinaFile Conversation," *China File*, November 12, 2013, http://www.chinafile.com/conversation/spiked-china.

[75] Truex (2016).

Even in democracies, expression is limited by laws that threaten punishment. Defamation laws exist in most countries, though they vary considerably in the extent to which they are used. South Korea has recently come under criticism for using criminal defamation laws to target journalists. In November 2014, then President Park Geun-hye of South Korea filed a criminal lawsuit against six journalists for reporting on a leaked government document.[76] Special interests, too, have been successful in a variety of democracies in advocating for lawmakers to pass laws that limit expression on particular issues. In a handful of states in the United States, agriculture lobbies have passed anti-whistleblower bills, often referred to as "ag-gag" bills, that make documenting anything inside an animal facility with the purpose to commit defamation illegal.[77] Other recent examples of criminal defamation laws in democracies include those in Indonesia, where social media users and journalists have spent time in jail for alleging political corruption or questioning the existence of God.[78]

2.7.2 Intimidation

Fear not only originates in legal deterrence, or the threat of state punitive action, but can also take the form of extra-legal intimidation or threats, where government actors or other authorities can dissuade citizens or journalists from consuming, expressing,

---

[76] Haggard and You (2015); "South Korea: Stop Using Criminal Defamation Laws," *Human Rights Watch*, December 14, 2014, http://www.hrw.org/news/2014/12/14/south-korea-stop-using-criminal-defamation-laws.

[77] Oppel, Richard, "Taping of Farm Cruelty is Becoming the Crime," *The New York Times*, April 6, 2013, http://www.nytimes.com/2013/04/07/us/taping-of-farm-cruelty-is-becoming-the-crime.html.

[78] Cochrane, Joe, "Defamation Law Reminds Critics of Indonesia's Past," *New York Times*, September 22, 2014, http://www.nytimes.com/2014/09/23/world/asia/23indonesia.html.

or collecting particular types of information. These types of threats are less observable to the public than censorship laws, which are often explicitly laid out in government documents and publicly enforced. Intimidation can be more specifically targeted toward particular people or entities, often toward public figures, journalists, and academics who could potentially influence the opinions of large groups of people.

In China, local government officials are known to intimidate journalists and social media users who, while typically operating within the law, sometimes uncover and print information that reflects badly on of local officials. Although at times the central government actively encourages investigative journalism, local officials find investigative work particularly threatening because it brings their failings to the attention of their central government bosses.[79] As such, local government officials employ intimidation tactics, extra-legally assaulting or kidnapping journalists who try to expose local corruption, land grabs, or local riots.[80]

In many semi-authoritarian countries, democratic institutions do not allow censorship to be explicitly codified into law, and therefore government officials often take it upon themselves to deter activists and journalists from reporting on particular issues. Mikhail Beketov, a Russian journalist, advocated for the resignation of the government in the Russian city Khimki. His car was blown up and his dog beaten to death shortly after his story was published. Continuing to write, Beketov was beaten by thugs so badly in 2008 that he was confined to a wheelchair and

---

[79] Tong (2011, pg. 49–79).
[80] "14 Police Suspended After Beating Up Journalists," *Global Times*, January 27, 2015, http://english.sina.com/china/2015/0126/777177.html; Iritani, Evelyn, "Beating Death of Journalist Spurs Inquiry," *Los Angeles Times*, January 25, 2007, http://articles.latimes.com/2007/jan/25/world/fg-chideath25.

died from his injuries in 2013. An investigation of the beating was suspended "for lack of evidence."[81] Reporters Without Borders estimates that in 2013, 71 journalists were killed, 87 kidnapped, and 2,160 threatened or physically attacked.[82] Along with countries that are notorious for threatening journalists, such as Syria, democracies such as Mexico and Brazil have significant numbers of missing or murdered journalists, as well as countries that have seen large protest events, like Turkey and the Ukraine. In India, eight journalists were killed in 2013, and more were threatened by police. In short, even in countries where censorship laws may not exist, intimidation still can be a tool for inducing fear-based self-censorship.

2.7.3 Reward

Fear tactics can come with carrots, not just sticks. A government may facilitate the promotion of a journalist who refuses to say negative things about the government or may pay off a media outlet for keeping particular information secret. An employer may promote employees who do not speak out on particular political positions. In this book, I will consider such rewards a form of fear because the implied opposite of reward is sanction. If failing to criticize the government as a journalist means you will be promoted, the implication is that you will not be promoted if you criticize the government. Like threats, rewards must be observable to work—citizens must know there is a payoff to be incentivized to limit their speech. In this case, the fear is in failing to receive the reward.

---

[81] Barry, Ellen, "Journalist in Russia, Badly Beaten in 2008, Dies," *New York Times*, April 8, 2013, http://www.nytimes.com/2013/04/09/world/europe/mikhail-beketov-russian-journalist-beaten-in-2008-dies.html?_r=0.

[82] "71 Journalists Were Killed in 2013," *Reporters Without Borders*, January 25, 2016, https://rsf.org/en/news/71-journalists-were-killed-2013.

2.7.4 When Does Fear Affect Access and Expression?

In order for fear-based methods of censorship to deter the production and consumption of information and affect the flow of information up the pyramid, citizens and the media must (1) be aware of the consequences of consuming or producing information, and (2) believe that these consequences will be administered. The threat or law in conjunction with the probability of punishment must also be significant enough to outweigh the expected benefit of the production, dissemination, or consumption of information.

Although it may seem obvious that for deterrence to work one has to know about a threat, this point is central to understanding the differences among the three censorship mechanisms. The requirement that citizens be aware of a threat of punishment means that governments must either target individuals whom they would like to deter—which can be time consuming and costly—or alert the public at large about the threat by making laws or "examples" well known to the public. That fear works by making punishment observable distinguishes it from friction and flooding, which can affect citizens without their being aware of government interference.

Second, it must be credible that the threat will be enforced. Enforcement of laws and the carrying out of threats is expensive, and it may not always be optimal for authorities to enforce.[83] Citizens may try to evaluate the willingness of the authority to follow through with punishment by evaluating how costly the information is to the authority. The more the authority's survival is threatened by the information, the more the media and citizens might be concerned that it will be worthwhile to the authority to punish those who spread it. Therefore, citizens may think that punishment might be more likely the more damaging the information they intend to spread is. If others,

---

[83] See Becker (1968) for a discussion of the economics of crime enforcement.

who they believe are in many ways similar to themselves, have been punished for similar crimes, citizens may believe that they also are susceptible to punishment.

Citizens and the media may also try to determine whether the authority has the capacity to punish, or what the costs to the authority are for punishment. First, authorities have direct costs of punishing. For example, if many citizens and journalists in the country are violating the censorship law, the state's capacity to punish everyone violating the law is less than in a society where only one person has violated it. Citizens and the media may feel more comfortable speaking out if many others are doing so.

Authorities may also pay external costs for punishments that citizens and the media will take into account when evaluating their capacity to punish. In the case of the blogger Raif Badawi in Saudi Arabia, the government incurred international costs from outraged Western governments in terms of diplomacy and international press coverage.[84] Some types of censorship may not be politically viable internally, and could cause outrage and public backlash. Threats of punishment for dissemination of information will be less credible when the costs of censorship are higher for the political authority.

In other cases, it might be clear that authorities will incur costs if they *do not* punish citizens and the media for violating censorship laws. In these cases, authorities' censorship laws are more credible. For example, in countries where substantial consensus exists over censorship laws, such as child pornography laws in the United States or religious blasphemy laws in religiously devout countries, the government would face public outcry if enforcement were lax. In other cases, where the government has promised extensive enforcement of censorship

---

[84] Black, Ian, "Global Outrage at Saudi Arabia as Jailed Blogger Receives Public Flogging," *The Guardian*, January 11, 2015, https://www.theguardian.com/world/2015/jan/11/flogging-global-outrage-saudi-arabia-silent.

laws, failing to follow through on enforcement could hurt its future credibility and reputation.

If the threat is credible, fear-based methods can have an enormous impact. If fear-based methods can intimidate all people who know a piece of information, they can effectively keep information secret and reduce trust and coordination among citizens.[85] Ambiguity of fear-based approaches can silence third parties who are not even on the radar of the government, simply because these third parties do not know whether they could be targeted or what would happen to them if they were.[86]

However, governments face many trade-offs when implementing fear-based methods of censorship. Restricting speech may make it more difficult for governments to understand the opinions of the public, which has in the past led to the surprise demise of regimes.[87] Speech can reveal corruption of local officials or bureaucrats, which can be beneficial to central leaders and the effective functioning of governments.[88] Limitations on freedom of speech can also limit scientific discussion or the spread of information about disasters, which can have damaging consequences for the economy and for the safety of the population.

Further, when the threat is not credible, fear tactics are dangerous methods of censorship for governments. Because awareness of the threat is necessary for its efficacy, the paradox of fear-based censorship is that these methods create awareness of censorship. Because information is an experience or credence good, citizens assess whether or not to consume it based on signals of its importance. Therefore, by articulating which types

---

[85] Friedrich and Brzezinski (1965, pg. 169–170); Young (2016) shows evidence of how fear can impact the probability of dissent in Zimbabwe. Pearce and Kendzior (2012) estimate the impact of fear in Azerbaijan.

[86] Stern and Hassid (2012), Bahry and Silver (1987, pg. 1068).

[87] Kuran (1989).

[88] Tong (2011, Chapter 1), Tong and Sparks (2009), Lorentzen (2013); Liebman (2005).

of information are off-limits, governments bring attention to the issues that could undermine them, a phenomenon popularly known as the "Streisand effect" for Barbra Streisand, who sued the California Coastal Records Project for posting pictures online of her coastal mansion.[89] Instead of protecting her privacy, her suit drew more attention to the photos, which were widely circulated online after news spread that she was suing the project.

Censorship may act as a signal to citizens or the media that the information is important and in this way might motivate them to go looking for or write more about the censored topic than they would have had they not experienced intimidation. Just as Kepler was assured that having his book banned would only "make it read more attentively"[90] and as books that are censored in China sometimes receive more attention than those that are uncensored,[91] prohibited material where punishment is not credible might be more interesting to producers and consumers of media because it signals importance. Fear may alert citizens to subject matter of importance, which may make them more aware of the issue subsequently.[92]

The government may also pay a reputational cost of censorship if the censorship law itself is unpopular. If the individual believes that the law or threat is unjust or that censorship signals weakness, then support for the authority may decrease among the censored. This could particularly be true if censorship itself signals that the political authority is not secure enough to

[89] "What is the Streisand Effect?" *Economist*, April 16, 2013, http://www.economist.com/blogs/economist-explains/2013/04/economist-explains-what-streisand-effect.

[90] Eisenstein (1983, pg. 254).

[91] Wong, Chun Han, and Olivia Geng, "Book Ban Rumors Boost Authors in China," *Wall Street Journal*, October 13, 2014, http://blogswsj.com/chinarealtime/2014/10/13/rumors-of-book-ban-boosts-authors-in-china/.

[92] A general model for this reaction is explained in Marcus, Neuman and MacKuen (2000), where emotions like fear alert citizens of something new and important, inspiring them to gather more information about the subject.

withstand the spread of sensitive information. Since authorities will often target those who disagree with them in the first place, signaling such weakness with threats that are not credible could be very dangerous, since it essentially alerts the enemy to the authority's lack of capacity.

2.7.5 The Internet Has Made Fear-Based Censorship More Costly for Governments

The costs to governments of fear-based methods of censorship are more severe in the information age, as there has been an increase in the number of producers of information in the public domain.[93] Whereas before, authorities only had to target the traditional media to influence what information became widely known to the public, because social media has introduced the possibility that the public find and broadcast stories without the traditional media, fear would need to be credibly targeted toward the widespread public to be similarly effective. The more people writing critiques of the government online, the more costly it becomes to punish them all, in terms of both the physical and reputational costs of repression. Credibly threatening punishment for millions of online users who are simultaneously sharing information with one another is—even by the most sophisticated censors' accounts—currently impossible.[94]

---

[93] See Mossberger, Tolbert, and McNeal (2007) and Conroy, Feezell, and Guerrero (2012) for a description of how the Internet has influenced political participation.

[94] "美记者质疑中国 "网络审查" 鲁炜:内容审查用词不当" December 9, 2015. Available at: http://news.china.com/domestic/945/20151209/20903585.html. Note that as surveillance technology improves, the crediblility of fear-based methods of censorship may increase. Yet, the other costs of censorship, including backlash, information gathering, and economic costs will still impact censorship decisions.

The "Streisand effect" is also exaggerated in the age of information. Overwhelmed with information on the web, the challenge of the consumer in the information age is knowing what to read. Awareness of censorship without credible threats of punishment signals which topics might be more interesting to seek out and write about. Whereas a person may not find information about a particular corrupt official if they simply type in "corruption" in a search engine, if they realize they have been censored talking about a particular official, then they will know that this information is somehow important to the government. If these writers are not deterred by government threats, they may be incentivized to continue searching and possibly continue writing on the topic, backfiring against fear-induced methods of censorship.

Moreover, the Internet is a more useful conduit of information for governments when individuals are not fearful about speaking out. Social media does not only provide a forum for individuals to speak to each other, it also serves as a way for authoritarian regimes to monitor public opinion.[95] If individuals are fearful of expressing themselves online, the value of online information for understanding citizen concerns is lessened.

Authorities take into account the credibility of their threats to citizens, their reputation, the possibility for backfire, and censorship's effects on the government's future access to information about the population when deciding the circumstances under which they should use fear-based methods of censorship. If censorship laws are very popular, rarely violated, and quickly enforced, fear-based methods of censorship will be credible and will have their intended effect. But when censorship laws are unpopular and threats of punishment target large numbers of

---

[95] Lorentzen (2015); Meng, Pan and Yang (2014); Chen, Pan and Xu (2015); Chen and Xu (2017a).

people who are already violating censorship laws, the threat of enforcement is less credible and instead reminds the population of unpopular policies. In these cases, authorities may focus on targeting fear-based censorship toward those who are most likely to find and synthesize damaging information: the political elite and the media.

2.8 FRICTION

On January 12, 2010, Google publicly alleged that it had been hacked by Chinese sources. In response, it threatened to stop obeying laws required of foreign businesses operating in China to censor particular content from its search engine. The resulting conflict between Google and the Chinese government came to a head in March 2010, when Google began redirecting its mainland users to google.com.hk, Google's unfiltered Hong Kong search site.[96]

Reacting to Google's refusal to filter content, the Chinese government began blocking the unfiltered Hong Kong site. In addition, throughout mainland China, the government throttled access to Google services, allowing access to Gmail and Google's social media site Google Plus for only about 75 percent of requests.[97] China Unicom announced that it had removed Google search from its search platform, further restricting its

---

[96] In a talk at Google headquarters, Google founder Sergey Brin claimed that the motivation behind Google's actions in China were based on his own experiences with information control growing up in the Soviet Union. Gustin, Sam, " Google's Sergey Brin Leads Charge Against Chinese Web Censorship," *Daily Finance*, March 24, 2010, http://www.dailyfinance.com/2010/03/24/googles-sergey-brin-leads-charge-against-chinese-web-censorship/.

[97] Millward, Steven, "Google+ Not Actually Blocked in China, Just Being Slowly Throttled," *Tech in Asia*, June 30, 2011. Available at: https://www.techinasia.com/google-plus-china.

accessibility for Chinese users.[98] Mainland users could access Google, but doing so required more work and more patience. For years, traffic to the search giant creeped along slowly, until Google was finally completely blocked in 2014.[99]

Google spends millions of dollars a year making search faster because research has found that faster search means more users. Google market research shows that slowing search by one second creates approximately a one percent drop in search volume. A video stalling can be aggravating enough that 80 percent of Internet users will become frustrated and leave Google's YouTube.[100] Consistent with this research, when China began slowing Google's services in China, Google lost a large portion of the Chinese market. Since 2010, Google's market share in China has declined precipitously. In 2010, Google accounted for over 10 percent of page views among search engines in China, but its share had dropped to less than 2 percent by 2013.[101]

Despite its failure to comply with Chinese censorship, Google was never illegal to Chinese users. Throttling and later blocking Google with the Great Firewall is a form of friction, which affects the accessibility of information. Friction does not create consequences for successful access; there is no downside for an individual for having accessed that information. Instead, it taxes information by imposing costs on the process of accessing

[98] Hille, Kathrin, and Justine Lau, "China Unicom to Drop Google Search on Phones Using Android," *Financial Times*, March 25, 2010, http://www.ft.com/cms/s/0/22975096-37b0-11df-88c6-00144feabdc0.html.

[99] Levin, Dan, "China Escalating Attack on Google," *New York Times*, June 2, 2014, https://www.nytimes.com/2014/06/03/business/chinas-battle-against-google-heats-up.html

[100] Hoelzle, Urs, "The Google Gospel of Speed," *Google Think Insights*, January 2012, http://www.thinkwithgoogle.com/articles/the-google-gospel-of-speed-urs-hoelzle.html.

[101] Millward, Steven, "Baidu down, Qihoo up, Google dead: 2013 was a year of drama for China's search engines," *Tech in Asia*, January 6, 2014, https://www.techinasiacom/how-baidu-qihoo-google-performed-in-china-in-2013.

information—frustrating individuals by requiring more time, money, or resources, or by simply preventing them from coming across the information by reducing the probability that it will be found. Friction can impose small or large taxes on information; it can impose very small costs in terms of time and money or can make information very difficult to find. As I show in subsequent chapters, for those with little time, patience, or resources, even small frictions—not to mention costly frictions—can have significant effects on whether citizens consume particular types of information or whether the media will collect particular types of data.

Friction affects access to and expression of information by making certain facts, data, social media posts, or news articles difficult to obtain. In doing so, it reduces the likelihood that a particular viewpoint will be communicated to the public or a particular fact revealed. Just like sales taxes reduce the number of products a person can buy on a limited budget, friction imposes constraints on what can be written within the short period of a news cycle because the media and citizens have a finite amount of time to gather and synthesize information.

As such, friction reprioritizes consumption and production of information by affecting its price. As discussed earlier, both citizens and the media are affected by the cost of information when deciding what to read and what stories to undertake. As I will discuss in more detail later in this section, this is particularly true in the digital world, where media competition is fierce and citizens are overwhelmed with the amount of information they could potentially consume. In this type of environment, the costs and inconvenience of access will be one of the most important factors in prioritizing the consumption and production of information.

Of course, there are certain types of information that by their nature have lower costs of access than other types of information. For example, readers are more likely to consume news that is printed in their native language. Collecting data is easier for some types of measurements than others: a day with severe air pollution is easier to observe than knowing that your food or water is contaminated with trace amounts of lead. Even though such "natural" frictions can have large implications for politics, to the extent that these costs of access are not manipulated by an interested party these frictions are not knowingly orchestrated and thus are not a form of censorship.

However, to the extent that convenience can by manipulated by interested authorities, friction is an important form of censorship. Costs of access do impose restrictions on public access and expression of information and have surprisingly strong effects on the public's and media's consumption of information. Even though the public is not prohibited from sharing or accessing information that is affected by friction, the time and money it takes to do so affects the likelihood that this information will spread.

Friction is also distinct from fear because it does not have to be observable to be effective. Like taxes, citizens will be aware of some frictions; for example, they may run across an error page that was obviously taken down by the government, or be told that an online search cannot be run because of government regulations. However, like value-added taxes of inputs to a product or sales tax that is priced into a product, many frictions will be hidden from the public. The citizen will simply experience more difficulty in accessing or spreading information, without knowing or understanding that access to that information is affected by the government.

Friction and fear are not mutually exclusive and can overlap. Which mechanism stops or throttles the flow of information may also be person-specific. For example, when a person comes across a webpage that has clearly been removed by the government, they might experience both friction, because the information is more difficult to find, and fear, if the removal of the website is paired with a threat of punishment for continuing to search for that information. However, another person who is more oblivious to signals of censorship or less easily frightened of the government may just experience friction and not fear.

Relatedly, fear-based censorship can create downstream friction. Fear imposed on the media might make stories about sensitive topics more difficult to find for the public, even if the public is not aware of punishment or does not experience fear themselves. Importantly, however, friction does not require fear and is often imposed without any fear. Slower Internet, throttled websites, or purposefully uncollected data are all common examples of friction that do not require fear but still affect the flow of information. As we will see later in this chapter, friction is often used as a substitute for fear when fear is too costly for the authority.

2.8.1 Friction Imposed on Distribution of Information

The most direct form of friction is cost applied to communication between the media and the public—between the middle and top levels of the information pyramid. These frictions require individuals to spend extra time or resources consuming or sharing news, social media, books, or opinion pieces that have already been written. Costs on the distribution of information are distinct from frictions between the lower levels of the information pyramid in collecting primary data or information that could then be analyzed and later printed in news, social media, books, or other forms of media. I will first discuss direct frictions on the dissemination of information, and in the next section explore frictions on the initial collection of information.

Perhaps the most infamous type of friction is the Great Firewall, China's sophisticated mechanism for blocking foreign websites that the government finds objectionable, including eventually Google. For people who are physically in China, websites such as Voice of America News (voanews.com), Facebook (facebook.com), and Twitter (twitter.com) return an error page instead of the website itself.[102]

Although the Firewall is technologically sophisticated, it is relatively easy to circumvent. Users simply have to download a Virtual Private Network (VPN), which allows them to log onto a computer outside of China and access the blocked site indirectly through that computer. Depending on the technological capabilities of the person, the Firewall is a large friction or very small friction imposed on foreign information. Simply knowing that the Firewall exists and can be jumped is a first step to overcoming the friction imposed by the Firewall, and not every person in China realizes that the Firewall exists. Even if a person knows that the Firewall can be jumped, using a VPN imposes small costs on a user's paycheck and time. VPNs can sometimes cost money—typically only a few dollars a month, but such costs would be prohibitive for many Chinese citizens. They also are invariably slower than using a computer directly, with costs of logging in and waiting for two computers to load a website. Sometimes, too, VPNs are shut down by the Chinese government; in these cases, users have to spend time finding an alternative VPN before they can jump the Firewall. As I will show in later chapters, for the typical consumer uninterested in politics, these small costs can be sufficient to significantly affect their behavior.

China is not the only country that filters access to particular sites—countries all over the world block content from reaching IP addresses within their borders. Both Saudi Arabia and Iran have sophisticated blocking systems that filter websites deemed immoral or with political content the government finds objectionable. Other countries block particular websites; for example,

---

[102] For a list of websites currently blocked by the Great Firewall from China, visit GreatFire.org.

Turkey has blocked YouTube and Pakistan has blocked Google's platform Blogger.[103] Other countries use temporary measures to block websites, such as denial of service attacks to shut down websites during particularly sensitive periods or protest events.[104]

When authorities do not want to use a Firewall to filter information, they can impose friction by simply slowing information transfer to make it more annoying for citizens to access. Internet blackouts can be strategically timed to prevent reporting of repression or protests.[105] Countries can also throttle websites, making them slower to load or unreliable. These types of methods are intended to aggravate the user, while not outright blocking the site. Iran has been known not to black out the Internet but simply make it slower during periods of unrest.[106] The recent debate in the United States about net neutrality fundamentally concerns the same issues of speed and friction. Proposals supported by telecom companies would make fast "lanes" on the Internet for content providers that agreed to pay more. Essentially, this would make the relative speed of some information slower than others. For impatient consumers waiting for websites to load, marginally faster websites would gain a larger audience and therefore more revenue and influence. If the selection of which content could move through fast lanes were political, this could act like online political censorship in more authoritarian environments.

Another example of online friction is search filtering and keyword blocking, where Internet search engines reorder the search results or disallow particular searches for political

---

[103] Rosen, Jeffrey, "Google's Gatekeepers," *New York Times*, November 28, 2008, http://www.nytimes.com/2008/11/30/magazine/30google-t.html.

[104] "State Blamed in LiveJournal Attack," *Moscow Times*, April 5, 2011, https://themoscowtimes.com/news/state-blamed-in-livejournal-attack-6116.

[105] Gohdes (2015).

[106] Aryan, Aryan and Halderman (2013, pg. 5).

purposes. In China, search engines such as Google and Baidu were originally required to block particular searches that include sensitive people or events. Social media sites such as Sina Weibo were required to do the same when users were searching for social media posts related to sensitive people or events. However, recently, Chinese websites have moved past simply prohibiting some searches and instead search services reorder search results in a way that obscures the omission of certain results to the user.[107] By burying sensitive webpages in the depths of the results, these search filtering methods of censorship create friction for particular types of information, and users may be completely unaware that this information is being de-prioritized. Similar concerns have been launched against U.S. social media companies that control the prioritization of information to users. While unverified, Google and Facebook have been accused of prioritizing particular types of news for users for political purposes.[108]

While there are many examples of frictions online, friction is not new or unique to the Internet age. In print publications, governments also try to de-emphasize certain types of information so fewer people come across them.[109] In China, government information agencies often mandate that particular pieces of news be published on the back pages of the newspaper, or below the fold, so as to reduce the total number of people who will come across that piece of information. Leaked directives show

[107] Knockel, Ruan and Crete-Nishihata (2017).

[108] Bump, Philip, "Did Facebook Bury Conservative News? Ex-staffers Say Yes." *Washington Post*, May 9, 2016, https://www.washingtonpost.com/news/the-fix/wp/2016/05/09/former-facebook-staff-say-conservative-news-was-buried-raising-questions-about-its-political-influence/. Shultz, David, "Could Google Influence the Presidential Election?" *Science Magazine*, October 25, 2016. http://www.sciencemag.org/news/2016/10/could-google-influence-presidential-election.

[109] See Gang and Bandurski (2011, pg. 56) for how the CCP tries to "grab the megaphone," or set the agenda, within traditional media.

explicit directions for placement within newspapers.[110] These government directives also mandate particular titles that are intended to be less sensational and attract less attention than newspapers might print otherwise.

Even authorities without direct access to media infrastructure, for example companies, politicians, and interest groups, can use the news cycle to make it more difficult for consumers to come across bad news. "Bad news Fridays," as media advisors in the field frequently refer to it, is when groups announce their bad news at or after 5:00 PM on Friday, when most journalists have gone home and most citizens are not paying attention to the news.[111] Because citizens may have stopped paying attention to news for the weekend, and the story is unlikely to run three days later on Monday, they are less likely to come across this negative piece of information.

Controversies over the material within libraries or in textbooks also reflects conflict over friction, as student access to this public information is nearly costless, whereas outside information takes initiative and resources for students to procure. These controversies are widespread, including controversies over the portrayal of historical wars,[112] the portrayal of race and class,[113] or ideology and nationalism,[114] and occur in countries around the world.

---

[110] "Ministry of Truth: Personal Wealth, Income Gap," *China Digital Times*, February 6, 2013, https://chinadigitaltimes.net/2013/02/ministry-of-truth-personal-wealth-income-gap/.

[111] Patell and Wolfson (1982).

[112] Fackler, Martin, "U.S. Textbook Skews History, Prime Minister of Japan Says," *New York Times*, January 29, 2015, http://www.nytimes.com/2015/01/30/world/asia/japans-premier-disputes-us-textbooks-portrayal-of-comfort-women.html.

[113] Turner, Cory, "The Great U.S. History Battle," *National Public Radio*, February 24, 2015, http://www.npr.org/sections/ed/2015/02/24/388443955/the-great-u-s-history-battle.

[114] Chen, Te-Ping, "Protest Over 'Brainwashing' Schools," *Wall Street Journal*, September 2, 2012, https://blogs.wsj.com/chinarealtime/2012/09/02/thousands-protest-hong-kongs-moral-and-national-education-push/.

2.8.2 Friction on the Collection of Primary Information

In the previous section, I described instances of information friction where access to media or information that had already been written and collected was throttled or made more costly. In these cases, friction throttled information traveling to the top level of the pyramid. In this section, I describe when the data necessary to write a story, book, or social media post is difficult to access, or when information is censored at the bottom of the pyramid. This is a deeper form of friction because it occurs at the initial stages of story discovery. Like a value-added tax on an input to a product that shows up in the price of the good, but is invisible to the consumer, this friction on collection of primary information can often be more invisible because it is further removed from the public.

Data collection has a natural cost—certain types of information are more difficult to collect than others, even without political manipulation. For example, it is less costly to go outside and observe the weather where you are than to collect information about the weather in an unoccupied part of Antarctica, thousands of miles away. It is less time-consuming to conduct an interview in your native tongue than in a foreign language. However, these frictions can be exacerbated by authorities (the government, political parties, interest groups, etc.) who have an interest in making particular types of information even more difficult to collect.

In this section, I will outline three different types of friction-based censorship that apply to the collection of data. First, authorities can throttle access to information they have already collected, making the information they collect more difficult for secondary sources to gain access to. Second, authorities may simply refrain from collecting particular types of information, even information that would be natural for them to collect. Last, for journalists, academics, or citizens interested in collecting particular types of data, authorities can throttle access to the collection of data, even if they themselves do not collect it.

2.8.2.1 Friction on Data Access

In the first case, groups and governments can slow access to information they already have, making it more difficult for citizens and journalists to collect information necessary to complete an article, social media post, or study on their topic of interest. In the United States and many democracies, Freedom of Information Act (FOIA) requests are meant to reduce friction in citizens' and the media's access to information. However, companies and interest groups lobby for exceptions from FOIA requests. For example, in 2003, data collected by the Department of Transportation about safety defects in cars was made exempt from FOIA requests obstensibly to prevent one auto manufacturer from gaining an advantage over another. In another example in the United States, the Tiahrt Amendment, passed in 2003, made private a government database that traced guns used in crimes back to dealers. Making this information impossible to access has made lawsuits against gun dealers and research about gun violence more difficult to conduct, as other sources of information must be used.[115]

Even without banning information, government agencies can make information harder to access under FOIA laws. When a bureaucracy does not want to release information, it can quote exorbitant prices for FOIA requests for copying and sending the information to citizens, the only aspect of a FOIA request a bureaucracy is allowed to charge for. The ACLU, for example, has been quoted hundreds of thousands of dollars for access

---

[115] Grimaldi, James V., and Sari Horwitz, "Industry Pressure Hides Gun Traces, Protects Dealers from Public Scrutiny," *Washington Post*, October 24, 2010, http://www.washingtonpost.com/wp-dyn/content/article/2010/10/23/AR2010102302996.html. Gup (2008, pg. 12).

to police records.[116] Journalists have been quoted hundreds of thousands of dollars for FOIA requests to access information about FBI contracts with defense companies.[117] Such exorbitant costs have motivated a few states to put caps on the amount that can be charged for access to information under FOIA laws. In authoritarian environments, costs of access can be even more arbitrary. When a public disaster strikes in China, local government officials are quick to control the sources of information, ensuring government officials follow victims' families to control their interactions with the press, or placing victims and their families in a hotel or a place where officials can control press access.[118] Although the Chinese government has become increasingly transparent in providing data about governance online, these data are often subject to scrutiny before they are posted, making it impossible to know their veracity. Local governments in China are known to collect inaccurate GDP and environmental data, inflating numbers to make it seem as if their jurisdictions are growing faster, and with less pollution, than they are in actuality.[119] Such manipulation of government statistics makes estimating true GDP numbers in China difficult

---

[116] Gup (2008, pg. 57); Masnick, Mike, "Michigan State Police Say It Will Cost $545k to Discover What Info It's Copying Off Mobile Phones During Traffic Stops," *TechDirt*, April 20, 2011, https://www.techdirt.com/blog/wireless/articles /20110420/01070213969/michigan-state-police-say-itll-cost-545k-to-discover-what -info-its-copying-off-mobile-phones-during-traffic-stops.shtml.

[117] Sampson, Zack, "Want to see the work Booz Allen did for the FBI? Get ready to fork over enough to buy a house," September 30, 2015, https://www.muckrock .com/news/archives/2013/sep/30/want-see-work-booz-allen-did-fbi-get-ready-fork -ov/.

[118] McDonell, Steven, "Yangtze Ferry Disaster: Chinese authorities start righting capsized ship; death toll rises to 75," *ABC*, June 4, 2015, http://www .abc.net.au/news/2015-06-04/bad-weather-interrupts-work-to-find-china-ferry -survivors/6522012.

[119] Wallace (2016); Ghanem and Zhang (2014); Buckley, Chris, "China Burns Much More Coal Than Reported, Complicating Climate Talks," *New York Times*, November 3, 2015, http://www.nytimes.com/2015/11/04/world/asia/china -burns-much-more-coal-than-reported-complicating-climate-talks.html?_r=0.

for investors, the media, and researchers.[120] Archives in China are not consistently open to academics and are often subject to gatekeepers or dependent on the sensitivity of the time period. The government will sometimes allow researchers more access to historical information that supports their current political agenda.[121]

2.8.2.2 Failure to Collect Data

Authorities can fail to collect information, thereby making it very difficult for the media to access. The logic behind the failure to collect data is often obscure—does the authority simply not have the resources for collection, or are they purposefully trying to hide information? For example, in the aftermath of the Ferguson police shooting in 2014, where an unarmed man was shot and killed by the police, the media attempted to print statistics reflecting the number of Americans killed by police each year. In fact, police do not collect these data, and the Justice Department only has statistics on "justifiable" police killings, which rely on voluntary statistics from police departments, where "justifiable" may be defined differently across departments. Data on unjustifiable police killings are not collected.[122] Scholars have found that discrepancies between sources of the number of police killings is due to the failure of police to report the data or the misclassification of police killings as homicides that were not

---

[120] Bradsher, Keith, "Chinese Data Mask Depth of Slowdown, Executives Say," *New York Times*, June 22, 2012, http://www.nytimes.com/2012/06/23/business/global/chinese-data-said-to-be-manipulated-understating-its-slowdown.html?pagewanted=all.

[121] Cunningham, Maura, "Denying Historians: China's Archives Increasingly Off-Bounds," *Wall Street Journal*, August 19, 2014, https://blogs.wsj.com/chinarealtime/2014/08/19/denying-historians-chinas-archives-increasingly-off-bounds/.

[122] Fischer-Baum, Reuben, "Nobody Knows How Many Americans The Police Kill Each Year," *Five Thirty Eight*, August 19, 2014, http://fivethirtyeight.com/features/how-many-americans-the-police-kill-each-year/.

due to the police.[123] Whether these failures to report are a result of error or a result of incentives is subject to speculation.

Autocracies are also notorious for refraining from collecting or for mis-collecting information that makes access to data more difficult for journalists, citizens, and researchers. For example, in Beijing, until 2012 the Chinese government consistently refused to collect data on fine particulate matter (PM 2.5), a particular type of air pollutant that is thought to have damaging effects on health. While the U.S. embassy posted PM 2.5 data for Beijing on its blocked Twitter feed, the Chinese government posted pollution data without PM 2.5 included.[124] Similarly, China has reported enormous progress in fighting crime over the past years after announcing a large anti-crime campaign. Yet the crime statistics reported from China are somewhat unbelievable— over two-fifths of counties reported "cracking" 100 percent of murders.[125] Many assume that local police simply omitted cases they thought were too difficult to solve.

2.8.2.3 Friction Imposed on Data Collection

When data are not collected by authorities, journalists and citizens may make an effort to collect the data themselves. Data collection by the media and citizens can be expensive and time consuming even without intervention by third parties, but authorities will sometimes try to make the collection of data itself more costly for anyone attempting it. For example, in China, lead poisoning is one of the major threats to public safety and in particular children's safety. At one point, estimates suggested

---

[123] Loftin et al. (2003).

[124] Wong, Edward, "On Scale of 0 to 500, Beijing's Air Quality Tops 'Crazy Bad' at 755," *New York Times*, January 12, 2013, http://www.nytimes.com/2013 /01/13/science/earth/beijing-air-pollution-off-the-charts.html.

[125] "Murder mysteries," *Economist*, April 6, 2013, http://www.economist.com /news/ china/ 21575767-official-figures-showing-sharp-drop-chinas-murder-rate -are-misleading-murder-mysteries.

that up to one-third of Chinese children could be affected by high levels of lead in their blood.[126] Interviews conducted by Human Rights Watch showed that political entities within China have made data collection on the severity of the problem extremely difficult. Hospitals, particularly in rural areas in Anhui, Hunan, Yunnan, and Shaanxi provinces, have repeatedly refused to give lead tests to parents and children.[127] Local hospitals have given misinformation about the health consequences of lead poisoning and the recommended treatment.[128] Although people are aware that lead poisoning is a problem, such lack of information collection has lessened widespread pressure on local governments, as local residents have found it difficult to organize because verifying that they are affected by the problem is difficult.[129]

Making data collection more difficult is not unique to the authoritarian context. For example, in war zones, the U.S. government has been accused of impeding journalists' access to particular sites, allowing journalists only in "approved" areas of the war zone. In the Persian Gulf War, journalists were escorted to parts of the war zone based on U.S. military decision making. The U.S. military made it difficult to access other types of information about the war outside of the perspectives of these "press pools," meaning that the U.S. media largely saw the war from one perspective. Those who were found violating press pool guidelines were removed from the area, which meant that

---

[126] LaFraniere, Sharon, "Lead Poisoning in China: The Hidden Scourge," *New York Times*, June 15, 2011, http://www.nytimes.com/2011/06/15/world/asia/15lead.html?pagewanted=all; "My Children Have Been Poisoned: A Public Health Crisis in Four Chinese Provinces," *Human Rights Watch* June 2011, http://www.hrw.org/sites/default/files/reports/china0611WebInside_0_0.pdf.

[127] Cohen and Amon (2011), Human Rights Watch, pg. 25–27.

[128] Human Rights Watch, pg. 25–27.

[129] Human Rights Watch, pg. 21–22.

journalists could sometimes not collect information needed to corroborate the U.S. government's account of the war.[130]

While we have only touched on a few examples for illustration in this section, authorities have myriad methods for imposing anything from small to significant costs on data collection. This censorship often does not involve punishment but can still have significant effects on the spread of information. Further, these frictions are often difficult for the public and media to observe—the lack of information is often less noticeable than its existence. It will typically not be apparent to the public that a story is not covered because of data unavailability. The few times it is made clear to the public that this information cannot be accessed, often the underlying intent is also opaque: are FOIA requests expensive because of politically motivated manipulation of information or because of true administrative costs? Does China not collect PM 2.5 data because they lack the technological capabilities or because they hope to mask the true levels of pollution? Unlike fear, where censorship must be explicit to deter, the intent behind friction is less apparent and can be explained away by authorities and observers, offering the cover of plausible deniability.

2.8.3 When Does Friction Affect Access and Expression?

Friction-based methods of censorship are more easily implemented by the authority the more the authority has control over information generation at the lower levels of the information pyramid. Information that can be collected only by the authority, either because they alone have access to the information or because only they have the expertise to collect it, can easily

---

[130] Boydston (1992); Apple, R.W. Jr, "War in the Gulf: The Press; Correspondents Protest Pool System," *New York Times*, February 12, 1991, http://www.nytimes.com/1991/02/12/us/war-in-the-gulf-the-press-correspondents-protest-pool-system.html.

be made more costly: the authority can simply fail to collect it, or if they do decide to collect it, they can make sure it is unavailable to the public. Control over information also enables the authority to provide reasons for information restriction. For example, if the government restricts where the military can provide journalists access to war zones, it may provide safety reasons for keeping journalists out of particular locations. Since authorities can control access at the data-collection stage, these types of actions are also more difficult for the public to detect, as the public will not always notice the *lack* of a story in the media. In contrast, when the authority does not control sources of information, such as events that happen quickly and are highly observable to large numbers of people, friction-based methods of censorship will be difficult to use. Information about events like environmental crises, large accidents that may implicate the government, or natural disasters that occur in large population areas will spread quickly, before information friction can be imposed. In these cases, high levels of censorship or the lack of reporting may be indications that the government is ignoring or repressing the issue, which could backfire and cause more, not less, consternation among the public.[131]

Once information has already been collected or is already known to some number of people, control over the information environment through friction requires political power or access to the media infrastructure and distribution of media.[132] The more control the government has over Internet content providers, newspapers, or television stations, the more successful it will be at creating friction. The more tools that the government has to control search engines or slow the delivery of particular types of information, the more the government will be able to impose friction on already created media articles.

---

[131] Jansen and Martin (2003).

[132] This point is made by Edmond (2013) who shows that the more centralized control is over media, the easier it is to control.

Governments of smaller countries, where many citizens rely on foreign news sources or Western Internet content providers like Twitter and Facebook, will have fewer options for imposing friction because they do not have direct jurisdiction over the outside media content.[133] Similarly, governments in areas where television or newspaper broadcasts span international borders will have trouble controlling information from outside.

Even if information is not particularly well known initially, it may be difficult for the authority to create friction if another organized entity has a strong incentive to seek out the information and publish it. For issues where there is a stronger civil society, more factionalism, or other types of political competition, it will be more difficult for authorities to hide information since it will likely be collected, published, and promoted by the competing entity.[134] Such competition also makes friction harder to justify—for example, the Chinese government had trouble justifying publishing pollution numbers that did not include levels of PM 2.5 because the U.S. embassy in Beijing was publishing these numbers on its own Twitter feed.

Citizens and the media will be more susceptible to friction if the cost added by censorship to the information is enough to offset the benefits of consuming or disseminating information. Importantly, how citizens and the media are affected by friction will depend on their *elasticity of demand for information*; in other words, how much their behavior changes in reaction to small changes in the price of information. In general, the more elastic citizens' and the media's demand for information—the more affected they are by changes in the price of information — the more effective friction-based methods will be since citizens

---

[133] Pan (2016).

[134] One of Wolfsfeld (2011, pg. 23–25) five principles of political communication is that when "authorities lose control over the political environment, they lose control of the news." This is because once political control is lost, more competing sources are able to leak and report information that the media can use to contradict the authority.

and the media will be more likely to substitute lower-cost information for that which has become higher-cost. As a result, friction will have a greater impact the less citizens and the media are willing to seek out the political information.

Because of the importance of elasticity of demand for information, friction will have a stronger impact when it is invisible—if the friction induced by the authority becomes known to its target, the citizen or media may take it as a signal that the information is important and their demand for this information might become more inelastic. If the observation of censorship creates more inelastic demand for information, more people will be willing to overcome costs to find the information because it was censored, creating the "Streisand effect" discussed earlier.[135] Relatedly, friction-based methods are more effective when censorship can be obscured or blamed on another cause. Plausible deniability will muddle the signal of the importance of information and citizens may explain friction away or ignore it. Like in contexts of direct repression, "plausible deniability" on the part of the government might be more credible when friction is implemented by an agent—a private company or a local level of government—rather than the central government itself.[136]

Citizens' and the media's demand for information may become more inelastic when external events make them attune to politics or when censorship disrupts their habits. During political crises, the public may sense threat and therefore be more likely to overcome barriers to seek out information. As I'll show in chapter 5, when an explosion shook Tianjin during August of 2015, many more people were willing to search out information across the Great Firewall. Similar research has shown that during revolutions and political crises, citizens may be

---

[135] See Jansen and Martin (2015) for a discussion of how authorities seek to mitigate censorship backlash.

[136] See Mitchell, Carey, and Butler (2014) for a discussion of plausible deniability of human rights violations.

more willing to seek out media to inform themselves of ongoing events.[137] Similarly, in democracies, heightened attention that results from crises or protests can draw attention to the limits on government data, or underreporting of events within the media.[138]

Similar to the economic observation that addictive goods are less price-sensitive, friction that suddenly disrupts habits will be less effective because people are generally more willing to spend time and money to continue habitual behavior. If friction gets in the way of something a user needs—for work or for entertainment, for example—they may be more willing to pay the costs of censorship evasion. As I'll discuss more in chapter 5, when the very addictive social media website Instagram was blocked in China, millions of people evaded the Firewall to access Instagram because they were accustomed to doing so,[139] and were subsequently exposed to censored political information.

Those who learn to overcome frictions during political crises or in reaction to habit disruption may have non-linear effects on the information environment. Once a user has learned to overcome friction, they may more easily be able to do it again in the future, or apply it to other types of information. For example, when someone learns to evade the Great Firewall, they may more easily jump it again in the future. As more people learn how to evade censorship, they may be more likely to share this information between their friends. Friction will therefore be less effective if it is broadly applied to both political information and entertainment or other types of information that citizens are highly motivated to access; in such cases, people may learn

---

[137] Ball-Rokeach and DeFleur (1976), Loveless (2008).
[138] Fischer-Baum, Reuben, "Nobody Knows How Many Americans The Police Kill Each Year," *Five Thirty Eight*, August 19, 2014, http://fivethirtyeight.com/features/how-many-americans-the-police-kill-each-year/.
[139] Hobbs and Roberts (2016).

how to overcome frictions in order to access entertainment and once they do, they will be able to apply it to other forms of information, such as political information.[140]

Of course, friction—like all forms of censorship—can have economic and political consequences that are detrimental for authorities. Blocking websites that could potentially be useful to economic growth (like Google, GitHub, or Dropbox) is like imposing a tariff on valuable inputs for local Internet companies. However, because taxes on information are more easily disguised than a prohibition that has to be communicated and enforced, censorship by friction is less likely to have the same backfire effects as fear. Friction will also not make citizens fearful of speaking their mind and therefore will allow the government to monitor public opinion. For these reasons, friction solves many of the dilemmas inherent in the imposition of censorship through fear.

2.8.4 The Impact of Friction Has Strengthened in the Information Age

The Internet has decreased the absolute per unit cost of information substantially. According to Internet Live Stats, there are more than one trillion individual webpages on the Internet.[141] With a known URL and a good Internet connection, information from all over the world can be accessed within seconds. As a result, many scholars thought that censorship in the age of the Internet would be futile—in President Clinton's words, "like nailing jello to a wall."[142] Easily copied or added to the trillions of

---

[140] This is similar to the argument made in Baum (2003), when entertainment and news are paired they may be more easily consumed by citizens. This is also true in a censored information environment.

[141] "Total Number of Websites," *Internet Live Stats*, accessed May 2, 2017, http://www.internetlivestats.com/total-number-of-websites/.

[142] "A Giant Cage," *Economist*, April 6, 2013, http://www.economist.com/news /special-report/21574628-internet-was-expected-help-democratise-china-instead-it -has-enabled.

websites online, many suspected that information simply could not be controlled.

However, despite the overall decrease in the cost of information, the relative cost of competing information is still relevant for consumers of information. Because information is easily substituted and citizens have a limited amount of time, the relative costs of information drive consumption patterns. Having more near-equivalent copies of information on the web increases the substitutability of information because if one piece of information entails costs, consumers are likely to be able to find something similar enough more cheaply elsewhere. Many recent studies have documented consumers' extreme impatience on the Internet. Google research has shown that even small, micro-second delays in searches can significantly decrease user search.[143] Krishnan and Sitaraman (2013) find that with each one second delay in video start-up, 5.8 percent of users switch to something else. Viewers who experience slow video equal to one percent of the duration of the video watch five percent less of the video than those with no delay. Mark, Voida and Cardello (2012) find that users on average switch windows on a computer 37.1 times an hour, with time staying on one window on average just over one minute. Yeykelis, Cummings and Reeves (2014) find that sympathetic arousal increases right around switching between tasks and windows on the computer, suggesting physiological reasons for impatience and distraction on computers. As a result, small changes in search algorithms have been shown to drastically shift consumption of websites and news.[144] As the elasticity of demand for information increases because of the Internet, censorship methods that rely on the friction mechanism become more potent.

[143] Brutlag (2009).
[144] Athey and Mobius (2012).

Unlike fear, which is more costly as more people become producers of information, the price of friction is scalable for increased numbers of Internet users. Search filtering one website many people use, for example, takes only one manipulation to affect all consumers. Removing a post from the Internet affects all people who would potentially look for that post. A dataset that is removed from a government website affects access for the entire public.

Friction, particularly in the digital age, facilitates plausible deniability and is less transparent than fear, which must be observed in order to function. Because a search on the Internet is ordered by algorithms and Internet errors frequently occur without censorship, even if the user comes across evidence left behind by friction, it can be difficult to know whether a technical issue or an authority purposely manipulating the web was the cause. Algorithms for search are protected intellectual property and difficult for the public to understand—an Internet user could not tell you whether the search results were ordered in a particular way because of an algorithm acting in the interest of the public, or because of an algorithm censoring in the interest of the authority.[145] If a user clicks on a link that is blocked by the Great Firewall, it is difficult to know whether that page is down because of the government or because the website itself is undergoing maintenance. Indeed, many websites in China "go down for maintenance" around the anniversary of the 1989 Tiananmen Square protests.[146] A link may be broken because it has been moved or because it has been intentionally broken by authorities. The intricacies and complicated technology of the Internet disguise friction-based censorship.

---

[145] Tufekci (2014).
[146] "Websites to 'Close' for China's 'Internet Maintenance Day'," *Register*, June 4, 2013, http://www.theregister.co.uk/2013/06/04/chinas_internet_maintenance _day_shutters_sites/.

The costless nature of the Internet has caused traditional journalism to be more susceptible to government frictions. Because of the "24-hour" nature of the news cycle, the fast pace of the Internet, and the fleeting nature of stories, costly investigation has become less profitable. In the United States, full-time professional staff at newspapers dropped 27 percent between 2000 and 2010, due to rapid declines in advertising revenue.[147] In particular, resources for investigative reporting and international reporting have been cut, and newspapers are more reluctant to allow their short-staffed journalists covering daily news to invest in high-cost stories.[148] These costs and uncertainties involved in story creation are more important in an era where competition between media outlets is more fierce and subscriptions to papers are being substituted with access to the Internet. Economic models of media show that advertising revenue is one of the most important components of independent press, as when the media has more advertising revenues, it is more difficult for the government to capture.[149] Traditional media outlets are closing their doors, reducing resources for investigative journalism, and relying more on information from political entities, opinion articles, or the syndication of news, which are less costly to produce.[150]

Of course, traditional media have now been augmented by online news. In particular, "citizen journalists," who spend their own time researching and reporting news, have received significant amounts of attention in popular and academic presses.[151] However, citizen journalists typically have more stringent monetary constraints on reporting than traditional journalists.

[147] Edmonds et al. (2012).
[148] Nichols and McChesney (2009).
[149] Gehlbach and Sonin (2014); Petrova (2011).
[150] Nichols and McChesney (2009).
[151] Bulkley, Kate, "The Rise of Citizen Journalism," *Guardian*, June 10, 2012, https://www.theguardian.com/media/2012/jun/11/rise-of-citizen-journalism; Tufekci and Wilson (2012).

Without an institution funding their salaries and the costs of investigation, citizens have fewer resources to invest in their stories. They also typically have less training to help them determine which stories might be successful. Citizen journalists will typically be more affected by the costs of a story in terms of time and money. Social media written by citizen journalists are more likely to carry re-shares of stories or opinions, which have lower costs of production, than the news media.[152] The decline of the traditional media and rise of citizen journalists have therefore made the information distributed and shared online more susceptible to frictions imposed by governments.

2.9 FLOODING

The last type of censorship is flooding, the coordinated production of information by an authority with the intent of competing with or distracting from information the authority would rather consumers not access. Flooding occurs when groups systematically create information and disseminate it at low cost, to make it convenient for the media to print on a large scale or easy for the public to access. Although it seems counterintuitive that the production of information could be considered a form of censorship, by making a particular piece of information very easy to access, flooding raises the relative cost of information from alternative sources and therefore can have the same impact as censorship. Contrary to common wisdom that more information is always better, flooding with irrelevant or less valuable information reduces the amount of time that citizens can spend consuming more valuable information and taxes good information by requiring more time to separate good information from bad information.

---

[152] Carpenter (2008), Nichols and McChesney (2009).

Flooding and friction are tightly paired: flooding causes friction by making information contemporaneous to the flooding effort more costly to access. However, the mechanism of increasing the costs is different: flooding increases the relative cost of information indirectly through competing information, whereas friction directly increases the costs of information, raising the absolute costs of that information. As I will show throughout this book, flooding and friction are often used together as authorities try to slow the spread of one type of information and promote another. Like friction, flooding is not always mutually exclusive of fear—the observation of propaganda can create fear and cause people to self-censor.[153] However, fear is not necessary for the flooding mechanism to work—citizens may be completely unaware that flooding is happening and still be affected by it. In fact, flooding is often used by authorities when fear and friction are too costly or could create backlash.

Like friction, there are natural types of flooding that affect citizens' consumption of information. Reporting on the Olympics, for example, has been shown to compete with reporting on natural disasters—areas affected by disasters that occur during the Olympics receive less aid because people are distracted by the games.[154] Although such distractions have important political and economic consequences, I do not consider distractions like the Olympics to be flooding-based censorship, insofar as they are not designed to decrease the accountability of political entities. However, to the extent that distractions can be coordinated by political organizations, political entities themselves can have a similar impact on citizens' consumption of information, an effort I consider to be a form of censorship.

As discussed in more detail at the end of this chapter, flooding is an increasingly convenient form of censorship for authorities

---

[153] See Huang (2015) for a discussion of the signaling function of propaganda.
[154] Eisensee and Strömberg (2007).

because now that much of the media is digitized it is relatively inexpensive to produce distracting information in large quantities. Producing superfluous information is often less costly to the authority than trying to find a way to throttle information that is already produced or to intimidate individuals so much that they refuse to speak out. In countries where information is relatively free already and citizens are less likely to be intimidated, flooding is an increasingly attractive option for political entities interested in controlling information. Flooding is also easier to use to affect information systems across borders, where authorities have less control over legal punishment, intimidation, and infrastructure that could allow them to create fear or impose friction.

In this section, I consider two main types of flooding. In the first case, the authority produces information that it then disseminates directly to the public at the top of the information pyramid. In the second case, the authority provides prepackaged information to the media at the middle level of the pyramid, with the intent of reducing the media's costs for a story, thus encouraging the media to print the story the authority designed in exclusion of others. In each case, the flooding may not include content directly related to the information the flooding is trying to suppress, but rather might take the form of entertainment or distraction that might be more interesting to the consumer. Much like advertising, flooding always occurs in a competitive context, attempting either to distract from or to overwhelm another party's version of events.

2.9.1 Flooding Directly to the Public

The first type of flooding competes directly with information already available to the public. This type of flooding operates at the dissemination stage, where the flooded material competes for attention with information being disseminated by media or individuals. Many times, the information that is being used to compete is not attributed to the government, even though it is government-coordinated.

Flooding directed at the public can be used for persuasion, confusion, or distraction. In each case, the purpose of flooding is to crowd out alternative viewpoints or perspectives. Sometimes flooding can take the form of traditional propaganda; the government can use its control over the media to create an omnipresent perspective on an issue for which the government has come under criticism. A classic example in China is the TV program *Xinwen Lianbo*, which airs nightly across China and represents the viewpoint of the central government. This news show stands in direct competition with Western viewpoints that cast China in a chaotic light, in which the chaos stems from autocracy. Instead, the oft-repeated Chinese propaganda viewpoint is that chaos stems from democracy, as Chinese reporters often focus on protests or political conflict in democracies. The TV program is shown on all local TV stations every night during prime time, crowding out alternative prime time TV.[155]

Traditional propaganda has been augmented by an online environment where paid commentators are cheap and can spread information widely. Authorities all over the world have designed flooding strategies to compete with online information that reflects poorly on them. On Twitter, governments have amassed "Twitter armies," coordinating the promotion of their version of events, increasing the ratio of Tweets that reflect well on their own perspective, and thus increasing the probability that consumers of information will run into their version of events. The Turkish, Israeli, and Palestinian governments all hire or enlist people to promote their ideas on Twitter. Such flooding

---

[155] Bandurski, David, "China Announces 'Newsy' Changes for CCTV's Official Nightly News Broadcast," *China Media Project*, February 4, 2008, http://cmp.hku .hk/2008/02/04/china-announces-newsy-makeover-for-cctvs-official-nightly-news-broadcast/.

strategies have resulted in "Twitter wars," where each government produces an onslaught of its version of events.[156] Even political parties in the United States are beginning to employ online armies that defend their candidate.[157] Web browsing data show that during the 2016 presidential election there were millions of shares of false news stories, which may have contributed to significant confusion about the candidates.[158]

Flooding can be used to undermine competing sources, either by directly disparaging them or by confusing the public into discounting the traditional press. Authoritarian governments around the world are known to widely disparage the Western press, using their own control over media to caution readers about bias in independent media.[159] Contradicting facts or persuading citizens to question reality, sometimes known as "gas-lighting," can also be the purpose of propaganda in order to confuse or distort citizens' perceptions of reality and thereby undermine the free press.[160] Most recently, the Russian government has been accused by the U.S. government of spreading misleading news online about the candidates in the 2016 election, undermining facts reported in the free press in an attempt to influence the election.[161] These efforts tax the public's

---

[156] Zeitzoff (2017).

[157] Halper, Evan, "Be Nice to Hillary Clinton Online—or Risk a Confrontation with her Super PAC," *LA Times*, May 9, 2016, http://www.latimes.com/politics /la-na-clinton-digital-trolling-20160506-snap-htmlstory.html; Markoff, John, "Automated Pro-Trump Bots Overwhelmed Pro-Clinton Messages, Researchers Say," *New York Times*, November 17, 2016, https://www.nytimes.com/2016/11 /18/technology/automated-pro-trump-bots-overwhelmed-pro-clinton-messages -researchers-say.html.

[158] Allcott and Gentzkow (2017).

[159] Allen-Ebrahimian, Bethany, "How China Won the War Against Western Media," *Foreign Policy*, March 4, 2016, http://foreignpolicy.com/2016/03/04/china -won-war-western-media-censorship-propaganda-communist-party/.

[160] Pomerantsev (2014) describes this phenomenon in Russia.

[161] Flegenheimer, Matt and Scott Shane, "Countering Trump, Bipartisan Voices Strongly Affirm Findings on Russian Hacking," *New York Times*, January 5, 2017, https://www.nytimes.com/2017/01/05/us/politics/taking-aim-at- trump-leaders-strongly-affirm-findings-on-russian-hacking.html.

attention, either misleading voters, or requiring them to spend more time to separate out which information is credible from that which is false.

Governments also use online armies for the second purpose of flooding—distraction—hiring thousands of people to post distracting information during sensitive events, what analysts have called "third-generation" Internet controls.[162] During protests surrounding Russian elections in 2011, pro-Kremlin Twitter users allegedly flooded anti-Kremlin hashtags with slogans and meaningless tweets, making it more difficult for anti-Kremlin users to find useful information and coordinate action.[163] Similar tactics have allegedly been used in democracies—the Mexican government, for example, has been accused of trying to thwart protests with bots that flood Twitter hashtags with meaningless punctuation.[164] As I will discuss more in chapter 6, China's "Fifty Cent Party," social media users who post at the government's direction, often write positive social media posts to shift attention from negative events.[165]

Flooding is not a phenomenon specific to the Internet; it also appears in traditional and popular media. During sensitive periods, Chinese propaganda authorities mandate that newspapers write "positive news" to make negative events less salient.[166] Russian authorities are also known to employ this tactic—the Kremlin has been know to suggest that news and television should focus on positive stories.[167]

---

[162] Deibert et al. (2010, pgs. 6–7).

[163] Goncharov, Maxim, "The Dark Side of Social Media," *TrendLabs Security Intelligence Blog*, December 7, 2011, http://blog.trendmicro.com/trendlabs-security-intelligence/the-dark-side-of-social-media/.

[164] Suárez-Serrato et al. (2016).

[165] King, Pan and Roberts (2017), "China's Paid Trolls: Meet the 50-cent party," *New Statesman*, http://www.newstatesman.com/politics/politics/2012/10/china's-paid-trolls-meet-50-cent-party.

[166] Brady (2008, pg. 95), Stockmann (2012, pg. 82); Stockmann and Gallagher (2011).

[167] Pomerantsev (2014).

2.9.2 Flooding Directed at the Media

The second type of flooding occurs when the authority directs the information to the media. By collecting data, analyzing it, and presenting these results to the media in an easily reportable format, the authority can encourage the media to report on a particular story. The media then may present this story to the public using the prepackaged version to reduce media costs. The public, however, may not recognize that the source of the information is the government itself, but instead view the news as independent.

Politicians, companies, and interest groups sometimes spend money to support scientific research that can bolster their product or cause. Research findings generated by authorities are then often picked up by the media to present a "balanced" view of the issue, but often do not disclose their funders directly.[168] Infamously, Philip Morris sponsored research claiming that cigarettes were not damaging to health. According to prosecutors, the company created the Tobacco Industry Research Committee (TIRC) in 1954 "to refute, undermine, and neutralize information coming from the objective scientific and medical community."[169] In 1998, tobacco companies sponsored the Center for Indoor Air Research (CIAR) to counter research on the detrimental effects of second-hand smoke. Confidential documents released as part of a 1998 settlement show that Philip Morris used the 244 studies produced by CIAR from 1989 to 1999 to fight public perceptions that second-hand smoke causes cancer.[170] Although Philip Morris is one particularly pernicious example, research funded by special interests and companies

---

[168] Shapiro (2016).
[169] "Complaint for Injunctions, Mandatory Injunctions, Damages, Restitution, Disgorgement, Penalties, and Other Relief," *UCSF Truth Tobacco Industry Documents*, June 5, 1996, http://www.library.ucsf.edu/sites/all/files/ucsf _assets/wacomplaint.pdf.
[170] Muggli et al. (2001).

to balance scientific consensus is very common, with examples ranging from head injuries in the NFL to skepticism on climate change.[171] Authorities can also use press releases to try to drive media coverage.[172] Grimmer (2013, pg. 129–130) finds that local papers will often use large amounts of language from U.S. legislators' press releases directly in news articles. He argues that press releases are purposely written in the style of news stories, acting as a subsidy for newspapers because journalists do not even have to rewrite them in order to print. Similarly, beginning with the Clinton administration and accelerating under the Bush administration, dozens of U.S. bureaucracies regularly released video press releases that supported particular government policies. These press releases were directly aired on local news programs without acknowledging that the government itself had produced them.[173]

Countries can use their own news agencies to push their soft power abroad. China's *Xinhua* news agency's worldwide expansion reflects a strategy to promote China's view of political events in foreign papers, as *Xinhua* spins stories quite differently than Western media.[174] In many countries with a small domestic news presence, *Xinhua* is frequently syndicated.[175] By making *Xinhua* stories deliberately cheap, China promotes its perspective on world events, increasing its international audience.

---

[171] Kain (2009, pg. 700), Stone (2011, pg. 398).

[172] Cook (1989, pg. 108–109).

[173] Barstow, David, and Robin Stein, "Under Bush, a New Age of Prepackaged TV News," *The New York Times*, March 13, 2005, http://www.nytimes.com/2005/03/13/politics/under-bush-a-new-age-of-prepackaged-tv-news.html.

[174] See Roberts, Stewart and Airoldi (2016) for a quantitative analysis of media slant between Xinhua and Western news sources.

[175] Shambaugh (2013, pg. 230).

2.9.3 When Does Flooding Affect Access and Expression?

In order for the flooding mechanism to be effective, the media and citizens need to be likely to consume the low-cost information produced by the authority instead of the information with which it intends to compete. Like friction, flooding-based methods of censorship will be more effective when the media and citizens have a higher elasticity of demand for information, or when the cost of information is a primary determinant of whether the media uses the information or citizens consume it. When citizens and the media are very affected by the cost of information, low-cost information produced and disseminated by the authority will be readily consumed and citizens will be unwilling to sort through the distracting information to find its alternative.

When propaganda is too obvious, it can generate a "boomerang effect," where propaganda is discredited by the public.[176] Flooding will therefore be more effective if citizens are not aware that it is generated by the authority. The authority could achieve this in one of two ways. First, it could build trust in its own sources of media and discredit alternative sources of media so that citizens are more likely to turn to government sources for information. Chinese state-run news sources, for example, proactively discredit Western media, though they still struggle with maintaining credibility in the eyes of the public.[177] Alternatively, it could hide the fact that it is manipulating the information environment, using media or individuals who look as though they are not related to the authority to spread the information. Individuals hired to post pro-government content on social media are examples of authority-funded information that is supposed to appear spontaneous. The less that individuals and the media are aware that the authority is behind the information, the less they will be able to discredit it.

---

[176] Jansen and Martin (2003).
[177] Gang and Bandurski (2011).

However, unlike friction, it is less imperative for authorities that their efforts to flood remain invisible since the public typically has fewer objections to the production of information than its suppression. Further, awareness of flooding does not usually bring attention directly to the information that the authority is trying to hide, and therefore does not undermine the authority as much as awareness of efforts of friction or fear. In this way, flooding should be a less risky strategy than friction or fear because awareness of these methods will not be as likely to produce backlash.

2.9.4 Flooding Has Become Cheaper with the Internet

Most authorities can participate in flooding if they have sufficient funds to do so—authorities may not have control over information they are trying to hide, but almost always have some type of information that they can promote.[178] The cost of creating information with which to flood will depend on the medium through which the authority intends to promote the information. The cost of flooding to the authority has decreased substantially in the digital age—Twitterers working for the Russian government, for example, use opposition hashtags to make it more difficult for the opposition to coordinate. The content of these tweets does not matter as long as they use the correct hashtag, and therefore such messages are very low cost. This type of flooding can even be implemented by bots rather than humans.

Similarly, flooding is easier to disguise in the age of the Internet than before the information age. In the past, personal opinions were not frequently voiced in the public domain—newspapers distributed information and officials and community leaders could make speeches or write op-eds, but

---

[178] Gunitsky (2015) provides a useful overview of how regimes can take advantage of the Internet using online propaganda.

typical citizens did not announce their positions. Today, however, individuals share descriptions of even mundane aspects of their lives and personal views on issues. These individuals do not necessarily have a public reputation to protect. The prevalence of online opinion makes it easier to disguise those who are paid by the government as individuals who genuinely hold these views.

The ability for individuals to bypass the media to share stories directly with the public also can allow for flooding to be more effective. Whereas the media decides which stories to include by making editorial decisions, social media is prioritized to consumers through algorithms. Authorities interested in using flooding can reverse-engineer and take advantage of these algorithms and coordinate to prioritize their information to consumers. If propagandists can find ways for users to engage with information through "clickbait" headlines or by disguising themselves as news media, they may be more likely to filter to the top of a social media algorithm.[179]

In other more traditional media, flooding may be more expensive. If authorities hope to spread their message in ways that look like news articles in traditional media, they need to distribute press releases that newspapers are likely to pick up and print. If these messages are persuasive, not just distracting, then the autocrat might need to collect data or conduct research to make the flooded messages convincing. Flooding via television requires either some control of the media network or large amounts of money for paid programming and advertising. Alternatively, some authorities may host high-profile events or news conferences to attract attention, and these events themselves can be expensive.

---

[179] Roberts, Hannah, "Google made changes to its search algorithm that unintentionally made it vulnerable to the spread of fake news, sources say," *Business Insider*, December 10, 2016, http://www.businessinsider.com/google-algorithm-change-fake-news-rankbrain-2016-12.

Flooding is the least draconian mechanism of censorship and it is rarely illegal even in democracies, and therefore it is the least likely to cause backlash. However, like friction and fear, it can have long-term costs for governments. If citizens discover government flooding efforts, it may undermine the credibility of the information environment, making the spread of misinformation and rumors more likely. As with censorship by friction, authorities may also trick themselves with their own propaganda, assuring themselves that they have more support than they actually do by measuring the balance of online opinion.

Because flooding is the least objectionable to the public of all the mechanisms, it will be used relatively more than friction and fear in societies with strict information freedom laws and intense competition between groups, for example, in democracies. Flooding may be used to complement or substitute for methods of fear and friction in cases where the authority does not have complete control over information, such as during sensitive periods or sudden high-profile events that could endanger the existence of the authority. In periods of crisis, when friction breaks down because individuals are motivated to seek out information, governments may turn to flooding as the public may seek out information of an unfolding situation and come across government-flooded media.[180] However, these may also be moments when the public is willing to spend more time ascertaining the credibility of the source, and therefore flooding, like friction, may be relatively less effective during crises than during time periods where public demand for information is more elastic.

---

[180] Baum and Groeling (2010) show that the government has an informational advantage at the beginning of a crisis, when less information about the crisis is out, but the public is still attentive to the event.

2.10 CONCLUSION

Fear, friction, and flooding—the mechanisms of censorship—are not specific to information-communication technologies or media. Over time, regime types, and issue areas, we have seen instances of each of these mechanisms of information manipulation in this chapter. However, the blend of strategies will vary across government structures, depend on the threats the governments face, and change in new information environments. As the structure and flow of information changes due to new technologies, the way that citizens and the media react to censorship and the costs censorship has for authorities change. In particular, the nature of the trade-off between using fear or punitive methods to create censorship and more porous methods based on friction or flooding will depend on the goals of the state and the costs that censorship inflicts on governments.

The logic of fear, friction, and flooding all point to a strategy of porous censorship in the digital age. In particular, the Internet has made fear more costly for regimes and friction and flooding relatively cheap. As more people participate online, repression must be credible to a larger number of people in order to enforce self-censorship. Yet because information is easily duplicated, substituted, and replaced, small variations in the cost of access in the form of friction can have large impacts on what the majority of Internet users consume. Similarly, the Internet has made flooding relatively cheap as government propaganda efforts online can be more easily automated and masked.

CHAPTER THREE

Censorship in China

The mechanisms of fear, friction, and flooding introduced in the last chapter illustrate the ways in which censorship can affect citizens and the media. The impact of each of these mechanisms on the spread of information varies across contexts. Some political entities, like totalitarian regimes, have opted for fear-based forms of censorship when power is concentrated in the hands of the government and awareness of control does not thwart government objectives. In other periods, authoritarian regimes have opted for friction- and flooding-based censorship that slows, but does not completely prevent, access to information, in order to reduce the probability of backlash or allow for more economic growth and internationalization. The constraints political entities face, the goals of the government, and the technological environment affect the capability of authorities to use each mechanism of censorship and the ways in which citizens will react to censorship.

In this chapter, I describe how the theory of censorship applies to modern China. First, I follow information control in China from the Mao era to the present. I describe how the Chinese state has adapted its censorship strategy to the changing goals of the state and the technological environment to balance information control with economic development, information collection, and fear of popular backlash. I follow these trade-offs through the Cultural Revolution, reform and opening, to the turning point of the Tiananmen Square protests and the rise of the Internet. I delineate the current institutional censorship structure and strategy in China and describe how the censorship system's ability to control information consumption while minimizing the perception of control enables it to effectively prioritize information for the vast majority of the population while minimizing the economic and political side effects of censorship.

3.1 MODERN HISTORY OF INFORMATION CONTROL IN CHINA

In this section I describe how the Chinese government's information control apparatus has evolved since the Mao era. The modern history of China not only provides context for the current period but also illustrates the political trade-offs between censorship mechanisms. In particular, highly observable methods of censorship based primarily on fear in the Maoist era have shifted toward less complete mechanisms of censorship based on friction and flooding after reform in an effort to contain the negative side effects of fear-based censorship on the economy, government information gathering, and political backlash. Even after the Tiananmen crisis, a turning point in information control strategy in China, the government opted to strengthen methods of censorship that were less intrusive to the average citizen rather than revert to censorship based on overt control, an indication of how overt censorship methods conflicted with its goals of economic growth and internationalization. The government's emphasis on friction- and flooding-based methods of censorship has only accelerated with the advent of the Internet, and the government has developed institutions that create porous censorship, relying on citizens' high elasticity of demand for information instead of their self-discipline.

3.1.1 Censorship under Mao (1949–1976)

Under Mao Zedong, the Chinese government exercised extensive authority in all areas of citizens' lives.[1] The Party viewed

---

[1] Walder (1988, Chapter 1) describes patterns of authority under Mao.

information control as a central component of political control, and Party dogma, ideology, and doctrine pervaded every part of daily routine. Propaganda teams were located in workplaces and schools to carry out work and education in the spirit of Party ideology and to implement mass mobilization campaigns.[2] Ordinary citizens were regularly encouraged to engage in self-criticism—publicly admitting and promising to rectify "backward" thoughts.

Under Mao, the introduction of "thought work" (思想工作) into aspects of everyday life meant that fear played a primary role in controlling the spread of information, as each citizen was aware of political control over speech and fearful of the consequences of stepping over the line. Although the severity of punishment for transgressions varied throughout the Maoist era, everyday speech could land citizens in jail or worse— criticizing your cat (in Chinese, a word that sounds like Mao) or giving your children unpatriotic names could be considered criminal.[3] Drastic punishments for both formal and informal speech and a system that encouraged citizens to report their closest friends and family members to authorities led to an environment of extreme self-censorship.[4] Fear transformed personal relationships between individuals from "friendship" to "comradeship," where private information could not be shared even between friends as betrayal of friendship was encouraged and commonplace.[5]

Newspapers, which became entirely state-run soon after Mao took power, were seen as a mouthpiece of the state rather than a mechanism of government oversight.[6] The Chinese Communist Party (CCP) adopted a Leninist view of the media: newspapers

---

[2] See Shambaugh (2007) for a summary of propaganda under Mao and Unger (1982) for a detailed description of education under Mao.

[3] Link (2002).

[4] Shirk (1982, pg. 130–135).

[5] Vogel (1965).

[6] Zhao (1998b, pg. 19).

should speak for the Party. By promoting Party ideology, and encouraging mass mobilization and positive thoughts, Leninist principles encourage the media to simultaneously educate and speak for the working class. Media—including radio, newspapers, and television—were run by central, provincial, and municipal governments directly, and were guided by the Central Propaganda Department of the CCP.

During this period, China, which was closed off from the Western world in an information environment completely controlled by the state, had arguably among the most "complete" control of information a country could muster, akin to today's North Korea. Citizens were aware of political control of all of their actions in their work, personal, and public lives. Cut off from private or non-state media and with relatively little interaction with citizens from other countries, they had little choice but to obediently follow propaganda controlled by Party media for fear of stark repercussions.

But even with ideological uniformity and totalitarian control based on repression, the Communist Party and the Chinese people paid a high price for highly observable forms of censorship that controlled citizens through brainwashing and deterrence. First, citizens' and officials' awareness of political control stifled the government's ability to gather information on the performance of policies, contributing to severe problems of economic planning and governance. The Great Leap Forward, in which around thirty million people died of starvation in the late 1950s, has been partially attributed to local officials' fear of reporting actual levels of grain production to the center, leading them to report inflated numbers.[7] Even after the Great Leap Forward, the inability of the Chinese bureaucracy to extract true economic reports from local officials and citizens led to greater economic instability and failed economic policies and plans.[8]

---

[7] Li and Yang (2005).
[8] Huang (1994).

Such extensive control also imposed explicit constraints on economic growth. Large amounts of trade with other countries was not possible without loosening restrictions on the exchange of information with foreigners. Innovation and entrepreneurship require risk-taking, creativity, and access to the latest technology, all difficult under high levels of fear that encourage risk-aversion. Millions of people were affixed with class labels that made them second-class citizens or were imprisoned in Chinese gulags that prevented them from participating in the economy. Often those who were persecuted had high levels of education and skills that the Chinese economy desperately needed.[9] The planned economy in concert with high levels of fear stifled economic productivity and kept the vast majority of Chinese citizens in poverty.

Finally, even in a totalitarian society with little contact with the outside world, government ideological control over the everyday lives of citizens decreased the government's legitimacy and sowed the seeds of popular discontent. Mao's goal of ideological purity led him to encourage the Cultural Revolution, a decade-long period of chaos in China based on the premise of weeding out ideologically incorrect portions of society, which in the process killed millions of people and completely disrupted social order. The chaos of the Cultural Revolution, combined with resentment toward the extreme ideological left in the Chinese political system that had spawned it, created openings for dissent. In 1974, a poster written in Guangzhou under a pseudonym called explicitly for reform. Similar protests followed—during the first Tiananmen Incident in 1976, thousands of people turned out to protest the ideological left, and several years later, in the Democracy movement in 1978 and 1979, protesters explicitly called for democracy and human rights, including free speech.[10]

---

[9] Naughton (1996, pg. 89–91).
[10] Teiwes and Sun (2004); Brodsgaard (1981).

3.1.2 Censorship Reform before 1989

When Deng Xiaoping gained power in 1978, he initiated policies of reform and opening that were in part a reaction to the intense dissatisfaction of Chinese citizens with the Cultural Revolution and prying hand of the government in their personal affairs. One of the hallmarks of Deng's transition to a market economy, which began in 1978, was the government's retreat from the private lives of citizens and from control of the media. Important leaders within Deng's government realized the trade-offs between individual control and entrepreneurship, creativity, and competition required by the market and decreased government emphasis on ideological correctness of typical citizens in China.[11] In the late 1970s and early 1980s, the CCP rehabilitated those who had been political victims during the Cultural Revolution, removing class labels and releasing political prisoners, a process that enabled more than twenty million additional people to participate in the economy, many of whom had high levels of education.[12] As Gold (1985) describes, the "omnipresent fear" that had been common in the Mao era lessened and personal relationships again became primarily private and economic. Citizens began to criticize the government and express dissatisfaction, privately at first, but later more publicly.

The government not only retreated from the private lives of individuals to stimulate the economy and address dissatisfaction, but also loosened its control over the media in order to reduce its own economic burden in the information industry.[13] Media—which under Mao had been publicly funded—imposed large operational costs on the government. As other aspects of the Chinese economy privatized, the government began to

---

[11] Gold (1985).
[12] Naughton (1996, pg. 89–91).
[13] Lynch (1999, Chapter 2).

commercialize the media to lessen its strain on government resources. The commercialization of news allowed the news media to respond to citizens' demands for entertainment and economic, international, and political news, which proved to be extremely lucrative for Chinese media companies. The lessened control also allowed Chinese media to compete with the new onslaught of international information that began to pour in as international trade and interactions increased, and Chinese media companies were able to innovate to retain market share in an increasingly competitive information environment.[14]

The 1980s also witnessed an increasing decentralization of the economy from the central Party planning system to the localities.[15] As the government began to decentralize its control, it began to rely on the media to ensure that local officials were acting in the interests of the Party. A watchdog media could help keep local businesses, officials, and even local courts in check.[16] Investigative journalism on local corruption was first encouraged by members of the central government in the 1980s, a trend that accelerated in the 1990s. While investigative journalism serves citizens by exposing corrupt politicians or lax economic practices, it also serves the state by exposing the defective aspects of its own system. Freer media in a decentralized state, it has been argued, can serve the government's own interest as much as it can serve the interests of citizens.[17]

Although restrictions on the press were significantly relaxed, the CCP did not completely loosen constraints on speech or the media during the 1980s, and there was significant political conflict within the Party over how free the media should be immediately following reform and opening. High-level members of Deng's government Hu Yaobang and Zhao Ziyang

---

[14] Stockmann (2012, pg. 50–59).
[15] Naughton (1996, Chapter 3).
[16] Liebman (2011).
[17] Zhou (2000).

supported greater freedom of the press, while more conservative members such as Deng Liqun thought that more emphasis should be placed on government-controlled thought work.[18] Conflict between these two groups within the Party and Deng's vacillation between them were hallmarks of CCP politics during this period. For example, Deng Liqun was head of the Central Propaganda Department from 1981 to 1985, but was removed because of his conservative stances for the more liberal Zhu Houze, who was later replaced for being too open to reform.[19] This oscillation between stances on media reflected a larger internal dispute over the extent to which the Party should play a role in the press.

However, the CCP did take significant steps toward relaxing control over the flow of information in the 1980s to loosen enforcement over speech, particularly relative to the Maoist era. By 1982, the Chinese constitution began to guarantee free speech and expression for all Chinese citizens, including freedom of the press, assembly, and demonstration.[20] Commercialization of Chinese newspapers began in 1979 with the first advertisement and gradually the press began making more profit from sales of advertising and less from government subsidies.[21] Radio and television, which had previously been controlled by the central and provincial levels of government, expanded rapidly to local levels of government and was also commercialized.[22]

By the late 1980s, prominent citizens and officials were calling for even more expanded versions of free speech. Even prominent government figures, such as Hu Jiwei, former editor of the government newspaper the *People's Daily*, called publicly for more freedom of speech, emphasizing how freedom of speech could promote political stability by revealing citizens' grievances

---

[18] Brady (2008, pg. 40).
[19] Brady (2008, pg. 40–41).
[20] Zhao (1998b, pg. 44).
[21] Shirk (2011, pg. 1–9).
[22] Zhao (1998b, pg. 55).

rather than keeping them hidden from the government.[23] Hu was in the midst of drafting a press law to clarify the Party's role in the press when the student protests were sparked by the death of Hu Yaobang in April 1989. These pro-democracy protests centered in Beijing's Tiananmen Square spread all over China, culminating in an internal CCP crisis and a large-scale violent crackdown on protesters on June 4, 1989, that was condemned internationally.

The June 4 crisis marked a turning point in government strategy with respect to the media and the press. Whether or not a freer media had in fact contributed to the Tiananmen protests, there was widespread consensus among Party elites after the crackdown that the loosening of media restrictions had aggravated the student demonstrations. In particular, during the months of the protests, reformers within the Party had allowed and even encouraged newspapers to discuss the protests.[24] In the immediate aftermath of the crackdown on the protesters and clearing of the square on June 4, 1989, censorship ramped up quickly. A large-scale crackdown on journalists, activists, and academics reintroduced widespread fear into the private lives of influential individuals, particularly among those who had been involved in the protest events. Government officials were ordered to return to the model of the media serving the Party and expressing enthusiasm for government policies.[25]

3.1.3 Post-Tiananmen: Control Minimizing the Perception of Control

One might think that after an event as consequential as the 1989 protests in Tiananmen Square, the government might return

---

[23] Zhao (1998b, pg. 36). "没有新闻自由就没有真正的安定," 世界经济导报, http://www.64memo.com/disp.aspx?Id=9075&k=%E5%A4%A9%E5%AE%89%E9%97%A8.

[24] Gang and Bandurski (2011, pg. 71–72), Brady (2008, pg. 42).

[25] Zhao (1998b, pg. 45–46).

indefinitely to tight control and thought work that had existed under Mao, as many leaders thought that loosened control had culminated in a direct threat to the regime. Yet a return to complete restriction of information and pervasive fear to control private and public communication between citizens was also not consistent with continued expansion and internationalization of the market economy on which the regime sought to base its legitimacy. Although the belief among government officials that free media had contributed to unrest prevented the CCP from returning to the extent of press freedom before Tiananmen Square, Deng did not return to the version of pre-reform information control that relied on fear-based control of individuals' everyday lives and instead quickly reversed the post-Tiananmen crackdown on speech.

Instead, government policy evolved toward a censorship strategy that attempted to minimize the perception of information control among ordinary citizens while still playing a central role in prioritizing information for the public. In essence, the government strengthened mechanisms of friction and flooding while for the most part staying out of the private lives of citizens. A few years after the Tiananmen crisis, the CCP returned to an apparent loosening of control, and commercialization of the media resumed in the mid-1990s.[26] After Deng's famous "Southern Tour" in 1992, meant to reemphasize the economy, broader discussions and criticisms of the state were again allowed, even publicly and even about democracy.[27]

Even though the government did not revert to Maoist-era censorship, the government tightened its grip on the media, officials, journalists, and technology in a way that allowed targeted control: by managing the gatekeepers of information, the government could de-prioritize information unfavorable to

[26] Zhao (1998b, pg. 47–50).
[27] Ding (2001, pg. 33).

itself and expand its own production of information to compete with independent sources. Even though the media had already undergone significant commercialization, the government strengthened institutional control over the media.[28] First, the CCP created stricter licensing requirements to control the types of organizations that could report news. They also required that journalists reapply for press cards, which required training in government ideology.[29] Despite extensive commercialization that created the perception among readers that news was driven by demand rather than supply, the government retained control over the existence, content, and personnel decisions of newspapers throughout the country, allowing the government to effectively, if not always explicitly, control publishing.[30]

Deng also strengthened control over Party propaganda and strategies of flooding. In 1990, one of the Party's leading news agencies, *Xinhua*, was close to bankrupt.[31] The government proactively changed its propaganda strategies after Tiananmen Square, adapting Western theories of advertising and persuasion, and linking thought work with entertainment to make it more easily consumed by the public.[32] After Tiananmen, the CCP decided to instruct newspapers to follow *Xinhua*'s lead on important events and international news, much as they had done with the *People's Daily* during the 1960s.[33] In the 1990s, the Party also renewed its emphasis on "patriotic education" in schools around the country, ensuring that the government's interpretations of events were the first interpretations of politics that students learned.[34]

---

[28] Brady (2009).

[29] Stockmann (2012, pg. 60).

[30] Stockmann (2012, pg. 52).

[31] Brady (2008, pg. 113).

[32] Brady (2008, pg. 73).

[33] Brady (2008, pg. 113).

[34] Zhao (1998a).

3.2 CENSORSHIP OF THE CHINESE INTERNET

During the period following the Tiananmen crackdown, China witnessed the arrival of the web in 1995, which complicated the government's ability to control the gatekeepers of information as channels of information transitioned from a "one to many" model, where a few media companies transferred information to many people, to a "many to many" model where everyday people could contribute to media online and easily share news and opinions with each other.[35] Had the government been worried about complete control over the information environment, we would expect it to try to slow the expansion of the Internet within the country. Instead, China actively pursued it. The Chinese government aggressively expanded Internet access throughout the country and encouraged online enterprises, as the CCP saw these as linked to economic growth and development.[36]

Yet as it was pursuing greater connectivity, the government simultaneously developed methods of online information control that would allow it to channel information online. In 1994, the government issued regulations for the Internet, concurrent with the Internet's arrival in China, stipulating that the Internet could not be used to harm the interest of the state.[37] Immediately, the state began developing laws and technology that allowed it more control over information online, including filtering, registration of online websites, and capabilities for government surveillance.

Descendants of the post-1989 period, the institutions that now implement information control in China for both news media and the Internet are aimed at targeting large-scale media

---

[35] National Committee for Cadre Training Materials (2011, pg. 5).
[36] Hong (2014, pg. 11).
[37] "中华人民共和国计算机信息系统安全保护条例," State Council, http://www.lawinfochina.com/display.aspx?lib=law&id=12136&CGid=.

platforms and important producers of information in both traditional and online media to make it more difficult for the average consumer to come across information that the Chinese government finds objectionable. The CCP also retains control over key information channels in order to have the capacity to generate and spread favorable content to citizens. The CCP's direct control over these information providers allows them the flexibility to make censorship restrictions more difficult to penetrate during particular periods and to loosen constraints during others. This censorship system is essentially a taxation system of information on the Internet, allowing the government to have it two ways: by making information *possible* to access, those who care enough (such as entrepreneurs, academics, or those with international business connections) will easily bypass controls and find the information they need, but for the masses, the impatience that accompanies surfing the web makes the controls effective even though they are porous.

The Party's primary avenue for influencing information control is through the CCP Propaganda Department (中共中央宣传部), hereafter CCPPD. The CCPPD is the main institution that monitors and devises strategies both for what content should be censored and for what types of content should be disseminated across all information media in China, including the Internet, mobile phones, print publications, radio, television, art, and education materials used in schools or vocational training.[38] The CCPPD can issue directives to gatekeepers in any of these media, from TV producers to Internet content providers to those in charge of education, to either censor or spread particular types of information.

The CCPPD is the center of the Chinese information control apparatus, but it delegates to a variety of smaller institutions in the state branch of the government responsibility to carry

---

[38] Shambaugh (2007).

out censorship and propaganda in different media in China.[39] The State Council Information Office (国务院信息办公室; SCIO) and General Administration of Press and Publication (新闻出版总署) are responsible for published media, including the licensing of publishers and Internet publishers, monitoring news and foreign journalists, and banning and pre-screening books. The Ministry of Culture (文化部) and the Ministry of Education (教育部) are responsible for regulation of the arts and education, respectively. The Ministry of Industry and Information Technology (工业和信息化部) is responsible for regulating the information technology industry. In 2011, the State Internet Information Office was established specifically to regulate content on the Internet.[40] The CCP also has institutions in charge of punishing those who violate information laws. The Ministry of Public Security (公安部), the institution that overseas the police, enforces censorship laws from violations of the Internet laws to publishing licensing laws. The Ministry of State Security (国家安全部) is in charge of intelligence gathering, which includes Internet surveillance that may be used to enforce information control laws.[41]

In 2013, president Xi Jinping upgraded the State Internet Information Office to create a new, separate administration for regulating Internet content and cyberspace, called the Cyberspace Administration of China (国家互联网信息办公室; CAC), run by the Central Cybersecurity and Informatization Leading Small Group (中央网络安全和信息化领导小组) and personally chaired by Xi Jinping. Xi, allegedly worried that

---

[39] Because there are many institutions with authority over various aspects of the media, in practice this control can be redundant and fragmented. See Yang (2013) for discussion.

[40] Buckley, Chris, "China Sets Up Agency to Tighten Grip on Internet," *Reuters*, May 4, 2011, http://www.reuters.com/article/us-china-internet-idUSTRE7436SA20110504.

[41] See Wang and Minzner (2015) for a description of the recent history of China's security apparatus.

there were too many bureaucracies in control of regulating the Internet,[42] formed the CAC to streamline Internet control.[43] Even though the CAC duplicates some of the responsibilities of existing ministries for information control, the new administration also placed regulation of the Internet and the State Internet Information Office directly under Xi's control.[44] The CAC sought to more strictly enforce censorship online, including shutting down websites that do not comply with censorship regulations, and increasing the prevalence of the government's perspective online by digitizing propaganda. The creation of the CAC shows the importance the Xi administration has placed on managing content on the Internet.

The institutions described above use a variety of laws and regulations to control information in their respective purviews. In China, these laws tend to be relatively ambiguous to give the state maximal flexibility in their enforcement. Censorship laws disallow a wide range of political discourse, including anything that "harms the interest of the nation," "spreads rumors or disturbs social order," "insults or defames third parties," or "jeopardizes the nation's unity."[45] Although, due to widespread discussion of protest events and criticism of the government online, the government cannot possibly (and likely would not want to) arrest all those who violate a generous interpretation of this law, these institutions keep a close watch particularly on high-profile journalists, activists, and bloggers, developing relationships with these key players to control content and

[42] "习近平谈关于加快完善互联网管理领导体制," 人民网, *People's Daily Online*, November 15, 2013, http://politics.people.com.cn/n/2013/1115/c1001-23559689.html.

[43] Alshabah, Nabil, "Information Control 2.0: The Cyberspace Administration of China Tames the Internet," *Merics China Monitor*, September 16, 2016, http://www.merics.org/en/merics-analysis/analyseschina-monitor/information-control-20.html#c15313.

[44] Lam (2015).

[45] "Falling Short: Appendix II: Media Law in China," *Committee to Protect Journalists*, https://cpj.org/reports/2008/06/12ii-2.php.

arresting those they view as dangerous. These activities are facilitated by surveillance tools that require users to register for social media sites with their real names and require Internet providers to keep records of users' activities.[46] Since Xi Jinping became president in 2012, additional laws and regulations have been written to prevent "hacking and Internet-based terrorism."[47]

The government keeps a much closer watch on the media infrastructure itself than on typical citizens. The propaganda department issues directives to the traditional media ordering them either not to report on content or to promote particular types of content. Online news portals are not allowed to post news that is not from state news outlets unless they themselves have a journalistic license from the state.[48] The CCPPD issues censorship directives to social media companies to filter content, ordering them to delete individual posts that are about particular topics, most frequently topics related to collective action, activists, pornography, or criticism of censorship.[49] Some websites automatically filter content by keywords, preventing individuals from posting anything with a sensitive term before the post is reviewed by censors. Online search providers, such as Baidu and Yahoo, omit particular websites from being listed when a user searches for sensitive words. This process, known as search filtering, also occurs within social media firms, such as Sina Weibo, which omits references to sensitive trending topics and disallows users from searching for media posts that contain particular terms.[50]

---

[46] Deibert et al. (2010, pg. 465).

[47] Lam (2015), see: http://www.npc.gov.cn/npc/xinwen/2016-11/07/content_2001605.htm, http://www.gov.cn/jrzg/2012-12/28/content_2301231.htm.

[48] Wang and Faris (2008).

[49] See MacKinnon (2009); King, Pan and Roberts (2013, 2014); Cairns and Carlson (2016); Miller (2017); Knockel, Ruan and Crete-Nishihata (2017) for a discussion of what is censored.

[50] For a discussion of search filtering and keyword blocking see: Ng (2013); Knockel et al. (2015).

Not only can the government order traditional media to print particular articles and stories, but it also retains flooding power on the Internet. The Chinese government allegedly hires thousands of online commentators to write pseudonymously at its direction.[51] This so-called Fifty Cent Party, described more in chapter 6, is an army of paid Internet commentators who work at the instruction of the government to influence public opinion during sensitive periods. In other work, we have shown that these propagandists are largely instructed to promote positive feelings, patriotism, and a positive outlook on governance and are unleashed during particularly sensitive periods as a form of distraction.[52] This is largely in line with President Xi's own statements that public opinion guidance online should promote positive thinking and "positive energy."[53] Other scholars have posited that they are also sometimes instructed to defame activists or counter government criticism.[54]

In the case of international websites, where the government does not have the jurisdiction to directly control the media, the Great Firewall,[55] officially referred to by the Chinese government as the "Golden Shield Project" (金盾工程), blocks particular websites from IP addresses within China, preventing Chinese citizens from accessing websites the government deems objectionable.[56] The Great Firewall is sophisticated enough to censor particular pages or images from being accessed in China and also includes surveillance capabilities by tracking requests

[51] Han (2015).

[52] King, Pan and Roberts (2017).

[53] Bandurski, David, "The CCP's Positive Energy Obsession," *China Media Project*, December 15, 2015, http://cmp.hku.hk/2015/12/15/chinas-obsession-with-positive-energy/.

[54] Han (2015); Bandurski (2008); Miller (2016).

[55] The Great Firewall is under the purview of the Ministry of Public Security, but the implementation of the Firewall is overseen in conjunction with the Ministry of Industry and Information Technology. The CCPPD, public security, and other government agencies provide directives to these ministries with instructions on which sites should be blocked; see Tai (2014).

[56] For a list of websites blocked in China, visit greatfire.org.

from computers inside China to foreign websites.[57] It can also throttle websites, making them slower, instead of censoring them outright.

Because the government focuses control on gatekeepers of information, rather than individuals, from the perspective of an ordinary citizen in China the information control system poses few explicit constraints. Street stands sell tens of different types of newspapers, all competing for attention by pandering to the consumer. It is not obvious what stories have been redacted from the newspapers and which the editors have been ordered to print. Internet access is widely available in China, with a flourishing social media environment where even vitriolic criticisms of the Chinese government are common. As I will show in chapter 4, many Chinese citizens are not scared by censorship. Censorship does not interfere with most citizens' daily lives or perceived access to information. In fact, many citizens do not even know that certain types of censorship exist.

For those who are aware of censorship and are motivated to circumvent it, censorship poses an inconvenience rather than a complete constraint on their freedom. Even though some foreign websites are blocked, they can be accessed with a VPN. Foreign newspapers and banned books can be bought in underground bookstores or in Hong Kong. Social media posts can be written with slightly different keywords to evade censors who filter sensitive terms.[58] For the well-educated, well-to-do elite, censorship is annoying but rarely makes information impossible to obtain. The porous nature of censorship allows those who really care about finding the information to access it, while effectively prioritizing information for those who are less interested.

That information *can* be accessed sidesteps many of the trade-offs that were present in the Maoist era. The perception

---

[57] Tai (2014, pg. 68–69).
[58] MacKinnon (2008); Hiruncharoenvate, Lin and Gilbert (2015); King, Lam and Roberts (2017).

that information control in China is porous means that many citizens believe that they consume relevant information and this in part prevents widespread backlash that more repressive forms of censorship could create. Pervasive criticism of the government online and in the international and domestic media also provides the central government with access to information about its own performance. The technical ability to access information imposes fewer constraints on the economy than complete inaccessibility of information would, as companies and students can evade censorship to access information that is central to their education, business, or research.

Yet, the system provides effective control of the typical person. Typical citizens in China can access almost any information that they want to access, if they can find the time and the resources. But because they are uninterested in politics, busy, and often unaware of the existence of alternative information, most people in China do not go out of their way to find information that is difficult to gain access to. Instead, they consume information that is relatively easy to find, often that which is prioritized by the information control infrastructure of the government. The flexibility of the censorship system drives a wedge between technologically savvy, politically interested individuals who easily circumvent censorship restrictions and those who are more affected by them.

This is not to say that the Chinese government has perfected information control, or that its current strategy is without its own trade-offs and risks for the government. First, any type of censorship creates a drag on the economy. Many companies operating in China have reported that information friction like the Great Firewall has severe negative impacts on their businesses because it limits access to technologies.[59] Chinese websites are

---

[59] Zimmerman, James, "Censorship in China Also Blocks Business Growth," *Wall Street Journal*, May 17, 2016, http://www.wsj.com/articles/censorship-in-china-also-blocks-business-growth-1463504866.

burdened with hiring censors, which makes them less competitive in international business. For average citizens, even though censorship is less observable than it might be under censorship that employs high levels of fear, it is not without footprints. When citizens run into traces of censorship, it can decrease the legitimacy of the government regime and cause backlash, as I will show empirically in the next chapter. In this way, the government censorship regime can undermine its own stated purpose.

For the government, the strategy of porous censorship also entails risks precisely because it is possible to sidestep. Porous information control relies on citizens to be indifferent enough to be satisfied with the information the government prioritizes. Certain types of events—such as financial crises, natural disasters, or government scandals—may create sufficient incentives for citizens to search out and find information that they otherwise might not come across. Moments when enough citizens are motivated enough to learn how to outsmart government media control are those when the information management strategy comes under the most pressure.

However, the Chinese government has come a long way in managing information while avoiding many of its costs. Comparing the information management strategy under Mao, which micro-managed every aspect of citizens' lives, to today information management is less visible and less costly. Yet even while minimizing the perception of control, the government is able to wield significant influence over which information citizens will come across. I turn to measuring how censorship influences the spread of information in the subsequent chapters.

CHAPTER FOUR

Reactions to Experience with Censorship

On December 20, 2010, Fang Binxing, the architect of the Great Firewall, opened an account on Sina Weibo. Within minutes, Sina Weibo users began following and commenting on Fang's wall, deriding the censorship mastermind and encouraging users to "surround and watch" (围观), or subject him to public scrutiny.[1] Despite high-speed censorship of their comments, these users got their point across, with comments such as: "Old dog why don't you die?" (老狗何不去死?), "Destined to be nailed to the history of disgrace" (注定被钉在历史的耻辱上), and "SB" (short for a Chinese curse word). Ridiculed, Fang deleted his account and the comments with it within three hours.[2]

The history of the Internet in China is littered with examples of simmering public resentment against censorship boiling over publicly. In January 2013, journalists from the newspaper *Southern Weekly* took to the streets to protest what they saw as excessive censorship of a New Year's editorial. The journalists posted their concerns with censorship of the newspaper on their Sina Weibo accounts, prompting petitions advocating more freedom of speech that were circulated and signed by scholars, students, lawyers, and intellectuals.[3] In another example in

---

[1] "关注就是力量 围观改变中国," 南方周末, January 14, 2010, http://www.infzm.com/content/40097.

[2] "Netizens Force Fang Binxing (方 滨 兴), Father of the GFW, Off of Sina Microblog," *China Digital Times*, December 20, 2010, http://chinadigitaltimes.net/2010/12/netizens-force-fan-binxing-father-of-the-gfw-off-of-sina-microblog/.

[3] "Special Feature: The 'Southern Weekly' Controversy," *Freedom House*, January 18, 2013, https://freedomhouse.org/cmb/2013_southern_weekly.

2013, the Chinese government began blocking GitHub.com, an American-owned website that allows computer programmers to share code. Programmers around China protested the block online, led by former China Google executive Kai-Fu Lee, whose Weibo post concerning the block was forwarded 80,000 times: "GitHub is the preferred tool for programmers to learn and connect with the rest of the world. Blocking GitHub is unjustifiable, and will only derail the nation's programmers from the world, while bringing about a loss in competitiveness and insight."[4]

These examples are only a few among many in which awareness of censorship in China has inspired widespread backlash against the government. Censorship is costly to authoritarian regimes because it can create anger and reduce trust among the broader population, create economic inefficiencies, and complicate government efforts to collect information from the public. These costs have been exacerbated by the information age because as more people participate online, more people have firsthand experiences with censorship. Media training manuals provided to government officials in China emphasize that one of the main differences between online media and traditional media is that anyone can participate: "The capacity of individuals and societal organizations to broadcast has strengthened, the number of people broadcasting information has increased …everyone now has a microphone." The expanded number of people in the public sphere means that the structure of communication "has changed from 'few to many' to 'many to many,'" which means that a "small, mundane problem can quickly escalate into a political problem."[5] Autocrats have historically retained strict control over the few in traditional media, but controlling the many in the digital age is more difficult.

[4] Kan, Michael, "GitHub Unblocked in China after Former Google Head Slams Its Censorship," *Computer World*, January 23, 2013, http://www.computerworld.com/article/2493478/internet/github-unblocked-in-china-after-former-google-head-slams-its-censorship.html.

[5] National Committee for Cadre Training Materials (2011, 5–6).

Perhaps due to evidence of self-censorship of journalists, activists, and academics,[6] the academic literature has suggested that self-censorship may be the primary form of government control over the ordinary user of the Internet.[7] Fear, unknown threats, and arrests of typical citizens might persuade citizens to restrain their speech online. The implication is that if the government can be more threatening and make censorship more constraining, it could increase control of information, even in an online environment.

However, these common conceptions of the functioning of censorship in China have overlooked the risks that widespread repression entails for the government in the information age. Deterrence must be observable to work and the expansion of people involved in public discourse has reduced the credibility of government threats. Instead, potential backlash against censorship can create unrest that reduces the legitimacy of the regime. Thus, increases in observable online constraints for everyday users can counterintuitively *decrease* rather than increase control of information.

Aware of these costs, the government pursues two different censorship strategies: one for typical Internet users and another for activists, public opinion leaders, and journalists. For typical Internet users, the government uses the strategy of porous censorship to walk the fine line of controlling information while preventing censorship from backfiring. The goal of this strategy is to divert information with friction and through distractions in the form of flooding. This form of control generally does not make the information off-limits—typically it is still *possible* to access. For individuals who are intent on accessing information, porous censorship allows them to do so, limiting backlash and allowing the government to plausibly deny interference. For

---

[6] For discussions of self-censorship of journalists, activists, and academics see Stern and Hassid (2012); Link (2002); Lee and Lin (2006).

[7] Kalathil and Boas (2010, pg. 26), Wacker (2003, pg. 88).

those who are indifferent, the logic of porous censorship relies on citizens' busy schedules, relative indifference to politics, and numerous alternative sources of information and entertainment in Chinese media, wagering that, for the most part, citizens are not willing to go out of their way to gather information about politics.

The government reserves more traditional fear-based censorship strategy to target journalists, public opinion leaders, and activists. Government training manuals show that the government realizes that traditional media and a few public opinion leaders can control the online agenda in China. During public crises, the government advises focusing control over the news media and key online social media stories.[8] This, in turn, creates a secondary friction and flooding effect on the average Internet user by decreasing the prevalence of objectionable information and steering the conversation away from topics that are less desirable for the government without creating general awareness of censorship. This two-pronged strategy of censorship drives a wedge between key public opinion leaders and the public. Because these different groups experience different censorship tactics, the public is more likely to believe that key public opinion leaders are similarly unconstrained in posting and accessing media online.

In this chapter, I first describe China's two-pronged strategy of censorship, in particular how typical Internet users are less likely to be targeted with fear-based censorship than journalists, activists, and key opinion leaders. Using surveys, online experiments, and a unique set of social media datasets, I show that, despite government efforts to signal to the public the consequences of spreading sensitive information online, fear-based methods of censorship do not deter much of the large online population in China, which is accustomed to regularly

---

[8] National Committee for Cadre Training Materials (2011).

reading and discussing political information. Signals that particular information is off-limits do not persuade online users to avoid the topic. In fact, for ordinary citizens who consume and produce political information online in China, experience with censorship and awareness of censorship negatively affects their opinion of the state and may even make them more likely to read and write about topics that are viewed by the state as more sensitive, as they are alerted to topics the Chinese government deems dangerous.

4.1 CHINA'S TARGETED CENSORSHIP STRATEGY

As Internet use has expanded in China, the Chinese government has made efforts to minimize its potentially destabilizing political impact. Laws that govern Internet activity specify that a wide variety of information is not allowed to be written or re-shared on the Internet, including information that "harms the interest of the nation," "spreads rumors or disturbs social order," "insults or defames third parties," or "jeopardizes the nation's unity."[9] These regulations are sufficiently ambiguous that they give the state considerable leeway on the types of people they can punish for online behavior.

These laws apply to all Internet users, but journalists, activists, academics, and public opinion leaders are more likely to be punished than typical users of the Internet, even if they write similar information. In the recent crackdown on online rumors, many of those arrested were high-profile Internet users who hold disproportionate sway over the online community or were already involved in offline activities the CCP would consider subversive. Some Internet laws even state that information that is re-shared many times is more likely to be considered criminal

[9] "Falling Short: Appendix II: Media Law in China," *Committee to Protect Journalists*, https://cpj.org/reports/2008/06/12ii-2.php.

by the government, thereby targeting higher-profile social media users whose posts are more likely to be re-shared.[10] In one recent prominent example, Charles Xue, a Chinese businessman who was famous for his liberal commentary on social media and had more than ten million social media followers, was arrested in August 2013 and detained for almost eight months. Three weeks before his arrest, Xue and other prominent microbloggers attended a meeting where they were warned about the "social responsibilities of Internet celebrities," which included spreading positive messages on Weibo instead of negative messages. The government accompanies arrests with efforts to discredit these high-profile individuals—Charles Xue was arrested for and later confessed publicly to soliciting prostitutes.[11]

The government targets high-profile journalists, academics, and social media users in a way that obscures fear-based censorship to the rest of the online community. Individuals who have been subject to government censorship report experience similar to that of Xue's of being "invited to tea" by government officials, where they are sometimes asked for information, told to write or not write about certain topics, and offered threats or rewards for particular types of behavior. These private, targeted conversations are likely more influential because they are more credibly threatening—if the government is willing to sit down to tea with you, they not only care sufficiently to do something about your behavior, but can track you down. Because these conversations are private, they can also be concealed from a larger public who might object to such repression. Although even previously detained microbloggers sometimes show surprising persistence in continuing to write about topics that are

---

[10] "New Rules Create Online Rumor Straitjacket," *Xinhua*, September 9, 2013, http://news.xinhuanet.com/english/china/2013-09/09/c_125354622.htm.

[11] Feng, Wang, "Outspoken Chinese American Investor Charles Xue Detained in Beijing 'Prostitution Bust'," *South China Morning Post*, August 25, 2013, http://www.scmp.com/news/china-insider/article/1299448/outspoken-chinese-american-investor-charles-xue-detained-beijing.

off-limits,[12] we would expect that targeted individuals will be more likely to self-censor than those who do not feel singled out by the government.

However, for most people who violate these broad Internet laws in China, there is no punishment at all—thousands of social media users daily write content that could be considered in violation of these laws, and the vast majority of them are not punished. Fear for the typical Internet user is the knowledge that such enforcement *could* happen at any time, though for all practical purposes it is extremely unlikely. The Chinese government's own training manuals on how to control public crises provide evidence that it strategically uses targeted fear-based censorship of the media to control public crises on social media, rather than attempting to micromanage typical Internet users. Aware that they cannot control all social media users, the government warns against ignoring or disrespecting average citizens' opinions and encourages authorities to avoid ignoring the issue.[13] Focusing on controlling traditional media and public opinion leaders, who can set the agenda, rather than on control-ling typical social media users, can lead the conversation away from what is off-limits, but also will avoid incurring the large costs of widespread censorship documented in this chapter.

In recent years, China has sought to strengthen the credibility of the enforcement of these censorship laws for Internet users. First, to improve surveillance of Internet users, the government has begun to require that users provide official identification

---

[12] For example, Wang Gongquan, a microblogger whose account with more than one million followers was shut in 2012 and who himself was arrested for four months at the end of 2013, reactivated his account right after returning from prison, posting about his time in jail and attracting over 10,000 follow-ers in one day before it was shut down (Wertime, David, "Wang Gongquan: The mysterious return of the microblogger," *Sydney Morning Herald*, January 31, 2014, http://www.smh.com.au/world/wang-gongquan-the-mysterious-return-of-the-microblogger-20140131-hvamg.html).

[13] National Committee for Cadre Training Materials (2011).

when they register for social media accounts. In 2012, Sina Weibo, China's largest microblogging platform (similar to Twitter), began to require real name registration for users.[14] In 2015, real name registration became required on all Chinese social media sites.[15] Real name registration in combination with more invasive surveillance technologies make government efforts to hold Internet users accountable for their online actions more credible, since users can more easily be tracked and identified. These types of surveillance may increase in the future as the government is experimenting with more detailed tracking of users and online credit scores.[16] Better surveillance could allow the government to more credibly use fear on China's large Internet population.

Second, the government has increased the frequency of arrests of social media users. In 2013, under the new President Xi Jinping, the Ministry of Public Security conducted a campaign cracking down on online "rumors" and other information deemed illegal in China. Although many of the targets were famous microbloggers as described above, the crackdown also involved some typical Internet users who were thought to be spreading misinformation.[17] Exact estimates of the number of people arrested are unknown, but many suspect that during the crackdown thousands of people were arrested for their online writing.[18]

[14] Fu, Chan and Chau (2013).

[15] Chin, Josh, "China is Requiring People to Register Real Names For Some Internet Services," *Wall Street Journal*, February 4, 2015, https://www.wsj.com/articles/china-to-enforce-real-name-registration-for-internet-users-1423033973.

[16] Chin, Josh, and Gillian Wong, "China's New Tool for Social Control: A Credit Rating for Everything," *Wall Street Journal*, November 28, 2016, https://www.wsj.com/articles/chinas-new-tool-for-social-control-a-credit-rating-for-everything-1480351590.

[17] ""打击网络谣言" 台前幕后," 南方周末, September 5, 2013, http://www.infzm.com/content/93974.

[18] Wee, Sui-Lee, "Chinese police arrest 15,000 for Internet crimes," *Reuters*, August 18, 2015, http://www.reuters.com/article/us-china-Internet-idUSKCN0QN1A520150818.

However, even with real name registration and increasing numbers of arrests, enforcement against all users who violate China's broad Internet laws is difficult for the government, and this difficulty creates protections for Internet users on the Chinese web who push the limits of censorship. Because millions of users share political information with one another every second on the Chinese Internet, users are—at least for now— shielded by the masses from being the target of the government's censure, even if the government has perfect information about what each individual is writing, reading, and sharing online. Later in this chapter, I describe the behavior of typical Chinese Internet users when they experience censorship, either when they are consuming online content, or when they are posting. I find that signals of censorship do not deter the production or consumption of information, as one might expect if Internet users were indeed frightened by Chinese Internet repression. Instead, such experience undermines the Chinese government's online censorship laws and can inspire more criticism and discussion of sensitive issues online in China. If the Chinese government were to engage in widespread fear tactics online in the future, it would also have to deal with the very real possibility of widespread backlash.

4.2 THE COSTS OF OBSERVABLE CENSORSHIP

In this section, I show that users who experience censorship are more likely to be angered or intrigued by the experience than to be fearful of government reprimands. In the empirical tests below, I study instances where Internet users run into observable censorship on the web. Measuring individual reactions to experience with censorship is difficult, as it requires simultaneously measuring censorship and observing how citizens respond. First, I study pairs of similar social media users who shared identical posts, but where one was censored and the other was not. I find that experiencing censorship does not cause users to avoid the censored topic; if anything, they interact more with it—writing more about the topic and complaining about government censorship policies. I also provide survey evidence that corresponds to this behavioral evidence: social media users do not report being fearful after having a social media post removed by the censors, but instead report anger or indifference.

Next, using a lab experiment conducted in China, I study what happens when consumers of social media observe censorship online. I find that when consumers click on a link that redirects to a censored error page, they seek out more information about the topic and are subsequently less likely to support government censorship policies.

The following studies do not provide evidence that self-censorship in China does not exist. Certainly some individuals fear to write about particular topics online because of the risk of repercussions. What the findings in this chapter do show is that when censorship is obvious to citizens, they may push back against the government. The results suggest that draconian methods of censorship could negatively affect government legitimacy. They also explain why the government primarily targets gatekeepers of information, such as journalists, activists, and users with many followers, but for the most part has avoided directly threatening the typical user with fear-based methods of censorship.

4.3 MATCHED COMPARISON OF CENSORED AND UNCENSORED SOCIAL MEDIA USERS

How does experience with censorship affect social media users' perceptions of the government? One way that social media users may experience censorship is when their own social media posts are deleted by government censors. Government directives issued daily to social media sites indicate what types of topics should be deleted from social media websites. Censors at the social media company then delete individual posts in accordance with the directive. A user who experienced censorship by having their post deleted receives a signal of the kinds of topics that the government currently considers too sensitive for the Internet.

If social media users believe that they could have their account blocked, be the subject of a police visit, or at worse jailed if they continue writing on that topic, then they might take the signal of censorship as an indication that they should avoid that topic in future writings. Experience with censorship could cause a chilling effect if the user perceives censorship as a wider signal of a government crackdown. If, however, social media users do not feel that punishment of continued writing on the censored topic is likely, censorship could be a signal of government weakness, of what the government fears, or that the government objects to social media users' opinions, and it may instead motivate the social media user to write more on the topic.

4.3.1 Research Design and Social Media Data

We cannot simply compare users who were censored to users who were not censored to understand the impact of censorship. Users who are censored write about different topics and have different opinions than users who are not censored, and therefore we would likely be measuring the differences between those groups of people rather than the impact of censorship. A perfectly scientific approach to test how users respond to experience with censorship would be to conduct an experiment that randomly assigns censorship to a set of individuals to see how they react. A randomized treatment and control group would ensure that, on average, there were no other differences between those who were censored and those who were not censored that might explain the response to censorship. However, randomly administering censorship on the Internet for research purposes without the consent of users would be unethical to implement.

With observational data, however, we can approximate such an experiment. I find instances where two social media users write identical or nearly identical posts, where one was censored and one was not.[19] I ensure that they are similar in all other observable respects, including how frequently they post and how frequently they are censored. Using this "matched pair design" allows me to compare the subsequent writings of the matched pair to estimate the impact of censorship.

To find matched social media users, I use a dataset of Weibo posts that was collected and made available by Fu, Chan and Chau (2013). Fu, Chan and Chau (2013) created a list of Weibo users with more than one thousand followers using the Sina Weibo User Search Application Programming Interface (API), and then followed these users throughout 2012. Their project, Weiboscope,[20] provides data for 14,387,628 unique users during this period.

The Weiboscope project collected the microblogs from each of the users' timelines in almost real time—before the censors had a chance to remove them—and also revisited each users' previous posts at least once a day, and frequently more than once a day, to record whether the post had been censored. If the post was removed, the authors documented the last time the message was seen before it was removed.[21]

---

[19] Miller (2017) shows that censors may miss posts because they are overwhelmed or deliberately thwarting censorship directives.

[20] http://weiboscope.jmsc.hku.hk/datazip/.

[21] They also documented the error message related to the removed post. From the authors' own experiments, "Permission Denied" indicates that the post had been censored, whereas "Weibo does not exist" usually indicates government censorship but could also mean that the post had been deleted by the poster. While the team

The Weiboscope data provides an almost ideal dataset to test netizen reactions to censorship because many users were followed over a relatively long time. The approximate date and time of censorship is known, revealing the approximate time that users were "treated" with censorship.

To find matched users, I first preprocess the entire dataset by removing all non-textual data from the microblogs, including emoticons and user names. After preprocessing, I find all pairs of posts with identical text, but with different censorship statuses. I require that matches have more than fifteen characters to ensure that two identical posts do not have different meanings because of their context, such as posts that only include short context-dependent phrases such as "reposting Weibo" (转发微博). To further ensure that the posts were written in the same context, I require that the matched posts were posted on the same day.

The removal of social media posts by the censors happens very quickly in China, as reflected in Weiboscope data. The data indicate that 14 percent of the censored posts were not seen after they were first collected; that is, they were deleted before the automated scraper had time to return to them. Half of the censored posts were last seen only a half day after they were first posted and then were removed from the web. More than 80 percent of censored posts were last seen less than two days after they were written. However, for a few posts, censorship occurs significantly after the posts were written. Since I want to study the reaction of Weibo users to censorship and Weibo users are more likely to notice censorship the more quickly it happens, I remove all matches where the censored post had not yet been censored more than two days after posting.

anonymizes the identity of the user, they include a subset of information about the user, including whether the user was "verified." Verified users on Weibo are typically those whose identity has been verified by the online platform and are typically the most prominent or famous users, who have more followers.

I ensure that the matched users wrote posts with similar sensitivities in the past. I calculate the censorship rate for each user before they wrote the matched post. Using matching,[22] I remove pairs where the overall historical censorship rate and censorship rate in the most recent ten-day time period are very different for the two users. This ensures that users in my final group of matched posts will both have experienced similar amounts of censorship overall and will have similar recent experiences with censorship.

In addition to censorship history, I ensure that other attributes of the paired users are similar. Since verified users, who are typically more famous and have more followers, may be more salient to censors than users who are not verified, I only consider matches where matched users have the same verification status. The Weiboscope data also indicate whether the Weibo post contains an image: I match on the inclusion or exclusion of an image in the matched post.

With these restrictions, I find 174 matched posts, or 87 pairs of posts, one censored and one not censored, written by similar users. Matches appear in each month of 2012. Within each match, the users wrote identical posts (usually both reposted the same post) on the same day, have similar censorship histories, and have identical verification statuses. The matched posts discuss topics that we would expect to be censored during this time period, including posts about activists and human rights lawyers, posts describing the corruption of top leaders, posts describing land demolitions and subsequent protests, posts regarding protests in Hong Kong, posts mentioning the leaked online sex video showing official Lei Zhengfu, and many posts that talk about the removal of then Chongqing Party Secretary Bo Xilai from the CCP. Some matched posts are also complaints about censorship, ranging from complaints about censorship

---

[22] Iacus, King and Porro (2009).

of investigative journalism, to complaints about the deletion of microblogs, to complaints about the censorship of scenes of nudity in the screening of the film *Titanic* in 3-D.

4.3.2 Do Weibo Users Persist after Censorship?

Using these 174 matches, we are interested in analyzing how the censored user's behavior after being censored differed from the behavior of the similar user who posted the same content but was not censored. I test their reaction to censorship using four metrics: (1) How similar are their subsequent posts to the censored post? (2) How likely are they to use sensitive words after censorship? (3) How likely are they to complain about censorship after being censored? (4) How likely are they to be censored after the matched post?

Similarity of Posts to Censored Post

First, I test whether the users persist in talking about the censored topic. Do censored users take government censorship as a signal that they should avoid a topic, declining to write further about that topic and self-censoring? Or do they take government censorship as a signal of the topic's importance and persist in writing about the topic more than their uncensored counterparts?

Because the posts from the matched pairs cover a wide range of topics, we cannot measure simply whether the censored group or uncensored group talks more about one particular topic after censorship. What we want to measure is how *similar* the posts they write after censorship are to the matched post. If the censored group self-censors, we would expect them to avoid the topic of the particular post of theirs that was censored. If they rebel, however, we would expect them to continue to write about it.

To measure similarity between the text of the censored post and the subsequent posts, I use a measure of string similarity that estimates the number of overlapping pairs of characters between each of the users' subsequent posts and the matched posts.[23] String similarity of 1 means strings are identical, string similarity of 0 means they have no overlapping sets of two consecutive characters. The more overlapping characters the two strings have, the higher their similarity.

I chose this method because it is very simple and transparent, and it corresponds with words in Chinese, which are typically two characters long. It also is correlated with censorship— having a higher string similarity with the censored post increases the likelihood the post is missing. For each user in the matched dataset, I measure string similarity between the matched posts and each post that the user wrote during the period from ten days before to ten days after the match. Figure 4.1 plots average string similarity for matched censored and uncensored users by time before and after the post. Although the censored group does talk slightly more similarly to the matched post than the control before censorship, this, difference increases after censorship. The censored group writes more similarly to the matched post than the uncensored group does after censorship, even accounting for the small differences between the two groups before.[24] Being censored, at first glance, seems to inspire as much or more writing *similar* to the censored topic rather than a trend away from that topic.

Use of Sensitive Words

String similarity is a useful metric in this context because short posts such as microblogs that display high levels of similarity

---

[23] I use the string kernel similarity measure from the *kernlab* package in R.

[24] The difference-in-difference estimate of treatment after censorship on text similarity is positive and significant. Including user fixed effects and other controls also produces a positive estimate.

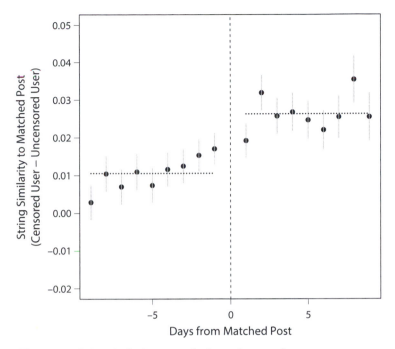

Figure 4.1: String similarity to matched post (censored users - uncensored users). Censored users are as or more likely to write posts similar to the matched post after censorship than uncensored users.

are also typically quite similar to each other in terms of topical content. However, it could be that the similarity that we are measuring is not related to the topic of the matched post, but rather the similarity is because of the ancillary words within the post. To ensure that we are measuring similarity of the *sensitive* content of the matched post, I estimate the words that most predict censorship in the matched posts by taking the one hundred words that are most related to the matched posts in comparison to a sample of uncensored posts written by the users.[25] These words are highly predictive of censorship

[25] This is measured by estimating the words with highest mutual information in the matched posts in comparison to a random sample of uncensored posts from the

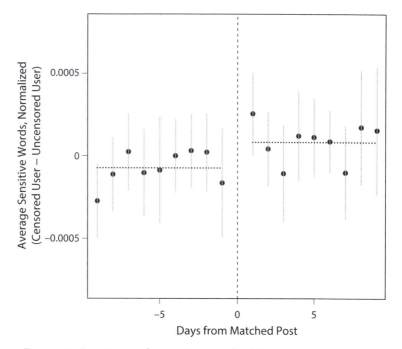

Figure 4.2: Sensitive words in posts, normalized (censored users - uncensored users). Censored users are as or more likely to use sensitive words after censorship than uncensored users.

and include such words as "punishment," "representatives," "miscarriage of justice," "stir up chaos," and "overthrow." For each post the users wrote in the ten days before and after censorship, I measure the number of times the user mentions a word within this list and divide by the post length to standardize across posts.

Figure 4.2 plots the average proportion of each post that is one of these one hundred words. Whereas on average the censored and uncensored groups use the words similarly before the matched post, the censored group is as or more likely to use

same time period; see Manning, Raghavan and Schütze (2008). A list of these words are included in the appendix.

these words after censorship, even though they had received a signal that these words are off-limits.[26]

Complaints about Censorship

Does the censored user complain more about censorship than the uncensored user? To study this, I sampled three thousand social media posts from the users on the second, third, and fourth days after the matched post. For each post, I recorded whether the post contained a complaint about censorship.

Censored users were twice as likely to complain about censorship after the matched posts than uncensored users—1 in 62 of the posts of the censored users complained explicitly about censorship, whereas only 1 in 100 of the posts written by uncensored users complained about censorship. This provides evidence that the censored users did indeed notice the censorship, as they talk about that experience in their subsequent posts. It also indicates that they feel more rather than less empowered to object to censorship directly to their censors after experiencing censorship.

Censorship Rate after Matched Post

Even though the censored and uncensored groups have identical censorship rates before the matched posts, the censored group was more likely to be censored in comparison to the uncensored group after writing the matched post. Figure 4.3 shows the before and after missingness of the posts. Although part of this effect may be due to the topical persistence of the censored group, these differences in censorship after matching may be too stark to be completely explained by the fact that the censored group tends to continue talking about the topic more than the

---

[26] The difference-in-difference estimate of treatment after censorship on sensitive word use is positive and significant. Including user fixed effects and other controls also produces a positive estimate.

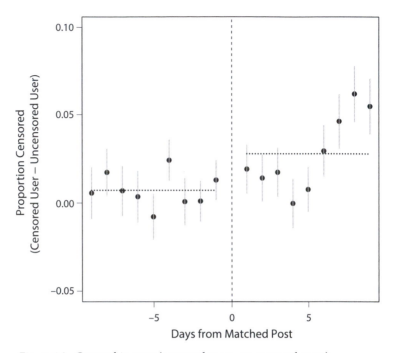

Figure 4.3: Censorship rates (censored users - uncensored users). Censored users are more likely to be censored after censorship than uncensored users.

uncensored group. I expect that the differences in censorship rates are partly due to increased attention by the censors, who may be flagging users after censoring them. This makes the results even more striking, since users are not only persisting after being censored, but are persisting in talking about the same topic in the face of increased scrutiny by the censors.[27] It also suggests that users who have been censored in the past subsequently become more targeted by the censors, providing

[27] The difference-in-difference estimate of treatment after censorship on missing posts is positive and significant. It is robust to including user fixed effects and other controls.

evidence that censorship focuses on those who the censors believe are more likely to disobey the rules.

4.3.3 Case Studies "Weibo is Democracy!"

Why would the censored group persist in writing about the censored topic when they have just received a signal that the topic is off-limits and they are under heightened scrutiny by the censors? A closer look at a few censored individuals provides some insight into the thought process of the censored users. Take the match between User Zhang and User Liu.[28] User Zhang and User Liu both shared identical posts on the same day, "voting" for a decrease in censorship of the Internet. User Zhang was, ironically, censored, while User Liu was not. Whereas User Zhang posted about the Internet only four times in the ten days before the post, he has twelve posts in the ten days after censorship that mention the Internet, six of which occur the day after he was censored.

Why would User Zhang be so relentless? User Zhang opposes censorship so strongly that he will do everything to defy the censors. He sees censorship as an indication that the government is trying to cover up corruption—he sees censorship as the direct result of corrupt officials. In the few days after being censored, User Zhang shares:

"//@经济抠门男：这是贪官们怕微博把他们都给爆料了吧，想挡住大伙的嘴，徒劳"

"It's because the corrupted officials are worried that Weibo will spill all their (negative) secrets, so they try to shut everyone up, it's useless."

---

[28] Names are pseudonyms; Weiboscope does not provide user names.

> "网络反腐，今天我们败了，但明天我们一定会迎来胜利。都贪污，你
> 不贪，你就没办法在官场混！"
>
> "Online anti-corruption, although we lost today, but we will
> have the victory tomorrow. Everyone is corrupted, if you don't,
> you can't survive in the government."

User Zhang's match, User Liu, also frequently writes about
corruption and the rule of law in China. User Liu also opposes
censorship, having written an identical post to User Zhang
"voting" for a decrease in censorship on the Internet. However,
User Liu is not reminded of how much he hates censorship
because, unlike User Zhang, his complaint was not censored.
User Liu therefore writes fewer posts about the Internet in the
period directly following the match.

In another example, User Zhu is censored when he posts the
following text about Lei Zhengfu, the Party official who was
caught on video with an eighteen-year-old woman, suggesting
that users watch the pornographic video:

> "【重庆雷政富同志，请辟谣！】资深调查记者举报，重庆市北碚区委
> 书记雷政富（正厅级），与重庆市开县赵家镇18岁女青年赵红霞发生不正
> 当男女关系后，又动用权力将赵红霞抓捕，试图封口。由于本人水平有
> 限，无法识别图片真伪，群众的眼睛是雪亮的，诚邀广大网友一起鉴定！"
>
> "Chongqing Comrade Lei Zhengfu, please tell me it isn't so! A
> senior investigative reporter reported that the Chongqing Beibei
> District Secretary Lei Zhengfu (at the department level), had an
> improper relationship with an Chongqing city, Kaixian county
> 18 year old woman Zhao Hongxia and used his power to arrest
> Zhao Hongxia to try to seal it. One person's ability is limited,
> can't validate the authenticity of the picture, everyone's eyes are
> good, we invite all the Internet users to try together!"

Despite being censored, User Zhu writes more about the scandal after censorship than before, outpacing his uncensored match who shared the identical post, User Li. Why is User Zhu so persistent? In User Zhu's own post, written after he was censored:

> "【微博就是民主！】微博（Twitter中国版本）的出现，彻底颠覆了中国的舆论格局，每个人都能发出声音，瞬间无限放大，传统媒体全跟在微博屁股后面做文章。微博本身具有"自净"功能 谣言必将被真相戳破，别封杀微博，赋予网友分自由，政府不用费心政改，媒体也不用呼吁新闻自由，只是，纪委要下岗了"
>
> "Weibo is democracy! The appearance of Weibo (the Chinese version of Twitter) completely overturns the public opinion structure in China, everyone can express their opinion, and it will escalate instantly and infinitely, all the traditional media are following Weibo to make stories. Weibo itself has a 'self-cleansing' function, myths will be busted by the truth, so don't block Weibo, give the Internet users enough freedom, the government does not have to worry about revising the law, and the media don't have to appeal for freedom of information, the Commission for Discipline Inspection can step down."

In essence, the act of censorship has been interpreted by this user as weakness—social media expresses truth and to censor social media is to hide the truth. In the ten days before the matched post, User Zhu's censorship rate was zero percent, the same as his match User Li. However, in the ten days after the matched post, User Zhu's censorship rate skyrocketed to 33 percent, while User Li's increased only to 4 percent. Despite being flagged by the censors, User Zhu persists, continuing to talk about the political topics he believes are important and criticizing censorship itself.

4.3.4 Survey of Internet Users in China

Why does experience with censorship embolden social media users and cause them to complain about their repression, despite increased scrutiny from government censors and indications that their writings are off-limits? Clearly, for the producers of online media studied in this section, the small increase in the probability of government reprisal was outweighed by countervailing forces that cause Internet users to persist in speaking about the topic that initially interested them and in some cases to write more about politically sensitive information in China.

To verify that the results presented here generalize to a broader population, following Dickson (2016, pg. 71–72), I included a question in a representative survey of urban residents in China conducted in the summer of 2015, asking respondents who were Internet users whether they had experienced censorship in the form of deletion of a social media post, removal of an account, not being able to post, or not being able to search for a term.[29] Eleven percent of the respondents admitted to having experienced one of these forms of censorship. Respondents were then asked: "Whether or not you have experienced [these forms of censorship], if you had experienced them, how would you feel?" Respondents were then given a set of emotions, from which they could choose none, one, or more than one.

The survey results presented in table 4.1 indicate that censorship does not inspire much fear. Very few of the respondents indicated that they would be worried or fearful after experiencing censorship—only 5 percent of all Internet users and 7 percent of users who admitted to having experienced censorship said they would be worried or fearful. The largest proportion of users said that they wouldn't care, 35 percent of all Internet users and 41 percent of those who had experienced

---

[29] More information about the survey methodology is provided in the appendix.

Table 4.1: Emotional reactions to censorship, urban survey in China.

	All users	Users with censorship experience
Wouldn't care	0.35	0.41
Angry or extremely angry	0.23	0.36
Sad	0.12	0.38
Worried or fearful	0.05	0.07
Proud or would brag to friends	0.03	0.10
Happy	0.00	0.00
Didn't answer	0.34	0.05

censorship. More than being fearful, users reported that they would be angry—23 percent of all users and 36 percent of users who had experienced censorship said they would be angry or extremely angry. This suggests that social media users could be pushing the limits of censorship because they disagree with it and hope to undermine it. Interestingly, the survey evidence indicates that the distribution of respondents' expected emotions among those who have experienced censorship and those who have not are similar, suggesting that the results in this study are more broadly applicable to the population of users who do not regularly post sensitive material online.

4.4 AN EXPERIMENTAL STUDY OF CONSUMERS OF SOCIAL MEDIA

Last, I study how online consumers of information react when they come across censored information. Although censorship in China is less obvious to consumers of social media than it is to producers, occasionally a consumer will come across a censored page. One way observation of censorship occurs is through a link, when a page that the person is visiting links to a page that has been censored. When the consumer clicks the link, the user will be taken to an error page generated by the Internet

Figure 4.4: Error page indicating that a post has been removed, from sina.com.cn.

content provider instead of the page with the original content. An example error page is displayed in figure 4.4.

Another way consumers of social media can observe censorship is within a forum or a discussion thread. When posts are censored within a forum, the content of the individual comment is removed, but the rest of the conversation still exists. Therefore, the user will see a removed post where the original post once stood. This can also occur on Sina Weibo, where sometimes when an individual post is removed, the rest of the thread remains uncensored.

Does the observation of censorship influence the likelihood that sensitive topics will be read? When consumers come across a censored page, they can often guess the topic of the censored post because of the context of the censorship. For example, if the user clicked on a link to a censored page, the title of the link will often give an indication of what the original post was about. Within a forum, consumers of information will see the discussion surrounding the missing post, and therefore may be able to guess the topic of the post's content, even though it is missing.

The observation of censorship may be a signal of what information that the government views as "in bounds" and thereby may affect the behavior of individuals. Many scholars have posited that authoritarian governments signal to citizens what they should be consuming and talking about and that these signals affect citizen behavior. For example, Singapore uses "out-of-bounds markers" to indicate what should and what should not be discussed.[30] Brady (2009) posits that a similar information control strategy is used in China, where "frames" or information norms show by example what should and should not be discussed in public. A netizen might observe censorship and infer Party guidelines, following the Party's lead in what information she should be consuming online. If the public does take the signal of censorship as an indication of what it should be consuming, we would expect this to have an important impact on the spread of information.

If consumers of information sometimes happen upon indications of censorship in social media, how do they react? If the consumer is primarily acting on fear or on the realization of norms produced by the censored post, interaction with a censored post will cause the reader to avoid further interaction with the topic. On the other hand, if censorship creates countervailing signals that undermine government legitimacy or enhance readers' curiosity, it might instead pique readers' interest, drawing them to more posts about the same topic and undermining the legitimacy of the government. These basic questions motivate an additional test: an experiment on the influence of awareness of censorship on consumers of social media posts in China.

Experimental Design

I conducted an experiment to study how consumers of social media posts react to censorship with two universities in China

---

[30] Benner, Tom, "Singapore's new generation wants a kinder, chiller country," *Global Post*, August 12, 2015, https://www.pri.org/stories/2015-08-12/singapores -new-generation-wants-kinder-chiller-country.

students at over the summer of 2013. Students were given a computer, either a laptop in a coffee shop or a computer in a lab setting, and were given access to the Internet. They were provided with a list of social media posts in a blog aggregator that I designed for the study. They were told to read whichever posts interested them, and told that they would be asked a few questions about the blogs they read after five minutes of reading, but they were not expected to cover all blogs or all the blog topics. The subjects were aware that their actions online were being watched, as the description of the process indicated that their behavior online was being recorded, simulating an environment of surveillance.

The social media posts covered four different topics about ongoing events in China: (1) protests over the construction of paraexlyne (PX) plants in Yunnan, (2) protests in Hong Kong against the Chinese government, (3) a scandal alleging that a Chinese Communist Party official's son, Li Tianyi, was involved in the gang rape of a woman, and (4) blogs speculating that the Chinese economy would soon descend into an economic crisis similar to the one that had occurred in the United States. Because this study was conducted within China, more sensitive topics could not be used, but pre-testing of the experiment suggested that these were all topics Chinese citizens expect to be sensitive and could be censored. All blogs within the study existed online and had not been censored at the time of the study.

Students were asked to read blogs that interested them and then told that they would be asked a few questions. They could judge which social media posts might interest them because the title of the post was displayed on the main page of the aggregator, and each title contained information that would allow them to determine the post's topic. It was clear that they could not cover all topics or read all posts during the time allotted.

For the treated group, the first post the reader clicked on in a randomly selected topic would not link to the blog itself, but instead to the error page associated with the blog's Internet content provider, indicating censorship. The student would then return to the blog aggregator and choose another post to read. For the control group, all links on the main page would direct to the full content of the post, and not to an error page.

The question of interest was: How does the experience with censorship influence the topic the reader selects next? Is the reader less likely to pick a post on that topic because she has received a signal from the government that that topic is off-limits? To measure this, I installed technology within the website to track the behavior of each individual. I could therefore observe when an individual was treated with a censored link and which link she decided to click on after encountering the censored page.

A comparison between the group that encountered censorship when they clicked on their initial topic of interest and those who did not encounter censorship on that topic is the causal effect of the awareness of censorship on the reader's consumption decisions. If the censored page created mainly fear and anxiety, we would expect participants to avoid the censored topic in the post they selected subsequently. If the censored page inspired curiosity or indignation, however, we would expect participants to be equally or even more likely to click on the censored topic. Finally, for those who were treated with censorship at some point during the course of their time on the blog aggregator, we can study how this affected their opinions on the validity of government censorship to explore how the observation of censorship affects government legitimacy.

Results: Participants Compensate for Censorship

The vast majority of the subjects recognized the error page as censorship. The last question in the survey following the experiment presented a screenshot of the censorship error page to the participants and asked them what they thought this error page indicated. An overwhelming 84 percent of the respondents said that the page was due to purposeful deletion of posts. Treatment was also successfully randomized—there was no difference between treated and control among other observed demographic covariates.

Censorship did not dissuade people from reading more about the same topic—instead it made people more interested in the topic. To estimate how the observation of censorship influenced readers in the most rigorous way possible, I selected the first post each participant had clicked on as the treatment post. This helps control for initial interest in the post, as presumably readers initially pick the topic that they are most interested in. The dependent variable of interest is whether the second post the participant clicked on discussed the same topic, or a different topic than the one that was initially deleted.

As shown in figure 4.5, readers who first clicked on a censored post were more likely to click on a post within the same topic next than those who first clicked on an uncensored post. This indicates that readers were not deterred by censorship, for if they were they would be less likely to click on the same topic having observed censorship. In fact, readers seem to compensate for the fact that they were censored by clicking on more posts about the topic overall than uncensored readers. I estimated on average how many total *uncensored* posts a person who had come across censorship initially would read in comparison to the person who initially did not come across censorship. The result was indistinguishable from zero: on average, a person who came across censorship initially would click enough subsequent posts to read between one and two uncensored posts about the topic by the end of the time period, about the same number as those who came across an uncensored post originally. This indicates that when readers are aware of censorship, they are willing and able to compensate for it.

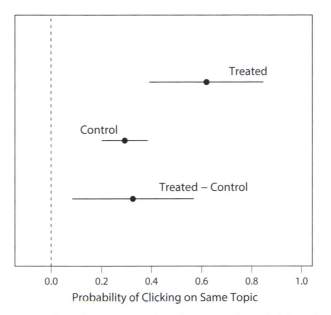

Figure 4.5: Effect of censored social media post on the probability of clicking on the same topic subsequently. The treated group (top) is more likely to click on a post of the same topic than the control group (middle). The difference in means is at the bottom of the plot.

Experience with censorship decreased treated users' agreement with government censorship policies. After the experiment, subjects were asked about whether they thought that particular categories of information should be regulated on the Internet, including online discussion, games, uncivilized language, ads, rumors, pornography, spam, violence, and false information. As shown in figure 4.6, when asked about how much regulation of the Internet there should be across these nine categories, subjects who observed censorship indicated that they thought the Internet should be less regulated across the board. This difference in opinion suggests that experience with censorship, instead of deterring social media users from seeking out information, may instead undermine the legitimacy of the government's information laws.

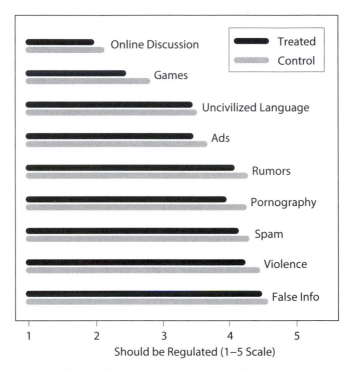

Figure 4.6: Effect of observing censored social media post on support for Internet regulation. Treated units (black) are on average less likely to support regulation across the board than control units (gray). A t-test of the overall difference between treated and control has a p-value of 0.08.

The implication of these results is that awareness of censorship on the part of consumers of social media posts does not dissuade these consumers from reading more about a topic. Instead, observing censorship interested readers in learning more about the topic and created disillusionment with government censorship laws. Inducing awareness of censorship in this case backfired to undermine government policy.

The findings presented in this chapter could explain why the Chinese government is constrained in implementing more draconian policies when censoring the Internet. If there were no cost to censorship, then the government might censor anything about itself that could be seen as unseemly. However, because censorship is costly for the government, it refrains from censoring too broadly and attempts to hide its censorship footprints online. In earlier work, my coauthors and I found that the Chinese government allows much criticism to go uncensored online, and instead focuses censorship on collective action—in other words, censoring the information that is a direct threat to the regime.[31] Internet content providers in China recently have tried to make censorship less observable by concealing error pages to the authors of censored blogs and simply reordering search results rather than throwing errors when search filtering, perhaps to lessen the backfire effect that censorship creates.

The evidence presented here suggests that government censorship policies are complicated by the fact that Internet users can compensate for censorship when they observe it. Topics the Chinese government would like to see removed online are constantly changing and developing as politics, international events, and protest events unfold. The government cannot simply signal what is off limits to online users because Internet users will not automatically avoid these topics and "purify" the information environment. Observable censorship instead can create more interest in the topic and undermine the reputation of the government.

4.5 CONCLUSION

In this chapter, I showed that signals of what topics are off limits do not induce typical Internet users to avoid topics. Using a matched pair design of microbloggers, evidence from a survey, and online experiments, I show that Internet users seem to read

---

[31] King, Pan, and Roberts (2013, 2014).

and share as much or more about topics that they believe to be censored. Further, the evidence suggests that experience with censorship may in fact undermine the government's reputation, inspiring social media users to complain about censorship, reevaluate their opinions on government censorship laws, and experience feelings of anger.

The evidence presented here is consistent with the incentives of online users in high information environments. In these situations, observable censorship attracts citizens to information, as it signals importance. Because so many people participate online, netizens are largely protected from punishment. Therefore, signals of off-limits information embolden users and reduce government legitimacy rather than inspiring widespread self-censorship.

If fear is not what is preventing typical Internet users from consuming off-limits information, then what control does the government have over the information environment? In the next chapter, I introduce more online data to show that when Internet users are not explicitly aware of what is off-limits, they are highly affected by the cost of access to information. Friction and inconvenience have a more significant impact on the typical Internet user in China than deterrence does.

CHAPTER FIVE

The Powerful Influence of Information Friction

In May 2011, I had been following news about a local protest in Inner Mongolia, where an ethnic Mongol herdsman had been killed by a Han Chinese truck driver in a dispute. In the following days increasingly large numbers of local Mongols began protesting outside of government buildings, culminating in sufficiently large-scale protests that the Chinese government imposed martial law. These protests were the largest that Inner Mongolia had experienced in twenty years.[1]

A few months later, I arrived in Beijing for the summer. At dinner with a friend, discussing ethnic divisions in China, I brought up the Inner Mongolia protest event. My friend struggled to recollect the event, saying that she had not heard of it. A few minutes later, she remembered that indeed a friend of hers had mentioned something about it, but when she looked for information online, she could not find any. Her assumption had been that the protest itself could not have been that important if she had not received word.

It was difficult by design for my friend to have learned of the protest event. Bloggers who posted information about the protest online had their posts quickly removed from the Internet by censors.[2] Local media were not reporting on the event, so news of the protest was reported mainly by foreign sources many of which had been blocked by the Great Firewall. Even for the media, information was difficult to come by, as reporting on the

---

[1] "China's Inner Mongolia 'Under Heavy Security'," *BBC*, May 30, 2011, http://www.bbc.com/news/world-asia-pacific-13592514.

[2] Evidence of censorship of this event is shown in King, Pan and Roberts (2013).

protests on the ground had been banned, and the local Internet had been shut off by the government.

Of course, information about the protest was not *impossible* to find on the Internet. I had been following the news from Boston, and even in China, the simple use of a Virtual Private Network and some knowledge of which keywords to search for had uncovered hundreds of news stories about the protests. But my friend, a well-to-do, politically interested, tech-savvy woman, was busy and Inner Mongolia is several hundreds of miles away. After a cursory search that turned up nothing, she had thought that the news was either unimportant or non-existent.

A few years later, in an interview in 2015, I asked a woman in China (henceforth referred to pseudonymously as Lina) to describe how she used social media. A young professional who had studied abroad in the United States, she used Chinese social media platforms like WeChat and Weibo and also frequently jumped the Firewall to connect with her friends in the United States on Facebook. Although for the most part she read news in Chinese from government newspapers like *People's Daily* and from more commercial Chinese newspapers like *Southern Weekend*, she also made time when she could to read the *New York Times* and the BBC's website.

Lina, unlike the average citizen, was very invested in politics and followed political events closely. She was involved in multiple organizations that advocated for gender equality and was an opinionated feminist. Because of her feminist activism, I asked her whether she had heard of the five female activists who had been arrested earlier that year in China, including in Beijing, for their involvement in organizing a series of events meant to combat sexual harassment.[3] The arrests of these five

---

[3] Branigan, Tania, "Five Chinese Feminists Held over International Women's Day Plans," *Guardian*, March 12, 2015, https://www.theguardian.com/world/2015/mar/12/five-chinese-feminists-held-international-womens-day.

women were covered extensively in the foreign press and had drawn international outcry—articles about the activists had appeared in the *New York Times* and on the BBC. Multiple foreign governments had publicly called for their release. Within China, activists had organized social media accounts to provide updates on their imprisonment, and lawyers and students had petitioned the Chinese government for their release. But posts about their detention were highly censored and the Chinese news media were prohibited from reporting on it. Lina, who participated in multiple feminist social media groups and made an effort to read Western news, still had not heard about their imprisonment.

In interviews, I kept encountering examples like these— where people living in China exhibited surprising ignorance about Chinese domestic events that had made headlines in the international press. People I interviewed had not heard that the imprisoned Chinese activist Liu Xiaobo had won the Nobel Peace Prize. They had not heard about major labor protests that had shut down factories or bombings of local government offices. Although this ignorance was widespread among Chinese citizens who had not traveled abroad, did not jump the Firewall, and rarely used the Internet, it was also surprisingly common among tech-savvy, globally traveled, well-educated Chinese citizens. Despite the *possibility* of accessing this information, without newspapers, television, and social media blaring these headlines, they were much less likely to come across these stories.

As Internet penetration has expanded, scholars have posited that the masses would be the beneficiaries of this new tech-nology, at the expense of the powerful.[4] The Internet creates transparency, providing minute-to-minute news on actions of

---

[4] Ferdinand (2000, pg. 5), Lynch (2011), Bellin (2012, pg. 138), Diamond (2010, pg. 70).

governments, politicians, companies, and interest groups. The Internet allows citizens to communicate with one another instantly, creating a new forum for civil society that can spread signals of discontent and organize action against the government, before bumbling censors delete this information.[5] According to these scholars, the Internet's ability to thwart government- and interest-group-led efforts of censorship makes it impossible for anything to be kept secret.[6]

However, as these interviews and the following empirical tests suggest, the perception that the Internet makes government control over information obsolete is fundamentally flawed. Although the Internet has made a lot of information *possible* to find, much information is still disaggregated or difficult for the public to access. Market research provides evidence that Internet users are for the most part lazy consumers of information, and consume only the most accessible information.[7] Governments and interest groups, which are the main actors gathering and providing access to information, determine what information consumers are most likely to read.

Porous censorship is surprisingly effective in the age of the Internet. The fact that information about these domestic events is *possible* to access creates the perception that information is free-flowing, and suggests that difficulty of access is due to lack of interest rather than government manipulation. However, the possibility of access does not mean that citizens will consume information. Even though censorship is easily circumvented, citizens often do not have the patience to circumvent it. Citizens are also often unaware of censorship, and therefore cannot counteract it. Although some citizens will take the time and spend resources to seek out information that is difficult to access, costs of access will have larger effects on the average

---

[5] Yang (2009*b*, pg. 30).
[6] Taubman (1998, pg. 266).
[7] Hoelzle (January 2012).

Internet user, who has fewer resources and little to gain from circumventing censorship.

In this chapter, I study the effect of two of these friction-based censorship methods on the spread of information on the Chinese Internet. I show that these methods of censorship have significant effects on the prevalence of information online and the regularity with which users access off-limits information. First, I study content filtering, the removal of social media posts online. Previous studies have estimated that anywhere between 1 percent and 10 percent of social media posts are removed by censors on Chinese social media sites.[8] Whereas in the previous chapter I studied the direct effect of the removal of social media posts on the users whose posts were noticeably deleted by the government, in this chapter I will study the indirect effect of content filtering, or how the removal of posts influences the vast majority of users who do not come across the error page but simply do not have access to the post. For these users, content filtering simply makes information about an event difficult to find—netizens do not know that information has disappeared; instead they simply have trouble finding it or do not run across it. I show that small perturbations in the timing of content filtering influences the spread of information about self-immolation events in Tibet. When censors are a bit slower, news about self-immolations spreads to more people on Sina Weibo than when the censors are a bit faster.

Second, I study the effect of the Great Firewall of China on the frequency with which Chinese citizens access foreign information. Outside of removal of social media posts, the Great Firewall of China is perhaps the most obvious example of online information friction in China. The Great Firewall blocks access from Chinese IP addresses to a list of foreign websites the government deems objectionable. Although the Firewall can be

---

[8] Fu, Chan and Chau (2013); King, Pan and Roberts (2013).

circumvented by logging into a foreign computer through a Virtual Private Network, which allows users to access the Internet through a third-party computer, seeking out VPNs and paying a small fee for using them increases the cost of information that can be accessed only by circumventing the Firewall.

Using nationally representative survey data and geo-located data on Chinese users of Twitter, I show that very few people in China evade the Great Firewall, despite the fact that during the time period of the survey, it was relatively easy to do so. I show that the types of users who are willing to circumvent the Great Firewall are more likely to reside in large cities, be technologically savvy, be interested in politics, and discuss sensitive political events than typical Internet users in China. I find that when a new website is blocked, its popularity in China is significantly reduced. In doing so, friction creates a small but effective wall between the general public, who are less interested in politics, and the well-educated and disillusioned wealthy class, decreasing the likelihood of anti-government mobilization.

5.1 THE EFFECTS OF CONTENT FILTERING ON THE SPREAD OF INFORMATION

This section will focus on one of the Chinese government's censorship methods: content filtering, which is the selective removal of social media posts online in China. While the Great Firewall blocks foreign websites, the vast majority of social media posts in China are written on the platforms of Chinese-owned Internet content providers (ICPs). As mentioned in chapter 3, the Chinese government devolves responsibility for content filtering of social media posts to each of these individual ICPs. When a user posts something that is objectionable to the government online, the website is responsible for removing this material from the Internet. If government censors find too much objectionable material on a website, they have the authority to shut the entire website down. Under threat of extinction, ICPs employ thousands of censors who remove content based on directives from government agencies.

Large-scale studies of content filtering in the past have shown that the government focuses the efforts of censors on removing posts related to protest events or those who could organize protests. Although censorship in China can be a relatively disaggregated process, King, Pan, and Roberts (2013, 2014) show that, surprisingly, the government largely does not target criticism of government policies, but rather removes all posts related to collective action events, activists, criticism of censorship, and pornography regardless of their support or criticism of the government. Consistent with this theory, Bamman, O'Connor and Smith (2012) show that censorship focuses on social media posts that are geo-located in more restive areas, like Tibet. The primary aim of government censorship seems to be to stop information flow from protest areas to other parts of China, or to prevent people from knowing about protest events. Since large-scale protest is known to be one of the main threats to the Chinese regime,[9] success for the Chinese censorship program is preventing the spread of information about protests in order to reduce their scale.

Despite extensive content filtering, if users were motivated and willing to invest time in finding information about protests, they could overcome information friction to find such information. First, information is often published online before it is removed by Internet companies. There usually exists a lag of several hours to a day before content is removed from the Internet. Therefore, even the most objectionable material will

---

[9] See Chen (2012) and Cai (2010) for a discussion of protests in China.

spend a period of time online and will be available to the public before it is removed.

Second, Internet content providers will occasionally miss posts related to an event. Automated methods of content filtering are not sophisticated or very successful, and therefore much of content filtering is done by hand. Since censors cannot read every post on the Chinese Internet, they may miss a fraction of objectionable material. Netizens who want to discuss a particular event may also find ways to trick the censors, either by finding websites that are less carefully watched (talking about politics on a dating website, for example), or by finding phrasing that makes posts about the topic difficult for the censors to find.

Last, if the event is reported in the foreign press, Internet users could access the information by jumping the Great Firewall using a VPN. Even if Chinese Internet content providers remove information about these events, Twitter, Facebook, or other blocked social media will often contain information describing the events. These social media companies do not filter content at the instruction of the Chinese government, and therefore, as long as a user has the know-how and money to access a VPN, they can access the entire unfiltered foreign web.

However, despite the possibility of accessing information in the face of content filtering, the slightly increased costs of information due to content filtering reduce the probability that netizens will come across information about protests, and therefore have a significant influence on the number of people who know about an event. This is primarily because content filtering reduces the prevalence of information on the Chinese Internet, meaning that fewer people encounter this information while searching the web. Content filtering particularly focuses on social media users who have large numbers of friends,[10]

---

[10] Zhu et al. (2013).

targeting those who are in positions to spread information about the sensitive event to the largest audience.

Content filtering not only decreases the accessibility of information; it also can disaggregate accounts of an event, reducing the salience of the event and increasing uncertainty about what exactly occurred. Users cannot tell whether the lack of information online about a particular event is due to government censorship or to general lack of interest in the event. If no one seems to be talking about protests in Inner Mongolia, for example, even people who know about them may assume that the protests do not have widespread support. They may assume that the protest was started by radicals, and that people they follow online, their "friends," do not support these people. Unless they subsequently spend time searching and aggregating multiple accounts of the event, netizens may not realize the importance of an event even if they simply happen upon one post related to it.

All of these small costs add up to create a multiplying influence on the inaccessibility and disaggregation of information about the protest. The more content filtering, the fewer people happen upon the information and the fewer new postings occur online. The fewer the new postings, the fewer people know about the event, and those who do are more likely to think the event has fewer followers than they would if there were more discussion online. The fewer people who know about the event, the fewer people know there is any reason to spend time searching for the information. The smaller the number of social media posts that are related to the event, the fewer people out protesting, and the smaller effect the protest has on governance.

Tibetan Self-immolation Protests

Between March 2011 and July 2013, 120 Tibetans self-immolated within China, the majority of whom died. Although the exact reasons for the self-immolations are unknown and probably vary, writings by self-immolators call for Tibetan independence, greater Tibetan autonomy, or the return of the Dalai Lama, all policy stances that the Chinese government opposes.

These protest events represented a major political problem for the Chinese government, as this spate of self-immolations followed large-scale protests in 2008, where thousands of young people protested in Tibet, some waving the Tibetan flag.[11] The self-immolations themselves were also sometimes followed by larger-scale protests. Since peaceful relations between minority groups and fighting independence movements are central to Chinese national security policy, the immolations were a direct challenge to the Chinese government. Self-immolations in other countries also have a history of causing political upheaval; for example, Mohamed Bouazizi, a Tunisian businessman, is credited with sparking the Arab Spring in 2010 after self-immolating in political protest.[12]

To discourage such protest events, the government responded rapidly to the self-immolation events, removing the self-immolator as quickly as possible and increasing police presence to prevent protests in the aftermath. Police punished villagers and families of Tibetans who self-immolated to discourage future events. Monasteries were often surrounded with police forces since many of the self-immolators were Buddhist monks.[13]

News of Tibetan self-immolations was uniformly and quickly censored on social media websites.[14] Unlike most political discussions, where one thread will generate thousands of re-shares in China, threads spreading news of Tibetan self-immolators

---

[11] Greve (2013).

[12] Lotan et al. (2011).

[13] Greve (2013).

[14] The experiment in King, Pan, and Roberts (2014) shows the high censorship rate of social media posts related to self-immolations.

are quickly cut off. Since information about self-immolations is scarce, social media accounts of self-immolations are often uncertain, for example, "I heard there was a self-immolation today in Tibet. Is it true?" News about specific self-immolation events is an example of a topic that is uniformly censored by all social media websites in China, and therefore fear of writing and reading about self-immolation events should be constant across events.

More Discussion of Self-immolations on the Weekends When Censorship Is Lower

To study how censorship influences the spread of news surrounding self-immolation events, I collected a random sample of social media postings from Sina Weibo, BBS websites, and Sina blogs related to self-immolations between March 2011 and July 2013 before the Chinese government was able to censor them.[15] Discussion about self-immolations on social media in China naturally clusters around self-immolation events. In this section, I define "bursts" of social media posts about an event as the spike in volume of social media discussion at the time of the event. Social media is characterized by bursts of activity,[16] but some events receive more attention than others. In this context, since I obtain posts *before* censorship, I am estimating how many posts were *written* about the event within my sample. However, depending on how quickly censorship occurs, many of these posts were *available* to readers only for a number of hours.

Of course, even after posts about the event are censored, it is possible for netizens to find information about any of these immolation events online. First, some posts are never

---

[15] I sampled by requiring the social media post to contain the words self-immolation (自焚) and Tibetan (藏) from the social media analytics company Crimson Hexagon.

[16] Ratkiewicz et al. (2010).

removed—they are missed by the censors. Second, netizens could jump the Great Firewall and read any number of foreign websites that report on these events. Censorship in this case is *not* an information blackout by any means. Instead, the degree and quickness of censorship will determine the effort a netizen would have to expend to find information about the event. As a result, this form of censorship functions through friction, a continuous variable that indicates the degree of difficulty in finding a piece of information, not a dichotomous variable that indicates complete availability or total unavailability.

Despite relatively high censorship across self-immolation events, some self-immolations receive more attention from social media users than others—some have longer bursts, or more discussion about the event. Figure 5.1 shows the variation in bursts within my sample across the 120 self-immolation events between 2011 and 2013. Some events receive barely any attention at all, while others have a large amount of social media discussion associated with the event.

Why would some immolations receive more attention than others? It could be that the nature of the event was such that certain events received more attention from the public than others. The age of the immolator is usually something people note when discussing self-immolation events, with younger immolators often discussed with more grief than older immolators. Monks who self-immolate might have a larger network of followers, leading to more attention about the event. Self-immolation events that appear in clusters might build on one another, generating more attention.

However, in an environment of high censorship, the fact that some immolators receive barely any online attention at all and that the spread of information about self-immolations is overall so stifled could be explained by variation in friction caused by the control of information. If differences in burst lengths between self-immolation events were due to variation

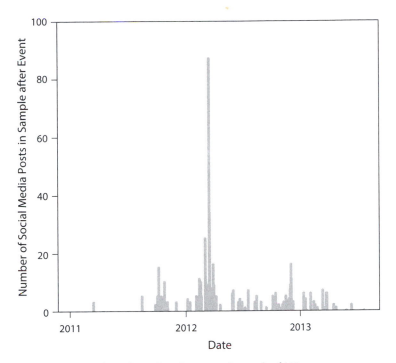

Figure 5.1: Number of social media posts after each of 120 self-immolation events between 2011 and 2013; sample from Sina Weibo, BBS, and Sina blogs.

in censorship, we would expect that social media posts that were online for a longer period would also have more time to be re-shared by others. The faster the censorship, the fewer people would know about the event, and the smaller the information available associated with it. The quicker that censors react to an event, the less online discussion about that event.

I do not have real-time data on censorship of self-immolation events because the infrastructure required to detect real-time censorship over such a long period is prohibitively large. However, real-time analyses of censorship over short time periods can be conducted, and a few authors have uncovered the regular schedule of censors. Using real-time data collected by King, Pan and Roberts (2013), which was collected around the same time that the posts within my sample were written, I find that censorship is low on the weekends relative to weekdays.[17] Typically, censorship occurs within one day of posting: a post written Friday is most likely to be censored on Friday. However, a post written on Friday is second most likely to be censored on Monday, not on Saturday or Sunday. This suggests that fewer censors are working on the weekends than on weekdays.

Self-immolations, however, can happen on any day of the week, and do. An analysis of all self-immolation events over the past two years shows that self-immolations are no more likely to happen on one day of the week than another. Since the act of self-immolation is so drastic, there is likely very little strategy involved in the particular day of the week chosen.

If information friction were effective in stopping the spread of information, we might expect that bursts related to self-immolations would be longer on the weekend, given that it might take longer for censors to locate and delete these postings and therefore provide a longer period of time for others to read and repost these social media posts. As shown in figure 5.2, bursts associated with self-immolations on the weekends are significantly longer than those associated with self-immolations that occur on a weekday.[18]

Of course, the length of the social media burst could be due to other variables besides censorship. Monks might be more likely to self-immolate on a weekend, and also are more likely to gain a larger following. The age of the self-immolator could be related to both the timing and the following. In order to control for

---

[17] The Weiboscope data provided by Fu, Chan, and Chau (2013) also show lower censorship on weekends in comparison to weekdays.

[18] Self-immolations that happen on Friday are considered weekend immolations because they often happen later in the day, and therefore discussion of these events often does not occur until the weekend.

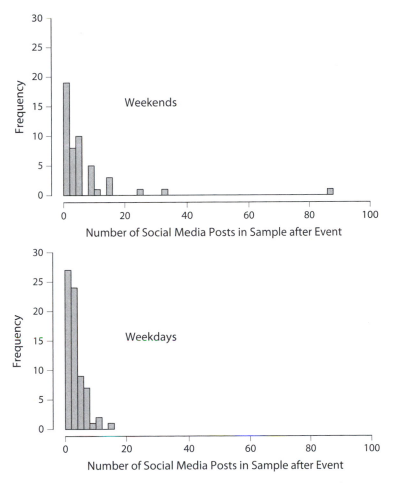

Figure 5.2: Weekend self-immolations (top) have more discussion than weekday self-immolations (bottom).

these variables, I collected data about the specific circumstances of each self-immolation event, including the age, whether the self-immolator was a monk, and the time since the last self-immolation to capture any clustering effects. The results are robust to these controls, and I show a full model controlling for these characteristics in the appendix.

To verify that this effect was not a result of people simply writing more posts on the weekend, I downloaded a random sample of blogs from the same source mentioning Tibet during the same time period. These posts are largely not sensitive; most talk about economic opportunities in Tibet, traveling in Tibet, or Tibetan culture. Surprisingly, people are significantly *less likely* to write about Tibet on the weekend than on a weekday.

The fact that the speed of content filtering influences the number of posts about a self-immolation event indicates that small costs of access to information, such as the timing of censorship, influence the spread of information about protest events throughout China. Even in this case, where fear and self-censorship should be constant across immolation events, the timing of censorship dictated by censors' schedules is correlated with the number of people who wrote about the event.

5.2 STRUCTURAL FRICTIONS AND THE GREAT FIREWALL

It could be that short-term frictions like the content filtering described in the previous section have short-term effects on the spread of information, but in the long run people can learn to overcome these frictions. Indeed, many scholars who have maintained that censorship cannot work in the age of information have argued that eventually users will discover the information because censorship is porous and they will learn to circumvent it.[19] Censorship in China has frequently been described as a "cat and mouse game," where citizens adapt to censorship technologies, which forces the government to change these technologies in an effort to prevent this circumvention.

---

[19] Yang (2009*b*, pg. 30).

Perhaps in a repeated game, netizens would learn to gain access to information that was off-limits.

In this section, I will show that, on the contrary, structural frictions can have persistent effects on the majority of the population, even over the long term. I focus on how a form of censorship that has persisted over years, the Great Firewall, affects the information citizens access in China. Even though the costs of evading the Firewall are relatively low and the technology to do so is available, not many people in China regularly jump the Firewall. Those who regularly jump the Firewall are exceptional in that they typically have more resources, more technical capabilities, and an unusual interest in politics, and therefore have lower costs of access and greater expected benefits of evasion. Thus the Great Firewall structurally separates activist issue publics in China from the Chinese public at large.

In this chapter I use two methods of measuring who in China "jumps" or evades the Firewall and who does not. First, I use a survey of urban users in China in which respondents were asked about their Internet behavior, including whether or not they circumvented censorship. Second, I directly observe Twitter users who are using a VPN to tweet from China. Twitter has been blocked from Chinese IP addresses since 2009. As such, it is difficult to know when a user on Twitter is from China, as their IP address is routed through a third computer so they typically cannot be traced to China. Although users in China must use a VPN to post on the blocked site, if they are using mobile phones or other geo-located devices, their location is recorded and sent to the Twitter API. Thus, many users record their location in China even if they are using a VPN. Using this information, I sample users who have tweeted at some point from China to estimate the effect of the Great Firewall on Twitter use and the differences in conversations among people in China who are evading censorship and those who are using Chinese alternatives to Twitter, like Sina Weibo.

5.2.1 "Jumping" the Great Firewall

The Great Firewall of China blocks particular foreign websites from Chinese IP addresses. These websites include a wide range of content that the Chinese government deems objectionable, from foreign news websites that regularly report on sensitive events in China, like the *New York Times*, to pornographic websites, to companies that compete with Chinese Internet companies and refuse to censor content at the direction of the Chinese government, for example, Twitter, Facebook, and Google.

"Jumping" the Great Firewall in China at the time of writing is not penalized and is not difficult, but it does involve time and money. First, a citizen in China must use the Internet in order for it to be possible to jump the Great Firewall. China has around 649 million Internet users, which is about 48 percent of the Chinese population. The vast majority of Internet users (about 85 percent) access the Internet from their mobile phone.[20] In the survey of urban residents conducted in China in 2015, 60 percent of respondents reported having used the Internet, a larger proportion because those sampled were urban residents, who are more likely to have access to Internet infrastructure.[21] Eighty-six percent report that one of the ways that they access the Internet is through their mobile device.

If a person in China uses the Internet, the first step to evading the Firewall is to actually realize that the Firewall exists and that evading censorship is in fact possible. Among Internet users, 48 percent did not know what evasion of the Firewall meant when asked whether they had jumped the Firewall. Ruling out those

---

[20] "CNNIC "发布第35 次 《中国互联网络发展状况统计报告》," Cyberspace Administration of China, February 3, 2015, http://www.cac.gov.cn/2015-02/03/c_1114237273.htm.

[21] More information about the survey methodology is provided in the appendix.

who do not use the Internet and those who do not know that evasion is possible, this leaves us with only 30 percent of the total sample who both use the Internet and recognize that the Great Firewall restrictions can be circumvented.

Next, a user has to find a Virtual Private Network that would allow them to evade the Firewall. As VPNs are periodically blocked by the Chinese government, this entails locating and downloading a VPN that has not yet been blocked from within China. To use a VPN, users sometimes have to pay small sums of money, typically a few dollars a month. Users also must be patient, since VPN access to the Internet also can be quite slow, as traffic is routed through a third-party computer first before reaching the user. VPNs are also regularly blocked and thwarted, and therefore "jumping" the Firewall sometimes requires several working VPNs. Even though these barriers are by no means insurmountable, of the people who used the Internet and knew that evasion of the Firewall was possible, only 16 percent stated that they had used a VPN to jump the Firewall. That means that, out of the entire sample, only 5 percent of urban residents reported that they had jumped the Firewall.

Why don't users who know that evasion is possible jump the Firewall? The survey included a question to ask users who knew that evasion was possible but reported not having evaded censorship why they did not jump the Firewall. Only 2 percent of these users said that they did not jump the Firewall because they were fearful and only 9 percent of the users said that they did not jump the Firewall because of legal concerns. The vast majority of users said they did not jump the Firewall because they didn't have a reason to (45 percent), they did not know how (15 percent), or it was too bothersome (14 percent). Small frictions that users have no reason to overcome, rather than fear or deterrence, seem to keep people from accessing information blocked by the Chinese government.

5.2.2 Who Evades Censorship? Evidence from the Survey

Who evades the Firewall and how are these netizens different from the rest of the population? In this section, I describe the correlates of Firewall evasion among Internet users in China. I find that citizens who jump the Firewall tend to be highly educated, concerned about politics, and have sufficient skills to evade censorship. Consistent with the survey respondents' own accounts of why they do not jump the Firewall, those who jump the Great Firewall have relatively more skills and resources at their disposal and can overcome the technical difficulties of acquiring a VPN. Those who jump the Firewall also have more reasons to evade censorship: they are generally more interested in international politics, participate more in politics both online and offline, and overall have a lower opinion of the government than those who do not use VPNs.

5.2.2.1 Those Who Jump the Great Firewall Are Younger and Have More Education and Resources

Most significantly, citizens who jump the Firewall tend to be much younger than those who do not. Survey respondents who grew up during the age of the Internet are significantly more likely to jump the Firewall than those who entered their twenties before the Internet was introduced to China. Figure 5.3 shows the propensity to use the Internet, know about the Firewall, and evade the Firewall by age. Chinese citizens in their fifties, sixties, and seventies largely do not use the Internet and do not know much about the Great Firewall. There is a significant increase in those who jump and know about the Great Firewall for those younger than 35: approximately 10–20 percent of those younger than 35 know about and evade the Firewall. Respondents around the age of 35 were younger than 18 when the first Internet cafés

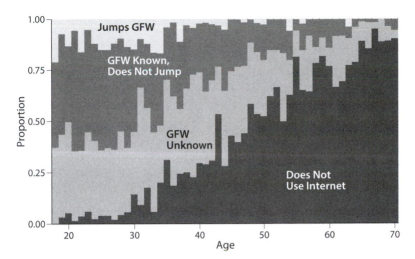

Figure 5.3: Internet use, knowledge of the Great Firewall, and evasion of censorship by age.

were appearing in major cities in China and therefore are the beginning of the generation who grew up with the Internet.[22]

In addition to being younger, those who jump the Firewall have attained far more skills through education than those who do not evade censorship. Seventy-five percent of those who jump the Firewall are either in college or have a college degree. In comparison, among those who do not evade censorship, only 25 percent have a college degree. Controlling for age, having a college degree means that a user is 10 percentage points more likely to jump the Great Firewall.

Technical capability is not the only thing needed to jump the Firewall. Access to VPNs cost a small amount of money. Individuals who jump the Firewall have an average family income of

[22] FlorCruz, Jaime A., and Lucrezia Seu, "From Snail Mail to 4G, China Celebrates 20 Years of Internet Connectivity," *CNN*, April 23, 2014, http://www.cnn.com/2014/04/23/world/asia/china-Internet-20th-anniversary/.

141,800 *yuan* per year, or $22,839.[23] Those who know what the Firewall is but do not jump it have an average family income of 87,100 *yuan* per year, or about $14,029. Those who do not use the Internet, in comparison, have an average income of 57,685 *yuan* per year, or $9,291. Those who jump the Great Firewall are also much less likely to be migrant workers in China—only 23 percent of those who jump the Great Firewall have a household registration in a rural area outside of the area, whereas 33 percent of all respondents had household registrations in rural areas and have migrated to the urban area where they were interviewed. Indeed, the Firewall exacerbates what scholars have called the digital divide by creating barriers to information that those with greater wealth and resources can more easily circumvent.[24]

Evaders of censorship are also more likely to be networked with foreigners, which would give them both more technological capacity to evade the Firewall and more reason to do so. Twenty-five percent of those who jump the Great Firewall say they can understand English, as compared with only 6 percent of all survey respondents.[25] Twelve percent of those who jump the Great Firewall work for a foreign-owned enterprise or foreign-based venture, compared to only 2 percent of all survey respondents. Forty-eight percent of those who jump the Great Firewall have been abroad,[26] compared with 17 percent of all respondents. Figure 5.4 shows a map of the proportion of Internet users in each province who indicated that they use a VPN. Unsurprisingly, the highest rates of censorship evasion

---

[23] Using an exchange rate from July 2015 http://www.x-rates.com/average/ ?from=USD&to=CNY&amount=1&year=2015 of 6.208627 *yuan* per U.S. dollar.

[24] Norris (2001); Schlozman, Verba and Brady (2010) show how the Internet serves the wealthy already; censorship exacerbates this.

[25] Questions about English ability were only asked to those with some college education, otherwise English ability is assumed to be zero.

[26] "Abroad" here includes Hong Kong and Macao.

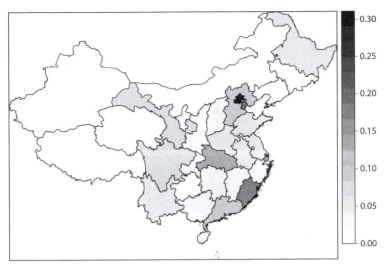

Figure 5.4: Proportion of internet users who evade censorship, by province. White indicates no data available.

are in large East Coast provinces with more connections to the outside world.

5.2.2.2 VPN Users: More Knowledgable about Politics with Less Trust in the Government

As described in the previous section, VPN users are typically better educated, have a higher income, and have more foreign connections than their counterparts who do not go to the trouble to evade censorship. Not only by their social standing, but also by their high levels of political knowledge, perceived efficacy, and participation, VPN users are part of the wealthy and educated class in China. However, VPN users on the whole have less trust in the government than users who do not jump the Firewall. Perhaps because they are very interested and participate in politics but do not trust the government, these citizens seek out information and social networks that the government blocks.

Those who evade the Firewall are more knowledgeable about politics than their counterparts. Forty percent of VPN users say they are interested in politics and 60 percent say they follow international politics, whereas only 28 percent of all respondents say that they are interested in politics and 30 percent say they follow international politics in the full sample. VPN users score higher than any other group on a political knowledge test within the survey—they are more likely to correctly name the Chinese president, U.S. president, and Japanese prime minister than those who do not use VPNs.

VPN users are also substantially more politically active and have high self-perceived political efficacy. They are more likely than any other group to have participated in political meetings, to have expressed their views to the government leadership, to have expressed their views through the media, to have participated in political protests, and to have petitioned the government.[27] Those who evade the Firewall also report much higher levels of political efficacy than their counterparts. When asked, "When you encounter unfair treatment, is your ability to solve the problem higher or lower compared with people you know?" VPN users are 11 percentage points more likely than those who do not evade the Firewall to report that they are much more or relatively more influential than people they know. These results hold up even when controlling for age, employment status, and college education, suggesting that VPN users see themselves as very capable in political situations, even in comparison to others within their social class.

Despite high levels of participation and political efficacy, VPN users are more distrustful of the government than even their well-to-do counterparts. Those who evade the Firewall believe the government is more corrupt than those who do

---

[27] Interestingly, VPN users are less likely to have voted in elections than other users.

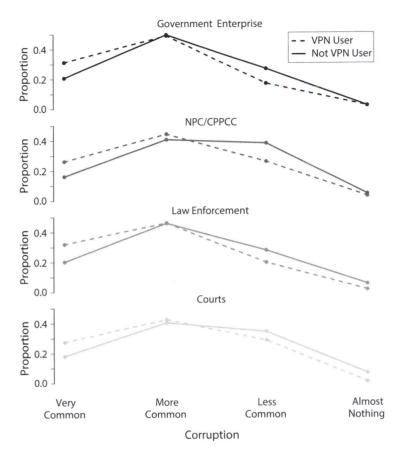

Figure 5.5: Evasion of the Great Firewall and perceptions of corruption in government.

not, even controlling for employment status, college education, and age. Figure 5.5 shows VPN users' and non-VPN users' answers to how vulnerable different levels of government are to corruption. VPN users, shown in the dotted line, consistently think that all types of government officials asked about in the survey are more corrupt than do their fellow citizens who do not jump the Firewall.

Naturally, VPN users are much stronger advocates of free speech and are more opposed to censorship than their fellow citizens who do not jump the Firewall. Seventy-two percent of VPN users in the survey disagreed with the statement, "The government should regulate the whole Internet," while only 60 percent of those who know about the Firewall but do not jump it disagreed with the statement, and only 57 percent of those who do not know about the Firewall disagreed with the statement. Eighty-five percent of VPN users agreed with the statement, "Internet governance should not violate individual freedom of expression," whereas only 77 percent of those who know about the Firewall but do not jump it agreed, and only 74 percent of those who did not know about the Firewall but were Internet users agreed.

Overall, the types of citizens in China who use VPNs are potentially threatening to the government. This set of people who jump the Firewall are well-endowed in terms of financial standing, education, technological sophistication, political and international connections, and political interest and knowledge. They frequently participate politically and know how to get things done, but overall they have less faith in government than their non-censorship-evading counterparts.

However, these users represent a very small fraction of the Chinese public. Conveniently, from the CCP's perspective, the Great Firewall separates this small group of political and well-educated users from the larger public simply by user selection, without resorting to repression or force. Because the broader public is less sophisticated and less politically interested, they will not take the time to enter into digital conversation across the Firewall.[28] Thus, the Firewall succeeds in creating a porous

---

[28] These findings are consistent with Chen and Yang (2017) who find that being given a VPN does not incentivize censorship evasion without attitional incentives to jump the Firewall.

but effective barrier between a skeptical class and the public they would have to connect with to have a bigger political impact.

5.2.3 Observations of VPN Users Using Geo-location

Of course, surveys rely on user-reported findings of evasion. These responses could contain measurement error due to social desirability bias, individuals rushing through the survey, or individuals misinterpreting questions. To retrieve a behavioral measure of evasion of the Great Firewall, in this section I identify Chinese users of the social media website Twitter, which is blocked in China. Although IP addresses that could locate individuals to China are masked by VPNs, the geographical location of the user is sometimes recorded by Twitter, particularly if the user is using a mobile phone or wants to publicly reveal their location by "checking in" at their location. In these cases, Twitter records the latitude and longitude of the user's Tweet and makes this information available for researchers through its API. If users geo-locate on Twitter to China, they must be using a VPN since Twitter is blocked from China.

To identify VPN users in China on Twitter, I use a random sample of approximately one-third of all geo-located tweets from China and Hong Kong (which is not affected by the Great Firewall) during September 2014 downloaded from the Twitter API. Geo-located tweets themselves are only a small subset of all Tweets; scholars have estimated that geo-located tweets are approximately 2–3 percent of the whole Twitter sample.[29] Therefore, the sample represents approximately .66 percent to 1 percent of total Twitter users from China and Hong Kong. My sample from the Twitter API returned on average 1,690 unique users per day tweeting from mainland China and on average 905 unique users per day tweeting from Hong Kong. As

---

[29] Leetaru et al. (2013).

the sample is approximately 1 percent of all Twitter users, a cursory estimate suggests that 169,000 unique Twitter users post each day from mainland China and 90,500 unique users post per day from Hong Kong. Given that there are about 5,388,354 Internet users in Hong Kong, this suggests that approximately 1.7 percent of Internet users in Hong Kong post on Twitter every day.[30] In comparison, in mainland China with about 675,131,785 Internet users, only .02 percent of Internet users post on Twitter every day.[31] Assuming Hong Kong provides an approximation for how much Chinese users *would use* Twitter *without* government censorship restrictions, this comparison suggests that China has about 1–2 percent of the Twitter users it would have without the Firewall restrictions. The Firewall, although easy to evade, is extremely effective at keeping Chinese users away from off-limits sites, even those that are popular in politically, culturally, and linguistically similar areas.

What types of users tend to jump the Firewall? To explore how Chinese Twitter users differ from typical social media users in China, we sampled geo-located Sina Weibo posts from the Beijing area in September 2014 and compared them with geo-located Twitter posts from the same area and time period.[32] After removing common Chinese words, figure 5.6 shows the fifty most frequently used terms on Twitter in China with their translations, and figure 5.7 shows the fifty most commonly used words on Sina Weibo with their translations. Consistent with the survey data, the most commonly used words on Twitter in China reflect the differences in the two user populations.

---

[30] Internet Live Stats, 2014 numbers. http://www.internetlivestats.com/internet-users/china-hong-kong-sar/.

[31] Internet Live Stats, 2014 numbers. http://www.internetlivestats.com/internet-users/china/.

[32] I remove posts by users who had indicated when they signed up for Twitter that their default language was a language other than Chinese to try to remove tourists and ex-pats from the sample. See Hobbs and Roberts (2016) for more details.

Figure 5.6: Fifty most common words after stopword removal, Chinese Twitter. Left panel, original words; right panel, English translation. Words are scaled in proportion to their frequency.

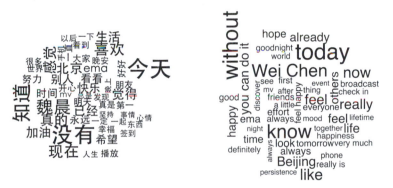

Figure 5.7: Fifty most common words after stopword removal, Sina Weibo. Left panel, original words; right panel, English translation. Words are scaled in proportion to their frequency.

Twitter users are more likely to use political words like "peace," "freedom," "country," and even to mention activists like Ilham Tohti, a Uyghur economist who was sentenced to life in prison in September 2014 for calling attention to repression in Xinjiang.[33] Chinese Twitter users are also likely to use words

---

[33] "China jails prominent Uighur academic Ilham Tohti for life," *BBC*, September 23, 2014, http://www.bbc.com/news/world-asia-29321701.

Figure 5.8: Fifty most common words after stopword removal, Hong Kong Twitter. Left panel, original; right panel, English translation. Words are scaled in proportion to their frequency.

about technology such as "Endomondoendorphins," a hashtag associated with the sports tracking application Endomondo. Chinese Twitter users—even those signed up in Chinese—are also much more likely to use English words, indicating that Chinese users of Twitter are more educated and internationalized. Weibo users, on the other hand, are starkly apolitical, most commonly discussing feelings and mood, or documenting the events of the day with words like "today," "tomorrow," "time," and "goodnight." They also are likely to discuss celebrities— one of the most popular words during this period is Wei Chen (魏晨), a popular Chinese pop star and singer.

Of course, these differences could be due partly to platform. Perhaps Twitter is simply a more political platform than Weibo and so Chinese citizens sign on to Twitter to discuss politics and use Weibo to chat with friends apolitically. However, mainland China users are conspicuously more political than their Chinese counterparts on Twitter who are not affected by the Firewall. Figure 5.8 shows the fifty most commonly used words on Twitter during the same period in Hong Kong. Instead of discussing politics, Hong Kong Twitter users are more similar to Sina Weibo users, discussing music, love, feelings, and celebrities. This suggests that the Firewall itself creates a barrier only particular types of users are willing to cross—users who tend to be highly educated, political, and technologically savvy. The Great Firewall creates two mostly disconnected social media communities—separating users who are dedicated to political activism away from the less engaged public.

5.2.4 Government Crackdowns on Websites

Despite the fact that the censorship imposed by the Great Firewall is incomplete and can be easily circumvented with a Virtual Private Network, small costs have large effects on which websites Chinese citizens are likely to access. In the last section, I showed that only a small fraction of the Chinese population regularly uses a VPN to evade the Firewall. In this section, I show that small costs of access also have dynamic effects on the types of information that Chinese users access. To do this, I show that when websites are blocked by the Great Firewall, fewer Chinese users access these sites. I focus on three cases of website blocks in China: (1) Google, which was slowly throttled but eventually completely blocked at the beginning of June 2014; (2) Wikipedia, which has been blocked intermittently by the Chinese government, but was completely blocked on May 19, 2015; and (3) Instagram, which was suddenly blocked during Hong Kong democracy protests on September 29, 2014. In each case, I use an interrupted time series analysis of website visits to understand how censorship influences Chinese traffic to the site.

Given the evidence provided in chapter 4 that observations of censorship backfire, it may seem contradictory that when a website is blocked in China it does not create more interest in the website. However, many users in China do not know that the Firewall exists and do not realize that the webpage is down due to censorship. Further, the government has developed ways to make censorship more ambiguous, throttling websites to make them slower instead of, or before, outright blocking them. I show at the end of this chapter that when Great Firewall blocks are more sudden and more obvious, more users download VPNs in an effort to jump the wall. The evidence provided here suggests that the more porous censorship is, the more easily it is disguised, and the more effective it can be at diverting access.

5.2.4.1 Case 1: Google

As I described earlier, Google entered into a conflict with the Chinese government in 2010, when it alleged that Chinese hackers had breached its servers. In March 2010, Google began redirecting traffic from the mainland to its Hong Kong website, which does not abide by mainland China censorship policies. Instead of outright blocking Google with the Great Firewall, the Chinese government began throttling the search engine, so it connected only part of the time. Finally, in June 2014, before the twenty-fifth anniversary of Tiananmen Square, the Chinese government blocked Google services outright.[34]

Even though Google was not completely blocked in China immediately after the dispute, the throttling of Google took an immediate toll on the number of Google users in China. Figure 5.9 shows the fraction of worldwide traffic from Chinese IP addresses to Google.com over the 2009 to 2015 period.[35] Initially after the alleged hack, Google received more traffic from China, perhaps as a result of increasing news about Google in China. However, immediately after the redirect, when the

---

[34] Levin, Dan, "China Escalating Attack on Google," *The New York Times*, June 2, 2014, https://www.nytimes.com/2014/06/03/business/chinas-battle-against-google-heats-up.html?_r=0.

[35] Data from Google's Transparency Report: https://www.google.com/transparencyreport/traffic/explorer/?r=CN&l=WEBSEARCH&csd=1235354784827&ced=1471030200000.

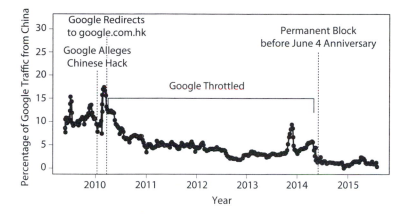

Figure 5.9: Proportion of Google traffic originating in China, 2010–2015.

Chinese government began throttling Google, traffic decreased precipitously. When Google was finally completely blocked in 2014, traffic from mainland China had already declined from an average of 10 percent of Google's traffic to 5 percent of its traffic. After the complete block, Chinese traffic made up less than 1 percent of the world's traffic to Google.com.

The Google case shows that the Chinese censors can control the popularity of websites by throttling them. Simply making a website slower frustrates users, giving them an incentive to switch websites. Such censorship also obscures the reason for the throttling. Was Google slow, or was this government censorship? In this way, porous censorship can diminish the backlash effects described in the previous chapter.

5.2.4.2 Case 2: Wikipedia

Like Google, Wikipedia has long had a fraught relationship with the Chinese government. Created in 2001 and first blocked in 2004, particular pages of Wikipedia such as descriptions of the Tiananmen Square protests have long been blocked. But

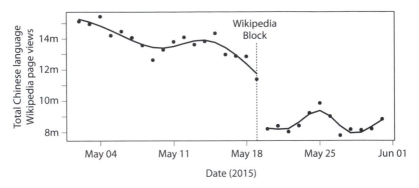

Figure 5.10: Chinese language Wikipedia page views, May 2015. All Wikipedia pages were blocked from mainland China beginning on May 19, 2015.

the entire Wikipedia website, too, has occasionally been made unaccessible from Chinese IP addresses.[36]

The entire Wikipedia site was again subject to the Great Firewall block on May 19, 2015.[37] To estimate the influence of the block on access to Wikipedia, I use data on the number of page views of Chinese Wikipedia (zh.wikipedia.org) during May 2015.[38] For each day, I summed the total number of page views on all Chinese-language Wikipedia pages. Figure 5.10 shows a sharp drop in the number of page views of Chinese Wikipedia pages, which occurred precisely on the day of the block—page views decreased from 11 million total page views per day to approximately 8 million.

From Wikipedia page views, we can't tell how many of the 11 million daily page views originated in China itself and

[36] Pan, Philip P, "Reference Tool on Web Finds Fans, Censors," *Washington Post*, February 20, 2006, http://www.washingtonpost.com/wp-dyn/content/article/2006/02/19/AR2006021901335.html.

[37] Fox-Brewster, Thomas, "Wikipedia Disturbed Over Fresh China Censorship," *Forbes*, May 22, 2015, http://www.forbes.com/sites/thomasbrewster/2015/05/22/wikipedia-disturbed-over-fresh-china-censorship/#6d046845f842.

[38] Page view data at http://stats.grok.se/.

which were accessed by users outside of mainland China—many of the page views may originate in Hong Kong, Taiwan, or from Chinese speakers living in other countries. If most of the 11 million page views per day were from mainland China the Wikipedia block decreased the number of mainland page views by 30 percent. However, it is likely that users of Chinese Wikipedia are more likely to originate from areas other than mainland China, which has its own Wikipedia-like website called Baidu Baike. Therefore, we expect that the block decreased the number of mainland users by substantially more than 30 percent. Regardless, the stark decrease in page views driven by the Wikipedia block reflects the amount of power the Chinese government has to affect the popularity of Chinese-language websites around the globe simply through friction.

5.2.4.3 Case 3: Instagram

Under very different circumstances, another widely popular social media website—Instagram—was also blocked in 2014. On September 26, 2014, pro-democracy protests broke out in Hong Kong over reforms to Hong Kong's electoral system initiated by the mainland Chinese government. Thousands of people took to the streets in what later became known as the "umbrella revolution." On September 29, 2014, the Chinese government blocked the social media website Instagram from mainland Chinese IP addresses, due to increased popularity among Hong Kong protesters.[39]

To study how the Instagram block influenced mainland users' access to Instagram, my coauthor and I sampled geo-located Instagram posts from across mainland China during September and October 2014. To do this, we used a geographical grid of China and randomly sampled locations in this grid. For each

---

[39] "Instagram Appears Blocked in China," *BBC*, September 29, 2014, http://www.bbc.com/news/technology-29409533.

randomly sampled location, we obtained all posts from the immediate area of the sample for the period, which we estimate reflects .25 percent of all Instagram posts.[40] The Instagram block halved the number of unique users accessing Instagram geo-locating to China overnight; only 53 percent of users continued to use Instagram after the block. Like Wikipedia, the Instagram block shows the powerful impact of filtering on traffic to popular social media websites.[41]

5.3 WHEN DOES FRICTION FAIL?

In the last section, I showed that by throttling and blocking websites, the Chinese government wields extensive power over the number of mainland Chinese users who frequent a website. Despite the ability to circumvent censorship, small costs of evasion generally decrease the number of people accessing the newly blocked website. However, this does not mean that Chinese Internet users are completely passive, at the whim of government censors. As I discussed in the previous chapter, Chinese users express substantial contempt for censorship, and make efforts to evade censorship when they are aware of it. In this chapter, I showed that particularly political and wealthy users with lower levels of trust in the government are likely to acquire Virtual Private Networks to evade censorship.

When will increases in costs of access change the behavior of citizens and prevent them from accessing a website? Users implicitly engage in a cost/benefit analysis when deciding whether to spend the time to evade censorship. They will be more

---

[40] If geo-located Instagram posts are 1 percent of all posts and the sample covered approximately 25 percent of all residences in China, then the sample reflects approximately .25 percent of all posts.

[41] For more detail on the study of the Instagram block in China, see Hobbs and Roberts (2016).

likely to spend the time and money to access blocked information when (1) blocked information is valuable to them, and (2) when censorship is applied suddenly, disrupting their short-term habits and raising awareness of censorship itself. In this section, I show how the circumstances of the block can have very different effects on user evasion behavior.

The value of blocked information depends partially on how easily information can be substituted by alternatives within China. The Chinese government has actively encouraged home-grown versions of foreign websites, and these homegrown versions are more easily controlled by censors than their foreign counterparts.[42] If the functionality of a foreign website can be easily substituted by an unblocked Chinese site, users may be unlikely to spend the time and resources to evade censorship.

Even if there are substitutes to the blocked website, the more suddenly a website is blocked, the more disruptive it will be to the habits of users, giving them incentives to seek out evasion technology to access the censored website rather than substitute with a Chinese version. If a citizen uses Gmail, a sudden block of Google may disrupt e-mail conversations or short-term projects, causing users to seek out a VPN to continue their short-term conversations. Slow, incomplete blocks, on the other hand, allow users to finish short-term projects with difficulty without seeking out a VPN, but eventually frustrate users enough so that they switch to the mainland Chinese substitute.

The three blocked websites discussed in the previous section—Google, Wikipedia, and Instagram—provide stark contrasts in the value and suddenness of each of their blocks. Instagram, an extremely popular photo site, does not have a direct Chinese analog and was blocked suddenly by the Chinese government during the Hong Kong protests, disrupting millions of users' photo sharing overnight. Google and Wikipedia, on

---

[42] Pan (2016).

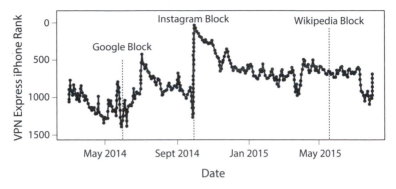

Figure 5.11: iPhone download rank in China of VPN Express, 2014–2015.

the other hand, both have mainland Chinese competitors—Google's analog in China is Baidu.com and Wikipedia's analog in China is Baidu Baike. Further, Google and Wikipedia have long been throttled by the Chinese government so not being able to access these websites was by no means sudden or unexpected.

These three blocks have very different implications for the number of people who sought to evade the Firewall because of the block. Figure 5.11 shows the download rank of the iPhone application VPN Express in mainland China on the days of each of the Google, Wikipedia, and Instagram blocks.[43] VPN Express increased in popularity only slightly after the Google block and was not more popular after the Wikipedia block than it was before—the block did not increase the popularity of evasion software. In contrast, the day of the Instagram block, the rank of VPN Express skyrocketed from the 1,229th most downloaded application in China to the sixth most downloaded application in China overnight. The Instagram block encouraged new users to download Virtual Private Networks, whereas the Google and Wikipedia blocks had few immediate effects.

---

[43] Information about download ranks obtained from App Annie, appannie.com.

The sharp increase in acquisition of Virtual Private Networks after the Instagram block highlights the difficulties the Chinese government faces in censoring suddenly during crises. Unlike Google and Wikipedia, where censorship was initiated from longstanding conflict between the companies and the Chinese government, censorship of Instagram was motivated by a protest event that the Chinese government was worried would affect political opinion of citizens in the mainland. Because of its quickly evolving nature, the government may have thought that it did not have time to slowly throttle Instagram, as it had done with Google and Wikipedia, before outright blocking it. Even though the government decreased citizens' overall access to Instagram, the Instagram block inspired more censorship evasion that facilitated user access to long-blocked websites such as Twitter and Facebook. Hobbs and Roberts (2016) show a spike in Twitter and Facebook downloads and user signups on the day of the Instagram block.

In general, crisis events complicate the government's ability to effectively use friction. Crises enhance citizen awareness of their political situation, which may make them more likely to spend the time and money necessary to find information, no matter how costly. As suggested by evidence in the previous chapter, sudden censorship that might accompany political crises may also alert citizens to the information that the government is trying to keep quiet, giving them incentives to seek out information that is not immediately available to them. Sudden censorship also disrupts habits, giving users incentives to seek out newly blocked informations.[44] Evidence from geolocated Instagram users during the Instagram block shows that users who continued to use Instagram through a VPN had significantly more likes and posts previous to the block than

---

[44] This is related to the "cute cat" theory of censorship proposed by Zuckerman (2014) where censorship that is blunt enough to include entertainment can create more backlash.

users who did not continue to use Instagram by evading the wall. It could be that the Instagram users downloaded a VPN simply to continue their habits, and in doing so were exposed to information already blocked by the Firewall.

Outside of VPN downloads before and after the sudden block of Instagram, the survey conducted in China in the summer of 2015 also suggests the Chinese citizens seek out censored information during crises. On August 12, 2015—which happened to fall in the middle of the survey of urban residents in China— explosions rocked the city of Tianjin, China, causing hundreds of deaths and injuries in apartment buildings nearby. Netizens uploaded to the web videos of the explosion—which was caused by a storage facility with overheated chemicals and could be seen from miles away—and the fire that spread from the explosion site to neighboring buildings.[45]

The enumerators of the 2015 survey happened to be between two waves of surveys in Tianjin when the Tianjin explosion took place. One of the starkest differences between the two waves of respondents in Tianjin was their propensity to have jumped the Firewall. For each day that the enumerators were in the field, figure 5.12 shows the proportion of those interviewed who jumped the Firewall. On the days before the explosion, only 5 percent of Internet users said they had jumped the Firewall. On the days following the explosion, almost 30 percent of Internet users admitted to having evaded censorship. Although we cannot be certain that these effects were directly due to the explosion, having been interviewed after the explosion in Tianjin predicts a 22 percentage point increase in the probability of jumping the Firewall, controlling for a battery of demographic and political characteristics. This evidence suggests that crises in which people have physical and financial incentives to seek out

---

[45] "China Explosions: What We Know about What Happened in Tianjin," *BBC*, August 17, 2015, http://www.bbc.com/news/world-asia-china-33844084.

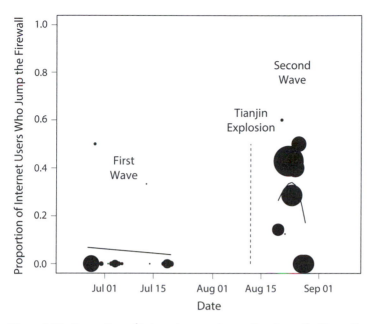

Figure 5.12: Proportion of Internet users who say they jump the Firewall, before and after the Tianjin explosion on August 12, 2015. Size of points reflects the sample size on each day.

information can undermine the effectiveness of friction-based censorship.

5.4 CONCLUSION

In sum, this chapter showed that small barriers to information access have important effects on the information consumption patterns of individuals in China. As I found first in the case of self-immolation events in Tibet, events that correspond to slightly quicker censorship are less likely to spread on social media than those that correspond with downtimes for the censors. Slight changes in the speed of censorship affect how much information is available to people in China about important political events within the country. Sudden censorship of websites starkly decreases how much they are visited by Chinese citizens. These blocks are particularly effective when censorship is porous—when governments throttle, but do not suddenly block, websites.

Even frictions that do not change over time have persistent effects on the online behavior of Chinese citizens. Very few people in China are knowledgeable and motivated enough to circumvent censorship from the Firewall, despite the fact that circumvention tools for the Great Firewall have existed for a decade. A back-of-the-envelope comparison to use of Twitter in Hong Kong indicates that Twitter use in mainland China is about 1–2 percent of what it would be were Twitter not blocked. This number is consistent with the results of our survey, which suggest that only 5 percent of urban respondents had jumped the Firewall. Those who do not jump the Firewall report that they have no reason to, that they do not know how, or that jumping the Firewall is too bothersome.

Those who take the time to circumvent the Firewall are from the upper class: are interested in politics, are highly educated, are networked with foreigners, and have high political efficacy and high incomes. While on blocked websites, they discuss sensitive topics like activists, the government, and human rights. The Great Firewall, therefore, separates the political discussion of the political elite from the rest of the public, strangling the potential for collective action by decreasing the following of those in the elite who are skeptical of the government.[46]

However, the very porous nature of censorship also means that there are limits on how much it can influence citizens. When there are few substitutes for blocked information, when information is blocked suddenly, or during crises when

---

[46] Barberá et al. (2015), Steinert-Threlkeld (2017), Chenoweth and Stephan (2011, pg. 39–40).

individuals have incentives to seek out off-limits information, citizens will be more likely to spend time and money thwarting the costs of access that the government has imposed on information. During these periods, the government will try to manage the conversation by dominating it, rather than by stalling it. In the next chapter I turn to the more indirect but increasingly popular method of censorship that functions through flooding. I show that the Chinese government uses flooding to distract from or compete with sensitive information in China, particularly during sensitive periods when friction may be less effective.

CHAPTER SIX

Information Flooding: Coordination as Censorship

In the afternoon of August 3, 2014, a 6.5-magnitude earthquake hit Yunnan province in China. The earthquake killed hundreds and injured thousands of people, destroying thousands of homes in the process. School buildings toppled and trapped children, reminiscent of the 2008 Sichuan earthquake, which killed 70,000 people, when the government was heavily criticized for shoddy construction of government buildings. Emergency workers rushed to the scene to try to rescue survivors.[1]

Eight hours after the earthquake struck, the Chinese official media began posting coordinated stories—not about the earthquake, but about controversial Internet personality Guo Meimei. Guo had reached Internet celebrity status three years earlier, in 2011, when she repeatedly posted pictures of herself dressed in expensive clothing and in front of expensive cars on Sina Weibo, attributing her lavish lifestyle to her job at the Red Cross in China.[2] Although Guo did not work at the Red Cross, her boyfriend, Wang Jun, was on the board of the Red Cross Bo-ai Asset Management Ltd., a company that coordinated charity events for the Red Cross. The expensive items that Guo had posed with on social media in 2011 were allegedly gifts from Wang. Attracting millions of commentators on social

[1] Jacobs, Andrew, "Earthquake Kills Hundreds In Southwest China," *New York Times*, August 3, 2014, http://www.nytimes.com/2014/08/04/world/asia/deadly-earthquake-in-southwest-china.html

[2] Hong, Haolan, and Jaime FlorCruz, "Red Cross China in Celebrity Crisis," *CNN*, July 6, 2011, http://www.cnn.com/2011/WORLD/asiapcf/07/06/china.redcross/.

media, the 2011 Guo Meimei scandal highlighted issues with corruption of charities in China, and donations to the Red Cross plummeted.

By 2014, when the earthquake hit, the Guo Meimei scandal was old news, long forgotten by the fast pace of the Internet. On July 10, 2014, Chinese officials had arrested Guo on allegations of gambling on the World Cup.[3] Then, out of the blue, on midnight of August 4, 2014, *Xinhua* posted a long, detailed account of a confession made by Guo Meimei that included admissions of gambling and engaging in prostitution.[4] On the same day, many other major media outlets followed suit, including major media outlets such as CCTV,[5] the *Global Times*,[6] *Caijing*,[7] *Southern Weekend*,[8] *Beijing Daily*,[9] and *Nanjing Daily*.[10]

The overwhelming number of newspapers sensationalizing the Guo Meimei confession on August 4 seemed too coincidental to be uncoordinated. Indeed, the *China Digital Times* received a government leak on August 4 that directed websites to "prominently display Xinhua and CCTV coverage of Guo Meimei, and to actively organize and direct commentary."[11]

3 "警方透露郭美美赌球犯罪细节：8人团伙 境外网站开户," *iFeng*, http://ent.ifeng.com/a/20140710/40171148_0.shtml.

4 "从炫富到涉赌，她为何堕入犯罪深渊？——郭美美涉嫌赌博犯罪罪被刑拘的背后," 新华, http://news.xinhuanet.com/legal/2014-08/04/c_111191 4547.htm.

5 "郭美美设赌局牟利数十万 "商演" 为名从事性交易," *CCTV*, http://news.cntv.cn/special/video/guomeimei/index.shtml.

6 "郭美美案引外媒关注:郭美美栽了 公权力莫再栽," *Global Times*, http://world.huanqiu.com/exclusive/2014-08/5095684.html.

7 "央视播出郭美美画面：素颜戴眼镜 戴着手铐下楼(图)," *Caijing*, http://politics.caijing.com.cn/20140804/3641759.shtml.

8 " "炫富女" 郭美美涉赌被刑拘 想对红会说声对不起," *Southern Weekend*, http://www.infzm.com/content/102888.

9 "王军谈包养郭美美:她是我一生的噩梦," *Beijing Daily*, http://news.sina.com.cn/c/2014-08-04/023930624032.shtml.

10 "郭美美: 23年素描: 20岁时因红会炫富事件走红," *Nanjing Daily*, http://news.sina.com.cn/c/2014-08-04/014130623848.shtml.

11 "Minitrue: Guo Meimei's Confession," *China Digital Times*, August 4, 2014, http://chinadigitaltimes.net/2014/08/minitrue-guo-meimeis-confession/.

The state propaganda apparatus seemed to be actively trying to engage the public with a story about a celebrity turned criminal and prostitute.

Why engage the public on Guo Meimei on that particular date? Many netizens and foreign media alleged that the Chinese government directed the coordination of news as a distraction from the Yunnan earthquake, which had the potential to reveal failings of the government's earthquake preparedness. Netizens noted that the Weibo account of the *People's Daily* posted a dozen times about Guo Meimei *before* reporting on the Yunnan earthquake—the major news story of the day—on the morning of August 4.[12] The focus on Guo, who had enraptured Chinese netizens years earlier, may have been a ploy to distract netizens from an unraveling crisis in southwest China.[13] In response, the Chinese Red Cross posted on its Weibo, "Rescue teams are working through the night, and time is of the essence. . . . So please, forget Guo Meimei."[14]

In the previous chapter, I showed that small costs that inconvenience online users can have important effects on citizens' online behavior, the spread of information about political events in China, and the potential for coordination between highly educated, internationalized citizens and the public. In this chapter, I focus on a different form of porous censor-

[12] Yuen, Lotus, "The Bizarre Fixation on a 23-Year-Old Woman," *ChinaFile*, August 6, 2014, https://www.chinafile.com/reporting-opinion/media/bizarre-fixation-23-year-old-woman.

[13] Boehler, Patrick, and Cece Zhang, 'I Like to Show Off': Chinese Celebrity Guo Meimiei Confesses to Prostitution, Gambling Charges on State TV," *South China Morning Post*, August 4, 2014, http://www.scmp.com/news/china-insider/article/1566142/i-show-guo-meimei-confesses-all-charges-cctv-broadcast; "Heavy Media Takedown of Guo Meimei Angers Chinese Netizens," *Offbeat China*, August 4, 2014, http://offbeatchina.com/heavy-media-takedown-of-guo-meimei-angers-chinese-netizens.

[14] Larson, Christina, "Stated Confession of Alleged Call Girl Guo Meimei Distracts From a Charity's Earthquake Relief Efforts," *Bloomberg*, August 5, 2014, http://www.bloomberg.com/news/articles/2014-08-05/guo-meimei-falsely-claimed-to-be-a-big-shot-at-chinas-red-cross.

ship, *flooding*, or the promotion of information, which changes the relative costs of access by making competing information cheaper and off-limits information relatively more expensive. The difference between friction and flooding can be explained by an analogy to taxes on something the government would rather people not buy, like gas-guzzling cars. If the government wanted fuel inefficient cars to circulate less within the economy, then it could either tax these cars directly, increasing the cost and therefore decreasing demand, or subsidize fuel efficient cars, which would increase the relative cost of fuel inefficiency and decrease demand. Similarly, the government can affect the cost of information by making the information harder to access (friction), or by promoting competing or distracting information (flooding). If successful, flooding-based censorship should have very similar effects to friction on the spread of information and the behavior of individuals.

The actual content of flooding can take a variety of different forms. As I show in the rest of the chapter, like the case of Guo Meimei, flooding in China often occurs when the government promotes information completely unrelated to a negative event the government would rather not be salient in the minds of the public. I will show a number of cases of flooding where government-flooded information is meant to distract. In other cases, governments use flooding to downplay or to control the narrative of an event by mandating the promotion of their own views on the event that compete with alternative views. This might be more likely to happen when the government has already lost control of a narrative of an event so that they cannot simply ignore it. Last, flooding sometimes has a more long-term goal, not in response to one event directly but with the intention to shape citizens' perspectives on politics. In these cases, flooding might be used to promote the government's overarching narrative about world events or encourage citizens to have a positive outlook on their own life. This latter type of flooding may not be in response to one event in particular, but may be meant to shape citizen perspectives on politics and their reactions to subsequent crises.

In addition to affecting the relative costs of information, flooding also acts as a less observable form of censorship because it does not bring attention to the information the political entity is trying to hide. Information flooding occurs when a group or government promotes its viewpoint by ensuring that a particular piece of information or a particular perspective is repeated from many different sources in the news media or social media. Because of the repetition, this information is highly accessible and may be virtually impossible for citizens to avoid. Citizens are likely to come across the information and are likely to share it with others, and the more citizens spend time consuming the information, the more it will distract them from other ongoing events.

As I noted in the previous chapter, friction is less effective for governments during crises, as citizens may be more willing to go out of their way to seek out censored information and information may have already spread to large networks of people, making it difficult to control. When the government has less control over information it would like to stall, the government will often resort to spreading alternative versions of events or distractions to de-emphasize the negative information, even when they cannot prevent citizens from accessing it. Flooding can also be an attempt to gain control of the narrative of a quickly escalating story, rather than preventing citizens from knowing it in the first place. Flooding might also be relatively more effective when the public is searching for new information, or early in an unfolding crisis.[15]

Unlike friction, which can be measured by observing post removal or website blocks, flooding is more difficult to measure

[15] Baum and Groeling (2010) have found that the public is more manipulable in democracies at the beginning of a conflict, when they have accumulated less information.

because it is often disguised as the typical spread of information. To empirically test how information flooding strategies implemented by the Chinese government influence the spread of information online, I describe coordinated efforts by the Chinese government to publish information in traditional and online media. Drawing on previous work,[16] I show that coordination of information is designed as a censorship strategy by the Chinese government, to provide news stories and viewpoints that overwhelm existing news stories or online information. I identify instances of propaganda in Chinese newspapers using plagiarism detection software and identify propaganda posts by using leaked e-mail archives from Chinese online government commentators.[17] I find that these flooding efforts reverberate in both the domestic and the international blogosphere, suggesting that the Chinese government is in fact effective in distracting from alternative news sources and promoting its own version of events.

In the next section, I review information flooding as a method of censorship and highlight how it differs from previous theories of propaganda. In the following section, I discuss the use of flooding strategies by the Chinese government. I then describe the data I use to identify the Chinese government's flooding efforts. In the last section, I estimate how information flooding influences the spread of information online.

6.1 WHAT EFFECT CAN PROPAGANDA HAVE IN THE DIGITAL AGE?

Using similar logic to scholars who maintain that censorship is impossible in a digital age, many scholars have argued that propaganda, or the promotion of information, is also outdated

---

[16] Roberts and Stewart (2016).
[17] King, Pan and Roberts (2017).

in the age of the Internet.[18] These researchers maintain that propaganda can be effective only when the state can control the agenda, or when the number of sources of information is constrained. As the number of media sources has proliferated with the advent of the Internet, consumers of information have more choices over the sources of information. In these environments, consumers of information select out of biased state media sources and into sources with more "reliable" information.[19]

A few authors oppose this view, arguing that although state media is recognizable, propaganda is a signal of government power and therefore is closely followed by citizens.[20] Propaganda, in these authors' views, creates norms that citizens are trained to follow.[21] Even if this propaganda is unbelievable, by inducing participation in propaganda, the state can create rituals and standards that encourage compliance.[22] In particular, in China, the government emphasizes propaganda to promote cultural governance, appealing to citizens' emotions to prevent protests and keep them in line with government policy.[23]

In this chapter, I show that propaganda can also be effective as a form of censorship in the online environment by influencing the relative costs of information. Political entities coordinate propaganda by repeating information from multiple sources so that it is low cost to citizens. Because such repetition increases the availability of information to citizens, the population becomes more likely to consume propaganda, regardless of whether they can identify the source. The "flooding" of information in the news media and blogosphere by political

---

[18] Lynch (1999, pg. 3–4), Lieberthal (1995).
[19] See Stockmann (2012, Chapter 8).
[20] Huang (2015).
[21] Brady (2008, pg. 134).
[22] Wedeen (1999).
[23] Perry (2013).

entities works not so much to signal power as to prioritize the consumption of government-produced news over news produced by other groups or by citizens themselves. Propaganda is effective because political entities have the resources to make it easy to access and low cost, and, for impatient online users, low-cost stories are more likely to be read and to reverberate throughout the blogosphere.

Coordination of propaganda has long been used by governments and other organized groups to promote information. China's 1977 Propaganda Directive explicitly directs the Propaganda Department to coordinate stories among the news media in order to "promote the CCP's current line."[24] More recently, governments and mobilized interests around the world have organized "Internet armies" to flood the blogosphere at the same moment. Notoriously, the Chinese "Fifty Cent Party" allegedly pays Chinese netizens to post at the direction of the government. Although the Chinese have been criticized for this strategy, other governments have adopted similar strategies, including Israel, where representatives have been recruited to post on blogs that are "anti-Zionist,"[25] and recently Turkey, which has a 6,000-member social media team to write pro-government posts.[26]

Not only the central government, but also individual Chinese government officials and companies use coordinated flooding strategies to bolster support. These groups pay public relations companies or unemployed citizens to post positive accounts of

[24] Brady (2008, pg. 15).

[25] Liphshiz, Cnaan, "Israel Recruits 'Army of Bloggers' to Combat Anti-zionist Web Sites," *Haaretz*, January 19, 2009, http://www.haaretz.com/print-edition/news/israel-recruits-army-of-blogers-to-combat-anti-zionist-web-sites-1.268393.

[26] Albayrak, Alya and Joe Parkinson, "Turkey's Government Forms 6,000-Member Social Media Team Volunteers to Promote Ruling Party's Perspective in Sphere Dominated by Protestors," and *Wall Street Journal*, September 16, 2013, http://online.wsj.com/news/articles/turkeys-government-forms-6000member-social-media-team-1379351399.

them online, like companies in the United States that will pay for positive reviews of their company on the web. Such actions have created scandals in China from time to time, because these local officials and companies regularly pay newspapers for articles that reflect positively on them.[27]

If governments, companies, and politicians were using such messages only to signal their own strength, they would want to take credit for these online messages. However, governments typically try to cover up the fact that they pay people to write online propaganda. Instead, they prefer that it appear as if "everyone" is writing pro-government comments or reporting a news story the government finds favorable or distracting. Part of the strategy of information flooding is issuing propaganda from many different sources, so as to disguise the fact that the information originated with the government.

Disguising the source of information flooding provides an added benefit to the government in that it has less potential to sully government credibility. Even though state news media already promote government versions of events, too much blatant government cheerleading may make the government media appear more biased. Except in obvious cases of coordination, like the Guo Meimei case described in the introduction, where netizens noticed the coordinated stories, most citizens may not realize that their local paper or the social media forums they visit are infiltrated with government propaganda. Incomplete control of the information environment allows the government to hide its own influence in the media by mixing with normal users.

By creating a multiplier effect in the news media and online, information flooding if successful can be worth the investment even though it is porous and cannot require readers to pay attention. The more sources a government or interest group can pay

[27] Chen, Wang, Shanshan Wang, Zhongyuan Ren, and Yishi Zhu, "Dirty Business for China's Internet Scrubbers, *CNBC*, February 19, 2013, http://www.cnbc.com/id/100472398.

to cover their story from their perspective, the more other news groups and other social media users pick up the story and share it with others. Flooding begets more flooding, and, if effectively done, this domino effect of information dissemination can be exponential. What began as a propaganda message can seem like an online event created by citizens as more and more people read and share the story.

Flooding creates friction for stories that are less desirable to the government. In interviews with Fifty Cent Party members, artist-dissident Ai Weiwei reveals that Fifty Cent Party members are often instructed to distract from current stories that are less desirable to the government.[28] This account is consistent with evidence from my work studying a leaked e-mail archive of online government-paid commentators that I describe later in this chapter.[29] Flooding of entertainment and "soft news" stories like the Guo Meimei confession brings these stories to the forefront at the expense of stories that could shed a negative light on the government. If citizens are distracted by the accessibility of flooded stories, they are less likely to read other stories.

6.2 FLOODING IN CHINA

Coordination of information to produce such flooding is key to the information strategies of the Chinese propaganda system. Like many organized groups, the Chinese government is in the perfect position to coordinate because it has the resources and infrastructure to do so. First, the institution of propaganda in China is built in a way that makes coordination easy. The Propaganda Department is one of the most extensive bureaucracies within the Chinese Communist Party, infiltrating every

---

[28] "An Insider's Account of the '50 Cent Party,'" *Freedom House China Media Bulletin*, May 12, 2011, http://www.freedomhouse.org/article/china-media-bulletin-issue-no-22/#2.

[29] King, Pan, and Roberts (2017).

level of government.[30] It is managed and led directly from the top levels of the CCP.

From the very top of the Party, messages are coordinated throughout the news media within China, through every medium of news, including television, print, and radio.[31] The government controls the personnel in every major media organization within China and requires each journalist to be government-certified. For day-to-day monitoring of content, the government issues propaganda directives to editors, who then decide what to include in the newspaper.[32] Postpublication monitoring is conducted by retired propaganda officials who make sure that newspapers are following the issued guidelines.[33]

The extent of newspaper coordination within China has waxed and waned throughout recent Chinese history. During the Maoist period and Cultural Revolution, articles within the *People's Daily* coordinated news around the country—smaller newspapers would reprint *People's Daily* articles when instructed.[34] With reform and opening after 1979, the coordination of news within China was significantly loosened and the Central Propaganda Department was weakened.[35] In the lead-up to the Tiananmen Square pro-democracy movement in 1989, newspapers were less coordinated, and several Chinese newspapers became well known as critics of the Party.

The events of 1989 caused a complete reversal in the CCP's strategy toward propaganda and coordination. After the crisis in Tiananmen Square, the government decided to strengthen its grip on propaganda. For example, in 1990, one of the Party's

---

[30] Lieberthal (1995, pg. 194–199)

[31] In this chapter, I focus explicitly on coordination within the print news and online media in China.

[32] Brady (2008, pg. 19).

[33] Brady (2008, pg. 22).

[34] Yu (1964, pg. 110–121).

[35] Brady (2008, pg. 40).

leading news agencies, *Xinhua*, was close to bankrupt. However, the government decided to use *Xinhua* as the coordinating agency following 1989, instructing newspapers to follow *Xinhua*'s lead on important events and international news, much as they had done with the *People's Daily* during the 1960s.[36] *Xinhua* is now one of the most profitable news agencies in the country because it leads the coordination of news.

Coordination of government media has now extended beyond traditional media to the blogosphere. As mentioned earlier, paid government commentators, or the "Fifty Cent Party," promote government-sanctioned news online. In addition, the government is known to contact high-profile social media users and important online opinion leaders before important events in order to coordinate political messages among highly followed social media users in China.[37]

6.3 DETECTION OF INFORMATION FLOODING IN NEWSPAPERS AND ONLINE MEDIA

In this section, I will show that coordination of information across government newspapers and online is often used for the purpose of censorship. In particular, coordination of information is used to distract from or prevent the dissemination of other types of information that the government would rather the public not see. I will show that the Chinese government uses newspaper and online propaganda not only to persuade, but also to throttle access to other forms of information. In the next sections, I will provide evidence that such coordination does indeed influence the spread of information online.

---

[36] Brady (2008, pg. 113).
[37] This strategy is described in case studies in propaganda documents, such as National Academy for Propaganda Cadres (2011).

To show that flooding is used for censorship, I must first identify propaganda. This is a difficult task because the spread of propaganda in China is a clandestine operation. For the most part, the government would rather that citizens not be able to distinguish propaganda from typical social media posts or the regular commercial news media. Stockmann (2012) describes how the commercialization of print media in China has allowed for propaganda to blend in with news, which may make it more believable and distracting for citizens, who may discount information that they believe originated with the government.[38] The government's online propaganda program is also a secretive enterprise where online propagandists attempt to blend into the normal social media environment. In this section, I use leaked propaganda directives from the government and leaked e-mail archives linked to online propagandists to reverse engineer general propaganda trends. I show that the instructions and trends in propaganda are consistent with an information flooding strategy intended to distract from alternative viewpoints or events that could negatively affect public opinion toward the government.

6.3.1 Identification of Propaganda in Newspapers

To identify newspaper propaganda in China, my coauthor and I combined leaked propaganda directives published online by the *China Digital Times*[39] with detection of coordination in a large collection of government newspapers.[40] Since the Chinese government uses propaganda directives to facilitate coordination, we reverse engineered propaganda by identifying days when all newspapers publish the same or nearly identical articles. We used the leaked propaganda directives to validate this measure

---

[38] See Stockmann and Gallagher (2011) for a description of how this phenomenon has impacted perceptions of Chinese legal policy.

[39] http://chinadigitaltimes.net/.

[40] Roberts and Stewart (2016).

and describe in more detail the kinds of instructions provided by the government to promote coordination. We found that large numbers of coordinated newspaper articles appear during sensitive political meetings and around sensitive political scandals, seemingly to distract or downplay the events.

To find coordinated newspaper articles, we collected every newspaper article from twenty-five provincial and city newspapers in China for the year 2012. The newspapers were scraped from each newspaper's "digital" website. These sites are different from the online news sites in that they contain only digital copies of the printed newspaper and do not include online advertisements. Although some Chinese newspapers' websites differ from their printed papers, the articles on the digital website reflect the content of the printed newspaper exactly. We recorded the date on which each article was published, the full text, and the page number of each of the articles. In total, the dataset contains 111,789 articles during the year 2012.

To identify moments of coordination, we grouped the articles by the date on which they were written. For each day, we compared each pair of articles written on that date to look for overlap between articles using open-source plagiarism detection software called Copyfind.[41] Copyfind works by identifying overlap between phrases of a specified length within the document pair. It then estimates the percentage of overlap in these phrases between the two documents, allowing for slight imperfections between phrase matches. High levels of phrase overlap indicate plagiarism, or in this case article coordination.

Of course, some forms of coordination between articles occur naturally, without directives from higher levels of government. Some newspapers may reprint *Xinhua* or the *People's Daily* not at the direction of the government, but to save on cost, a process called syndication. However, it is unlikely that coordination

---

[41] Copyfind software available at: http://plagiarism.bloomfieldmedia.com/z-wordpress/software/copyfind/.

of identical stories across the vast majority of papers would occur naturally simply because of syndication. Only seldom will editors of the majority of papers decide to report on the same story. In the cases where the story was important enough that all papers would want to print an article covering it, typically a subset of the papers will devote resources to printing their own version of the event. Therefore, syndication that occurs naturally, not by design, should occur across small subsets of papers, and almost never across every paper. If an identical story were printed across every paper, there is a high chance that coordination was designed by the Propaganda Department.

We found that reprints of newspaper articles across papers corresponded with this expectation. Among groups of article reprints, more than 50 percent of articles had a total of only two newspapers that printed overlapping stories. More than 95 percent of overlapping articles were featured in fewer than ten newspapers, or fewer than half of the papers. Less than 1 percent of overlapping articles had more than fifteen newspapers that were coordinated. Printing of identical news stories among large numbers of newspapers is a rare phenomenon.

To validate that the coordination among large groups of articles is by government design rather than by chance, we looked for leaked propaganda directives that correspond to the coordinated articles identified by the algorithm. The *China Digital Times* (CDT) contains a collection of both propaganda and censorship directives collected from journalists in China. These directives are posted on the CDT's website http://chinadigitaltimes.net.[42] If some of the highly coordinated days also correspond to leaked directives, this will validate that

---

[42] The vast majority of the leaked directives the CDT collects are censorship directives, detailing what the newspapers should not print rather than what they should print. Some of the CDT directives are a combination of censorship and propaganda directives, suggesting that if papers would like to write on a topic, they can only use the *Xinhua* or *People's Daily* version of events.

our algorithm is picking up moments of government-induced coordination.

Many of the coordinated events we found within the newspapers had corresponding leaked propaganda directives. In one example, a leaked propaganda directive on November 18, 2012, indicated that all media should emphasize a *Xinhua* article that urges readers to study and implement the 18th Party Congress's collective learning ideology.[43] In the newspaper corpus we collected, nineteen of the twenty-five newspapers printed a version of this article that had over 70 percent phrase overlap with others that had printed the same article, and all of the newspapers for which we could collect page numbers printed the article on their first page.

In another example, in March 2012, a propaganda directive indicated that newspapers should report the *Xinhua* version of a meeting between Wen Jiabao and reporters.[44] Nineteen out of twenty-three newspapers printed that day included the same version of this story. On November 28, 2012, a leaked propaganda directive indicated that newspapers should follow *Xinhua* in reporting on the death of Luo Yang, the main architect of the J-15 Chinese fighter jet.[45] Seventeen of twenty-three newspapers that printed that day had the same reprinted version of the story. The correspondence between these leaked directives and the coordinated articles with reprints across many papers provides

43 "【真理部】中央政治局集体学习," *China Digital Times*, http://china digitaltimes.net/chinese/2012/11/%E4%B8%AD%E5%AE%A3%E9%83%A8%EF%BC%9A%E4%B8%AD%E5%A4%AE%E6%94%BF%E6%B2%BB%E5%B1%80%E9%9B%86%E4%BD%93%E5%AD%A6%E4%B9%A0/

44 "【真理部】温总理记者见面会," *China Digital Times*, http://chinadigital times.net/chinese/2012/03/%E4%B8%AD%E5%AE%A3%E9%83%A8%EF%BC%9A-%E6%B8%A9%E6%80%BB%E7%90%86%E8%AE%B0%E8%80%85%E8%A7%81%E9%9D%A2%E4%BC%9A/

45 "【真理部】罗阳逝世," *China Digital Times*, http://chinadigitaltimes.net/chinese/2012/11/%E4%B8%AD%E5%AE%A3%E9%83%A8%EF%BC%9A%E7%BD%97%E9%98%B3%E9%80%9D%E4%B8%96/

strong evidence that highly coordinated newspapers are often the result of government efforts in propaganda.

6.3.1.1 Coordination: Sensitive Time Periods, on Sensitive Issues

Now that we have developed a measure of propaganda across provincial and city newspapers, we can identify when coordination is used by the government, to better understand the purpose of newspaper propaganda. Does coordination happen at regular intervals? Or during particular time periods? When does the Party decide it needs to control the information environment?

Figure 6.1 maps the number of coordinated events over time, where at least 70 percent of newspapers printed the same article. The largest numbers of coordinated articles occurred during Party meetings, particularly the extremely sensitive period of the power transition between Hu Jintao and Xi Jinping in November 2012. During this time period, there was extremely high coordination among papers—at the highest point, four separate articles were coordinated on one day across almost all papers. The coordinated articles that are printed during the meeting are about the proceedings of the events and Party ideology. By forcing all papers to print the same version of the event, the Party prevents alternative interpretations of the most high-level Party meetings and spreads the Party's perspective on its own governance.

The prevalence of propaganda during this period also aligns with journalists' own account of Party media control around important meetings. Journalists reported being required to avoid any negative news or commentary for the entire month of November 2012.[46] Further, many of the articles coordinated during this period were printed on the front pages of the

---

[46] Duggan, Jennifer, "China Internet Censored for Party Congress," *Al Jazeera*, November 17, 2012, www.aljazeera.com/indepth/features/2012/11/20121115105540550384.html.

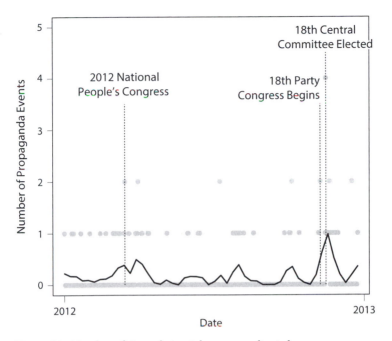

Figure 6.1: Number of times that articles are coordinated across more than 70% of papers by day, 2012. Highest levels of coordination appear during national meetings.

papers. The Party's interpretation of the meetings and news about the meetings were by design the first thing newspaper readers saw during the November transition of power from Hu Jintao to Xi Jinping, de-emphasizing other stories that could detract from the Party's spotlight or call into question the Party's power.

The other main cluster of coordinated news articles outside of the March and November meetings was in August 2012. This corresponds to an extremely sensitive event within the Party—the trial of the wife of the Party Secretary of Chongqing Bo Xilai, Gu Kailai, who was given a deferred death sentence in August 2012 for murdering a British businessman. The cluster of propaganda around this time may have occurred as a distraction from this sensitive event. Although not all of the articles discuss the event directly, some allude to it, urging Party members to understand the full meaning of "socialism with Chinese characteristics," and encouraging Party discipline.

Coordination seems to be not only a tool to distract from sensitive events within the Chinese government but also a means of control of newspapers so that alternative views of these events cannot gain traction in the media. Articles relating to the sentencing of Wang Lijun and Gu Kailai in 2012 are frequently coordinated across papers and appear in the leaked propaganda directives, but the message is to de-emphasize the event. The purpose of coordination in these circumstances is to prevent the newspapers from providing alternative accounts of the incident or sensationalizing it, thereby explicitly censoring the editorial leeway of the newspapers.

Similarly, discussion of policies on the environment, corruption, food safety, real estate prices, and relations with Japan are also sometimes coordinated, again perhaps to prevent sensationalist versions of these events. Leaked propaganda directives associated with these events tend to instruct that they should be de-emphasized to the back pages of the newspaper and not "hyped."[47] Coordination, in this case, is used not to distract, as it is during Party meetings or sensitive periods, but to control the number of alternative stories about the policy implementation or sensitive event.

Overall, in this section, I showed that newspaper propaganda is often used as a tool of censorship by filling the front pages of the newspapers during sensitive periods and controlling reporting and placement of stories within newspapers on sensitive topics. Rather than always being used to persuade or cajole the

---

[47] "Directives from the Ministry of Truth: Food Safety," *China Digital Times*, August 17, 2012, http://chinadigitaltimes.net/2012/08/directives-from-the-ministry-of-truth-food-safety/.

reader, as we often think of propaganda, the flooding strategy of the Chinese government is to affect the likelihood that readers come across particular articles or accounts of events. In the next section, I look to see whether these same strategies also appear in the Chinese government's approach to online propaganda.

6.3.2 Identification of Online Propaganda

To identify the online flooding strategy employed by the Chinese government, I turn to leaked e-mail archives from a local propaganda department. These archives, leaked by blogger "Xiaolan,"[48] provide several years of e-mail correspondence between a local propaganda department in Zhanggong county in Jiangsu province and government officials who had been tasked with posting online propaganda. Many of the e-mails include posts that internet commentators nicknamed the "Fifty Cent Party" made at the direction of the local propaganda department. Although we have no way of knowing whether the e-mail archive is complete, the leaked e-mails give us a window into the instructions and propaganda posts that were coordinated by government entities over this period.

In order to identify the online propaganda, a team of research assistants went through each of the 2,000 e-mails in the archive to extract the details and reports of the online propaganda posts. In total, the research assistants identified 43,757 online propaganda posts on around 2,000 accounts over a two-year time period.[49] A full description of the post collection process and full analysis of the posts are included in King, Pan and Roberts (2017).

---

[48] https://xiaolan.me/50-cent-party-jxgzzg.html.
[49] The archive's authenticity was verified by locating posts from the archive online.

6.3.2.1 China's Fifty Cent Party: Highly Coordinated Cheerleading

If propaganda were meant to persuade, online propaganda posts should address the political questions that are highly contested within the blogosphere. Current conceptions of online propaganda in China posit that the Fifty Cent Party is primarily tasked with countering anti-government rhetoric online. Social media users are accused of being Fifty Cent Party members when they defend government positions in heated online debates about policy, or when they attack those with anti-government views. In large part, scholars and pundits have viewed Fifty Cent Party members as attackers aimed at denouncing or undermining pro-West, anti-China opinion.[50] Fifty Cent Party members, for the most part, have been seen in the same light as traditional propaganda—as intending to persuade rather than to censor.

For the most part, however, the leaked online e-mail archive containing Fifty Cent Party posts does not suggest that the purpose of Fifty Cent Party posts is to take on critics of the Chinese government, or persuade people to support Chinese government policy. Very few of the thousands of posts in the archive were *argumentative* in nature or were aimed at defending the government against attackers or attacking its critics. Instead, the vast majority of Fifty Cent Party posts seem to be designed to distract from political arguments happening on the Internet. Like coordination among newspapers, the coordination of online propaganda serve as censorship or distraction, rather than for persuasion.

Instead of attacking, the largest portion of Fifty Cent Party posts in the leaked e-mail archive were aimed at *cheerleading*

---

[50] Bandurski, David, "China's Guerrilla War for the Web," September 24, 2008, https://blogs.law.harvard.edu/guorui/2008/09/24/chinas-guerrilla-war-for-the-web/; Lam, Oiwan, "When China Briefly Unblocked Facebook, Trolls Rushed In," *Hong Kong Free Press*, November 26, 2015, https://www.hongkongfp.com/2015/11/26/when-china-briefly-unblocked-facebook-trolls-rushed-in/.

for citizens and China—patriotism, encouragement or motivation of citizens, inspirational quotes or slogans, gratefulness, or celebrations of historical figures, China, or cultural events. Many of the posts were not even political in nature. For example, many remember heroes who sacrificed for China: "是你们抛头颅洒热血换来了我们今天的幸福生活，向你们致敬！你们永远活在我们心中!" "We salute you who shed your blood in exchange for our happy life today! You will always live in our hearts!" Others encourage citizens to keep trying to achieve their goals: "幸福不易须珍惜，明日振兴催奋进。" "Happiness doesn't come easily, so treasure it; tomorrow reenergize and advance with courage."

In order to measure the target of propaganda, we divided a random sample of 200 leaked Fifty Cent Party posts into five different categories. If propaganda posts were meant to persuade, the posts should fall into either (1) argumentative praise or criticism, including praise or criticism of the government that takes a position vis-à-vis another viewpoint; or (2) taunting of foreign countries, including comparisons of China to other countries with the sentiment that China is better, or insults toward other countries. These first two categories are how most pundits had described the purpose of the Fifty Cent Party in the past. If posts were meant to distract or change the subject, posts would fall into (3) non-argumentative praise or suggestions, including praise of current government officials, programs, or policies, which is not responding to an alternative viewpoint; (4) cheerleading for China, including patriotism, encouragement or motivation of citizens, inspirational quotes and slogans, thankfulness, gratefulness, inspiration or gratefulness for historical figures, or cultural references and celebrations; or (5) factual reporting, including descriptions of current government programs, projects, events, or initiatives, without praise or criticism.

We found that the majority of the leaked Fifty Cent posts, 85 percent, fell into the cheerleading category. The second most prevalent type of post was non-argumentative praise or criticism (11 percent). The last type of post we found within the sample were posts that contained factual reporting about government programs or policies (4 percent). In the random sample, we found no examples of taunting of foreign countries or argumentative praise or criticism. In King, Pan and Roberts (2017) we use automated methods to extend this analysis to the rest of the post and to accounts that we predict to be associated with the Fifty Cent Party in other provinces. We find similar results; overwhelmingly, the posts we identify cheerlead and distract, rather than argue online.

The observation that most of the posts seem to be intended to make people feel good about their lives—and not to draw attention to anti-government threads on the Internet—is consistent with recent indications from Chinese propaganda officials that propagandists attempt to promote "positivity." The Chinese Communist Party has recently focused on encouraging art, TV shows, social media posts, and music to focus on creating "正能量," or "positive energy," to distract from increasingly negative commercial news.[51] Although sources do not directly lay out the reasoning behind this positive energy strategy, reorienting the public toward the positive instead of trying to counter negative criticism is a way to distract the public from negative online discourse without drawing more attention to it.

Not only do the leaked e-mails show that online flooding in China is aimed at generating positive sentiment rather than countering criticism, the timing of the posts themselves provide

---

[51] "正义网：时代需要 "周小平们" 的网络正能量," 正义网 http://www.jcrb.com/opinion/zywy/201410/t20141023_1443348.html, "广电总局：鼓励拍摄正能量电视剧," 北京商报, http://it.sohu.com/20120904/n352242285.shtml, "媒体要准确把握舆论导向　传播社会正能量," 华商网, http://ehsb.hsw.cn/shtml/hsb/20141111/191042.shtml, "鲁炜：让网络空间清朗起来的 "六个具体目标"," 千龙网, http://news.ifeng.com/mainland/special/luwei/content-4/detail_2013_10/30/30805526_0.shtml

indications that online propaganda is used during sensitive periods and to distract from highly sensitive events. Figure 6.2 shows a timeline of the posts retrieved from the e-mails. Although the leaked archive gives us only a small view of the online propaganda system in China, the online propaganda effort like the coordination of articles in the newspapers is quite "bursty," or focused within particular periods. The two major bursts within the time period are focused on promoting Chinese patriotic festivals, including Qingming festival, which is a traditional Chinese cultural holiday to celebrate ancestors, and Martyr's Day, a new day created by the CCP to celebrate military heroes. A third burst is focused on the promotion of Xi Jinping's slogan the "Chinese Dream," which was a major focus of propaganda during the spring of 2013. A group of propaganda posts is also clustered around the Third Plenum of the 18th Party Congress, an important Party meeting in November 2013, and another group of posts comments on a local government development initiative.

However, outside of these cultural, slogan, and meeting bursts, there are two large bursts of propaganda posts—one at the end of June and beginning of July 2013, and another in May 2014—which do not have an obvious purpose. These bursts contain typical cheerleading posts, making it difficult to determine the reason the posts were concentrated within such a short period.

A closer look at the e-mails associated with the first burst reveals that this concentrated set of positive propaganda may have been aimed at distracting from riots against the government in Xinjiang, which occurred on June 26, 2013, and killed 27 people.[52] The posts at the beginning of the burst are associated with an e-mail from the Zhanggong propaganda department

---

[52] Forsythe, Michael, "Xinjiang Violence Leaves 27 Dead after Clash with Police," *Bloomberg*, June 26, 2013, http://www.bloomberg.com/news/articles/2013-06-26/xinjiang-violence-leaves-27-dead-after-attack-on-police-stations.

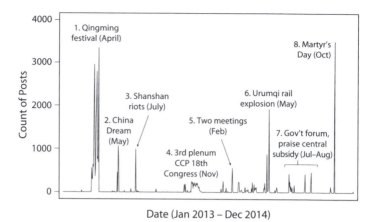

Figure 6.2: Timeline of Fifty Cent Party posts in leaked e-mail archive, reproduced from King, Pan and Roberts (2017).

written to a blind copied group of individuals only a few days after the riots with examples of online propaganda condemning terrorism in Xinjiang, promoting national unity, and promoting harmony between nationalities. One hour later, the Zhanggong propaganda department reported to the higher-level city of Ganzhou that its team had posted hundreds of microblogs promoting positivity, the Chinese Dream, tolerance, diversity, and revitalization. The timing of the e-mails suggests that the propaganda posts were a follow-up to the original posts that condemned terrorism in Xinjiang. It also suggests that when online propaganda is meant to react to a crisis only a small number of propaganda posts actually address the event directly. Instead, most posts are focused on distracting from the negative event with "positive energy."

The second burst of posts does not have an e-mail trail like the first burst, but its timing is also associated with an event in Xinjiang. On April 30, 2014, a knife attack and bombing in the Urumqi railway station killed three people and injured dozens immediately following a visit by Chinese President Xi Jinping.[53] In the days that followed, thousands of posts appear in the leaked dataset that cover a wide range of topics, including the people's livelihood and good governance. Although there is no direct evidence in the e-mail archive that the burst is a response to the bombing, the parallels between this burst and the one in June 2013 provide suggestive evidence that this burst, too, was created with the purpose of distraction.

6.4 THE INFLUENCE OF FLOODING ON THE SPREAD OF INFORMATION

Having described the logic behind flooding, I now show that government coordination of information has an important influence on the prevalence of information that appears within social media. Either because government efforts to spread information are high in volume or because netizens unwittingly pick up flooded information and reshare it, increases in coordination are associated with significant increases in the spread of government-sanctioned information online. As the ratio of government-initiated to citizen-initiated information online increases, citizens will be more likely to come across government propaganda relative to alternative viewpoints and will be more likely to share them.

To show this, I estimate the impact of both the coordination of newspaper articles and paid online commentators on the web. I find that the *particular wording* of the coordinated newspaper article spreads throughout both the domestic and also, more surprisingly, the international blogosphere, showing

---

[53] "Deadly China Blast at Xinjiang Railway Station," *BBC*, April 30, 2014, http://www.bbc.com/news/world-asia-china-27225308.

that information flooding strategies have a multiplicative effect on the spread of information. Next, I show that online discussions of Qingming festivals in recent years are many times more likely to reflect the government's framing of the festival, evidence that online propaganda indeed influences the tone of the conversation.

6.4.1 How Does Newspaper Coordination Influence the Spread of Information?

How does the coordination among newspapers in China influence the spread of information? If information is sufficiently coordinated, are others more likely to reprint these stories? Do social media users and other commentators pick up the same language used in the coordinated newspaper articles?

To answer these questions, I estimate whether newspaper articles that were more coordinated were more likely to appear on non-news sites and within individual social media posts. To do this, I take consecutive word strings from more coordinated articles to see if they appear more frequently on the web than those where there is less coordination among newspapers. For each unique cluster size of coordinated newspaper articles ranging from two to twenty, I sample 100 coordinated articles.[54] For each of these 1,290 articles, I sample five 30-character strings randomly from the text of the article. I then use the Google API to search each of these 6,450 strings on Google and record the number of search results returned.

I obtain three different search result metrics. First, I count the number of search results Google returned overall. I also count specifically the number of search results returned on sina.com.cn,[55] the most popular blogging site in China. Last, I

---

[54] For some coordinated cluster sizes, there were not 100 unique instances in my dataset. For these clusters, I took all of the coordinated articles.

[55] Using site: sina.com.cn within the search results.

count the number of search results returned on blogspot.com, the most popular blogging site within the United States, which is blocked by the Great Firewall in China.[56]

I measure the relationship between coordination and the number of search results, both within and outside of China. Figure 6.3 shows the number of coordinated papers on the x-axis, and the log of the search results on the y-axis. There is a very strong correlation between the degree of coordination across newspapers and number of search results containing the strings of the coordinated articles.

It could be that these results are simply a reflection of coordination by government propaganda workers who could repost the same wording as in the provincial newspapers at the direction of the Chinese government. However, within the leaked Fifty Cent posts, we did not see examples of the Fifty Cent Party reposting copies of traditional media stories on the web. We would also not expect the Fifty Cent Party to write social media posts on websites outside of the Great Firewall, such as blogspot.com, which are less likely to be frequented by the average Chinese citizen. The evidence suggests that the link between coordination and social media mentions is not simply through other coordinated measures initiated by the CCP. Instead, the multiplicative relationship between coordination and search results likely indicates that the propaganda is being reprinted by regular Chinese citizens and also by citizens abroad.

6.4.2 How Do Online Commentators Influence the Framing of a Holiday?

How do government online commentators influence the tenor and framing of online conversations? In this section, I study

---

[56] I used the Google API to do this, and close examination indicates that the number of returned search results is fairly accurate. The number of search results when you simply search Google from a desktop is often very inaccurate, which is why using the API (application programming interface) is important.

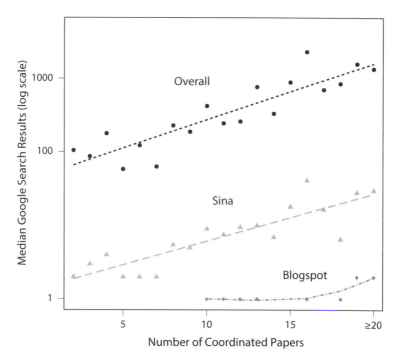

Figure 6.3: Relationship between average coordination and number of Google search results for all websites, sina.com.cn, and blogspot.com.

how the tenor of the online conversation about the Qingming festival in China has changed as the government's effort to affect online conversations through paid commentators has increased in recent years.

The Qingming festival, also known as the Tomb Sweeping Festival or the holiday of Pure Brightness, occurs every spring and is traditionally a time when Chinese pay respect to their ancestors by visiting their graves and presenting them with offerings. The holiday has its origins in ancient China, but was largely disallowed in the Maoist era. After reform, the Qingming festival has returned to China and is now widely observed throughout the country.[57]

[57] See Johnson (2016) for a discussion of the history of the Qingming festival and its current treatment today in China.

Qingming is problematic for the Chinese government because these rituals have frequently turned political. The Tiananmen Incident in 1976 originated in a gathering to remember former Premier of China Zhou Enlai on Qingming, but turned into a protest against government officials. The holiday brings attention to graves of those who were killed during sensitive political events, like the 1989 Tiananmen Square protest. In recent years, before the Qingming festival, in an effort to prevent instability, government police have detained outspoken family members of those killed on June 4, 1989.[58]

As Qingming has become more popular in recent years, the Chinese government has made an effort to take back the festival for its own purposes. In particular, the CCP has tried to link Qingming to the recognition of Communist martyrs by showing officials on television visiting the graves of famous revolutionary heroes.[59] This framing is consistent with an increasing emphasis on the CCP as a nationalist, unifying force by emphasizing the sacrifices the party has made to unify and provide stability and prosperity for the country and distracting from the more contentious history of the Qingming holiday.

The "martyr" framing of Qingming is reflected in the leaked Fifty Cent Party posts discussed earlier in this chapter. The largest volume spike in the leaked archive occurred on the Qingming festival (figure 6.2). Many of these posts link Qingming with revolutionary heroes. The burst contains posts such as: "Qingming is the day where we relive the fire of the revolution and we commune with the martyrs." ("清明是重温革命烽火,与先烈对话的日子"), "Mourn the martyrs, the great men who gave their lives for the birth of new China. Because of them we now have a happy life! Because of them we now have

[58] Laris, Michael, "Tiananmen's Edgy Proximity," *Washington Post*, April 6, 1999, https://www.washingtonpost.com/archive/politics/1999/04/06/tiananmens-edgy-proximity/bcb50b9f-9f7b-4bb6-9b22-d7badbded429/.

[59] Johnson (2016).

international status! Because of them the Chinese people can finally once again stand proudly among the nations of the world." ("深切悼念那些为新中国诞生 而献身的英烈和伟人们, 因为有了他们我们才有现在的幸福生活! 因为他们, 我们才有现在的国际地位! 因为他们, 中华民族才又一次傲立世界民族之林.")

Can the CCP be successful in changing the tenor of the tomb sweeping festival with its coordinated framing of the festival? To study how the online conversation has changed as the government has increased its focus on online propaganda,[60] I gathered a random sample of social media posts on baidu.com, sina.com.cn, and sohu.com that mentioned the word "Qingming" during April 1–April 5 of each of the years 2012–2016. In each year, I counted the proportion of posts that mentioned the word "martyr" (either "先烈" or "烈士") during that period.[61]

The results are plotted in figure 6.4. Since Xi Jinping took office, there has been a remarkable six-fold increase in discussion of martyrs online associated with the Qingming festival. Although the word "martyr" was used in less than 0.5 percent of posts that mentioned "Qingming" on these websites in 2012, in 2014–2016 almost 3 percent of all posts that mention "Qingming" also mention "martyr." The increase in prevalence of posts equating Qingming with martyr's day reflects a shift in the way that online information portrays the holiday and its purpose to the public. It also shows that the government can wield significant influence over the tenor of the online discussion through flooding.

---

[60] Bandurski, David, "A 'Year of Innovation' for Internet Controls," *China Media Project*, January 7, 2016, http://cmp.hku.hk/2016/01/07/39575/.

[61] Posts were sampled from the online social media analytics company Crimson Hexagon.

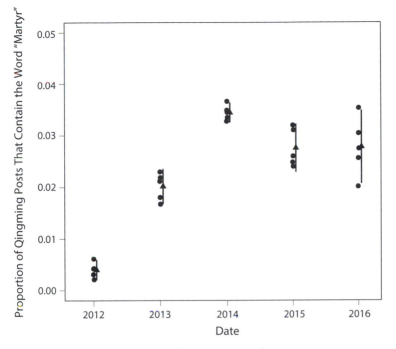

Figure 6.4: Proportion of posts about Qingming that mention martyrs, April 1–5, 2012–2016.

6.5 CONCLUSION

Information flooding is the least identifiable form of censorship of all the mechanisms described in this book. Particularly with the expansion of the Internet, the government can hide its identity and post online propaganda pretending to be unrelated to the government. Coordinated efforts to spread information online reverberate throughout social media because citizens are more likely to come across them and share them. Such coordination can distract from ongoing events that might be unfavorable to the government and can de-prioritize other news and perspectives.

We might expect that coordinated government propaganda efforts would be meant to persuade or cajole support from citizens on topics that citizens criticize the government about. However, the evidence presented in this chapter indicates that governments would rather not use propaganda to draw attention to any information that could shed a negative light on their performance. Instead, governments use coordinated information to draw attention away from negative events toward more positive news or their own overarching narrative, or to create positive feelings about the government among citizens. This type of flooding is even more difficult to detect, and dilutes the information environment to decrease the proportion of information that reflects badly on the government.

CHAPTER SEVEN

Implications for a Digital World

When I was in China in 2006, coming across blocked websites was less common than it is today. Some Wikipedia pages were blocked and some links in the *New York Times* website would return an error, but otherwise, I could access information I would normally use with no extra effort. I posted pictures on Facebook, I used Google. Twitter had not started yet, but I instant messaged through Skype. The paradigm of incomplete censorship had not yet been widely applied—the Great Firewall did not affect many websites and did not yet create major differences in the accessibility of online news between people living in the United States and those in China.

Each subsequent time I visited China, the government had added friction to information from the Western world. Google and Gmail can no longer be accessed without a VPN. Facebook, Twitter, Instagram, the *New York Times*, YouTube—so many of the Internet content providers from which Internet users around the world receive their news—are no longer available in China without evading censorship. When traveling to China, I have become accustomed to using a VPN to do simple things like keep up with e-mail, collaborate with coauthors on Google Drive or Dropbox, or wish a friend happy birthday on social media.

Despite being *able* to access websites from the United States, doing so was frustrating and time consuming. I have found myself increasingly turning to the vibrant and ever-expanding world of Chinese social media. I signed up for WeChat, Weibo, QQ, and 126 e-mail because these platforms were more convenient. These companies are some of the most exciting technology companies in the world, with innovative platforms that attract audiences in their own right. However, the politically inspired division between the networks, information, and online communities in China and in the rest of the world worries me. Although the difference between the Chinese and English languages naturally creates its own barrier and imposes friction on sharing information, understanding, and friendships across the Pacific, the seclusion of Chinese social media users from the rest of the world on the Internet as a result of censorship creates an environment that could exacerbate misunderstandings, nationalism, and differences in perceptions between the population of one of the most important and powerful countries and the rest of the world. Despite many pundits' characterization of porous censorship in China as "futile,"[1] this book provides evidence that typical users are affected enormously by these small costs of information without always realizing it, providing credence to worries of polarization not only within China but also between China and the rest of the world.

7.1 WHY POROUS CENSORSHIP MATTERS

This book has shown the surprising effects of porous censorship, or small but circumventable taxes on information, on what citizens read, share with others, and think about politics. The perception that the Internet allows us the possibility to access so much information reassures us that governments and political entities cannot completely hide information that could keep them accountable. But the impatience and indifference to politics inherent in the busy schedules of typical citizens mean that ease of access has strong effects on what information the

---

[1] August, Oliver, "The Great Firewall: China's Misguided—and Futile—Attempt to Control What Happens Online," *Wired*, October 23, 2007, http://www.wired.com/2007/10/ff-chinafirewall/.

majority of the public consumes and shares. With the decline of the traditional media, increases in hidden forms of censorship combined with the ability of governments to engage in online political propaganda have created an environment where political entities have a surprising amount of control over what information is easiest for their constituents to come across. Censorship that functions through friction and flooding can exacerbate divisions and reduce political entities' accountability even when they do not explicitly make any information off-limits.

In this book, I have described the ways in which citizens can be affected by censorship. Fear affects citizens through deterrence, by making individuals frightened to share or access information. Fear is effective only when it involves a credible threat, when governments are able to credibly commit to punishing individuals for speech. Fear without credibility can have unintended negative consequences for governments, by creating a public backlash against censorship or by creating incentives for citizens to conceal information the government would find valuable. Friction influences the spread of information by making it more difficult to access, and similarly flooding affects citizens by introducing information that distracts from the information the political entity would rather keep off-limits. Friction and flooding are more effective when citizens' elasticity of information is high, or when information has more substitutes. Users are even more affected when they do not know that censorship is happening because they do not have the awareness necessary to counteract it. Search filters, throttling, and paid online propaganda commentators can be explained away by a search engine's algorithm, too much Internet traffic, or a slew of concerned citizens. Friction and flooding, although technically easy for citizens to circumvent, divert and distract the public, particularly when their real purpose and potential consequences go unnoticed.

The influence of fear, friction, and flooding on individuals' consumption of information has clear implications for government strategies of censorship in the digital age. Porous censorship is useful to authoritarian regimes precisely because only some individuals circumvent it. Fear, which is difficult to use to credibly target millions of Internet users, can be primarily used against high-profile individuals and the traditional media who could influence large numbers of people. For the typical Internet user, censorship based on friction and flooding is used to nudge individuals away from conversations, focal points, and networks the government prefers they would not be involved in, separating potential support from the activist core.

This strategy of porous censorship mitigates many of the costs that fear-based censorship creates for authoritarian governments. Fear comes with the potential for backlash against censorship or, if applied too broadly, may limit the ability of governments to collect true information from citizens and discourage complaints that keep local government officials in check. Porous censorship, on the other hand, frustrates the vast majority of citizens from accessing information the government deems dangerous, while not making any information explicitly off-limits and allowing online consumers to feel as if all information is possible to access.

Using online experiments, large social media datasets, datasets of newspapers, leaked archives of propaganda, and a nationally representative survey, I provided evidence that supports this theory of censorship in the empirical sections of this book, showing that the vast majority of Chinese Internet users' consumption and production of information is not affected by fear and deterrence. As I showed in chapter 4, when citizens observe censorship, they become *more* interested in the information, seeking out information that is related to it and continuing to write about off-limits topics. Because online users are looking for signals of topics' importance, censored information draws attention to topics the government would rather not be discussed.

In contrast, in chapters 5 and 6, I show that censorship that taxes information has large effects on the typical individual's production and consumption of information. Internet users do not circumvent the Firewall because they do not know it exists, find it bothersome, or have no reason to. Small variations in barriers to access, like blocked websites, censors' schedules, or the timing of coordinated propaganda have large impacts on the amount of information about a topic online. Even though many people report being angered by censorship, when it goes unnoticed it can have surprisingly large impacts.

However, because porous censorship can be circumvented, it has vulnerabilities. During crises, or in periods when censorship suddenly disrupts their habits, even typical citizens are likely to search out information regardless of the costs. As I have highlighted throughout this book, moments of crisis and instability may make it difficult for authoritarian regimes to control access to and spread of information because citizens' demand for information becomes more inelastic. For authoritarian regimes that adopt these strategies, I expect that unexpected, sudden crises that draw large-scale public attention—like the Tianjin explosions described in chapter 5—will likely be the moments when information will be less affected by censorship and governments are more likely to be held accountable.

7.2 AUTHORITARIAN RESILIENCE

The findings in this book speak to a growing literature that puzzles over the resilience of authoritarian governments in the face of the third wave of democratization and the expansion of the Internet.[2] The evidence suggests that the resilience of

[2] Nathan (2003); Anderson (2006); Gilley (2003).

authoritarian regimes is due not only to repression and responsiveness but also to other tools used to slow down coordination of collective action. The friction- and flooding-based methods of censorship described in this book do not employ force, make information impossible to access, or respond to citizens' concerns. Instead, they nudge citizens away from activist circles and alternative viewpoints that could facilitate collective action that is dangerous for the regime.

The evidence presented in this book suggests that authoritarian governments may adopt this strategy of porous censorship in part because citizens themselves are strategic consumers of information. Consumers are faced with a problem of information overload and are therefore seeking signals of information importance. Awareness of censorship can draw consumers *toward* rather than *away* from information. Repression and responsiveness address issues directly, drawing attention to the issue the government would like to ignore. Throttling or distraction, in contrast, distract and divert citizens to other topics.

In comparison to direct repression, porous censorship bolsters authoritarian resilience by manipulating citizens' incentives so that they choose, rather than are forced, to engage in the desired behavior. As Aldous Huxley, author of *Brave New World*, writes in a forward to the second edition, "A really efficient totalitarian state would be one in which the all-powerful executive of political bosses and their army of managers control a population of slaves who do not have to be coerced." Rather than making books unavailable or information impossible to access, censorship taxes manipulate incentives so that most citizens *choose* to consume information palatable to the government. It provides distractions and alternative arguments that citizens select into because they are more readily available and more widely circulated among the population.

The contrast this book draws between repression and porous censorship can be applied to other areas of authoritarian control and could predict ways in which new technologies could be used in the future. For example, experts now worry that as improvements in surveillance technology make online behavior easy to track, governments will increase their ability to track dissidents. Many governments around the world are expanding their surveillance programs, though the details of these programs are shrouded in secrecy. The Chinese government is experimenting with a social credit score, which could include information about what users write on the Internet and could have implications for the ability to borrow money, get a job, or be granted a visa.[3] Although some say that such a credit system would provide a much-needed measure for lenders to evaluate potential borrowers,[4] others say the idea stretches too far into the political behavior of individuals and instead could act as a mechanism to punish individuals for engaging in political conversation online.[5]

A framework centered on repression would expect autocrats to use surveillance technologies to track individuals online and make punishment more credible. Indeed, authoritarian governments have used these technologies to infect dissidents' computers and phones.[6] Certainly, surveillance technology will make fear-based censorship easier for autocrats, and this is something that the wider academic and policy community should be greatly concerned about.

---

[3] Hamilton Gillian, "China's Social Credit Score Is Doomed to Fail," *Financial Times*, November 16, 2015, http://blogs.ft.com/beyond-brics/2015/11/16/chinas-social-credit-score-system-is-doomed-to-fail/.

[4] Tsang, Tim, "How New Credit Scores Might Help Bridge China's Financial Inclusion Gap," *Center for Financial Inclusion Blog*, June 6, 2016, https://cfi-blog.org/2016/06/06/how-new-credit-scores-might-help-bridge-chinas-credit-gap/.

[5] Chin, Josh, and Gillian Wong, "China's New Tool for Social Control: A Credit Rating for Everything," *Wall Street Journal*, November 28, 2016, https://www.wsj.com/articles/chinas-new-tool-for-social-control-a-credit-rating-for-everything-1480351590.

[6] Marczak, Bill, and John Scott-Railton, "The Million Dollar Dissident: NSO Group's iPhone Zero-Days Used against a UAE Human Rights Defender," *Citizen Lab*, August 24, 2016, https://citizenlab.org/2016/08/million-dollar-dissident-iphone-zero-day-nso-group-uae/.

But less acknowledged is that the enormous data-collection programs that accompany surveillance could be used to personalize friction and flooding to a wide range of users. Surveillance could make friction and flooding more powerful by allowing for targeting of individuals with information that makes them less likely to come across information that damages the regime. Just as Google targets advertisements to users, governments could use information gathered from surveillance to target distracting information to users who might have recently read or searched for sensitive topics. In this way, governments could use surveillance to exert influence over users without even revealing that they are interfering, much less resorting to coercion.

As I have shown in this book, governments are already taking advantage of online information to target censorship within the population. But as the Internet becomes more customized and more data about consumers becomes available, so will censorship be customized to the individual rather than be applied in a blanketed way to the whole population. Such targeted censorship will increase its plausible deniability, as citizens will experience censorship differently. It may also further increase the digital divide between wealthy and marginalized populations,[7] as those with less resources and education are less likely to be able to recognize and circumvent censorship when they encounter it.

7.3 IMPLICATIONS FOR FREE SPEECH IN DEMOCRACIES

The evidence and theory presented in this book have broader implications than just for information provision in autocracies. Traditionally, scholars have drawn a stark contrast between

---

[7] Norris (2001).

freedom of speech in autocracies and democracies by focusing on *freedom of expression*, or an individual's liberty to express themselves in the public sphere.[8] This perspective is based on the traditional structure of the media, where very few people expressed their views to the masses. Free speech theorists before the digital revolution worried that certain people would be excluded from broadcast media.[9] Autocracies banned particular voices from entering into the media, whereas democracies allowed more freedom in who could take the public stage.

However, the introduction of digital media has made the contrast between democracies and autocracies less stark. As more people have begun to participate in the public sphere, the bandwidth for public speech has widened. As Balkin (2004) notes, the contest over free speech is not so much anymore *whether* someone can take the public stage, but instead which voices will rise to the top and which will be lost in the cacophony. Censorship consists not only of preventing individuals from speaking but also of determining how their speech is prioritized and presented to the public, the contest over the "code" and structure of the Internet.[10]

In all societies, political entities have enormous amounts of power in how information is organized in the public sphere. Corporations wield significant power over the algorithms behind online search and there is evidence that the order of search results has electoral influences.[11] Bureaucracies have a significant say in what data they collect and how available they make it. Interest groups and political parties invest large amounts of money in flooding the Internet with their own interpretation of events, drowning out the concerns of skeptics. As the financial belt of traditional journalism tightens, political

[8] Scanlon (1972).
[9] Balkin (2004, pg. 6).
[10] Lessig (1999, Chapter 7); Stockmann and Luo (2017).
[11] Epstein and Robertson (2015).

groups have greater sway over affecting the content of articles by feeding journalists stories or refusing to respond to inquiries for interviews or data.

If the prioritization of information for political purposes has the impact of censorship, as this book suggests, then in democracies we have to rethink how we can protect free speech in a world of information overload. Perhaps the algorithms behind online search should be more transparent to the public so that we can have open debates about what voices get shuffled to the surface and what voices are buried. Perhaps we should concern ourselves more with competition between online search, social media, and Internet service providers to ensure that consumers are always provided a variety of perspectives. Maybe government data transparency should be standardized across bureaucracies to avoid selective, incentive-based transparency.[12] As democratic environments have shown that they too are susceptible to friction and flooding,[13] this book's broader perspective on censorship in the digital age demands that we at least ask questions about how we view freedom of information in democracies in the age of the Internet and what policies should be implemented to protect it.

7.4 A CALL FOR FUTURE RESEARCH

There is still much we do not understand about the political implications of censorship in authoritarian environments and the direction that these efforts are headed. As authoritarian governments develop sophisticated techniques to prioritize information for their citizens through porous censorship, we as

---

[12] Bertot, Jaeger and Grimes (2010).
[13] Byrnes, Nanette, "How the Bot-y Politic Influenced This Election," *MIT Technology Review*, November 8, 2016, https://www.technologyreview.com/s/602817/how-the-bot-y-politic-influenced-this-election/.

researchers must keep up with our own study of the political impacts of censorship to help understand and inform others of the potential political results of these efforts. From an academic perspective, understanding the future of authoritarianism will require understanding how effectively these governments can control the agenda. From a policy perspective, understanding how citizens are influenced by media will allow us to better predict political outcomes and develop technologies that promote freedom of information.

Scholars should increasingly seek to find ways to study government censorship and propaganda efforts so that these strategies can be uncovered and made public. Here I describe two directions researchers might take to explore the implications of the findings in this book: better understanding the long-term economic, educational, and ideological impacts of censorship, and extending the theory to other countries and theories of repression.

7.4.1 Long-term Economic and Ideological Impacts of Censorship

While this book focused on the short-term impacts of censorship on access to information, future research should focus on enumerating the long-term impacts of censorship, including its economic, educational, and international implications. Despite the surprising impact of porous censorship, which I have highlighted, the findings presented here also suggest that censorship is accompanied with important costs to the Chinese economy, even if it is easily bypassed. Friction and flooding in China act like tariffs and subsidies of information, skewing the market for information and creating inefficiencies. Like all international trade protections, some Chinese companies benefit from these market distortions. Sina Weibo, Renren, and Baidu are all protected from international competition because their competitors Twitter, Facebook, and Google are blocked by the Great Firewall. Arguably, censorship has created space for some local Chinese companies to innovate and prosper without foreign competition.

For many technology companies in China, however, the frictions associated with censorship impose large costs on innovation. Start-ups working on developing new technology in China must use VPNs to access important coding tools such as those provided by Google. Social media companies must employ tens, sometimes hundreds, of censors to ensure that their content is in line with government guidelines. These taxes undoubtedly slow innovation in China and retard the growth of the technology industry. Enumerating the economic costs of censorship on the Chinese economy will help us better understand its impact on international trade and economic growth in China and the types of companies that stand to win and lose from the censorship apparatus.

Beyond the economy, the costs of censorship are also dramatically felt in the area of education. As the Chinese school system is one of the primary conduits for information, the government can control accessibility of information by controlling educational materials. Banning textbooks[14] and censoring academics[15] may make foreign information less accessible and easier to control, but it also throttles information from the world's leading scholars from entering the Chinese school system. Budding computer scientists in China start with a penalty, as they must use a VPN to use some of the world's leading software. Frustrated with government censorship, academics are

---

[14] Chen, Andrea, and Zhuang Pinghui, "Chinese Universities Ordered to Ban Textbooks That Promote Western Values," *South China Morning Post*, January 30, 2015, http://www.scmp.com/news/china/article/1695524/chinese-universities-instructed-ban-textbooks-promote-western-values.

[15] Phillips, Tom, "It's Getting Worse: China's Liberal Academics Fear Growing Censorship," *Guardian*, August 6, 2015, https://www.theguardian.com/world/2015/aug/06/china-xi-jinping-crackdown-liberal-academics-minor-cultural-revolution.

likely to look for positions outside of China.[16] A better understanding of the long-term impacts of censorship on human resources in China will be important to understand China's transition to a high-skilled economy.

The long-term ideological effects of censorship are perhaps the most important. Censorship creates disparities in access to information across political classes in China, exacerbating income disparities and potentially sowing the seeds of long-term political conflict. The political elite, tech-savvy, internationally educated Chinese citizens jump the Firewall easily, while those in rural areas are more affected by censorship because they are less aware of it and do not have the tools to circumvent it. Censorship is regressive in that it exacerbates the digital divide between classes. Perhaps more problematic, it creates an information chasm between the poor and the political elite that could turn into political or ideological conflict in the future.[17]

Though the digital era has made large strides toward bridging gaps between countries and cultures, censorship in China throttles cultural exchange between China and the West. As the Chinese government increasingly manipulates the media to prioritize its own version of international events, it also ties its hands in how it can resolve international conflicts.[18] The bifurcation of media consumption between Chinese and Americans may slow the formation of common ground and common knowledge that may be essential to cooperation between East and West in the future. Future research seeking to understand how media bifurcation affects citizens' support

---

[16] Phillips, Tom, and Ed Pilkington, "No Country for Academics: Chinese Crackdown Forces Intellectuals Abroad," *Guardian*, May 24, 2016, https://www.theguardian.com / world / 2016 / may / 24 / academics-china-crackdown-forces-intellectuals-abroad.

[17] See Pan and Xu (forthcoming) and Wu and Meng (2016) for more discussion of potential ideological conflict in China.

[18] Weiss (2014).

of international cooperation is essential to understanding how censorship will affect the U.S.–China relationship.

7.4.2 Fear, Friction, and Flooding around The World

While the empirical sections of this book focused on the Chinese case, more work needs to be done to test the impacts of fear, friction, and flooding in other authoritarian environments. This research is increasingly imperative as evidence suggests that China's model of censorship is being exported to other regimes. How do other authoritarian systems of censorship differ and converge with the Chinese model? As the theory in this book suggests, the particular combination of fear, friction, and flooding will depend on the political structure, level of economic development, and technological capabilities of the regime. A better understanding of the predictors of the various incarnations of censorship would allow us to anticipate its implementation across political environments.

Similarly, are the reactions to the observation of censorship similar across authoritarian regimes? This book suggests that citizens' elasticity of demand for information varies by their interests, education, and information environment. Are there some countries and contexts where porous censorship is more or less effective? Are there political environments that tend to be more prone to backlash? Exploring the impact of censorship comparatively would allow us to understand how fear, friction, and flooding travel to other cases and environments.

CHAPTER EIGHT

Appendix

8.1 DESCRIPTION OF THE CHINA URBAN GOVERNANCE SURVEY

The 2015 China Urban Governance Survey was carried out by the Research Center on Data and Governance at Tsinghua University during the summer of 2015. Urban residents above the age of 18 were sampled via GPS Assisted Area Sampling (Landry and Shen, 2005) to ensure that both residents and migrants were represented within the sample. The survey sampled 50 county-level cities and urban districts in 24 provinces, excluding Inner Mongolia, Jilin, Guizhou, Tibet, Qinghai, Ningxia, and Xinjiang. The total number of respondents surveyed was 3,513, among 5,526 sampled–a response rate of 63.6 percent.

8.2 WORDS RELATED TO CENSORSHIP, MUTUAL INFORMATION

This table of words are those that have high mutual information and higher probability of appearing in a censored than an uncensored Weibo post written by matched users. These are the words used to understand how sensitive words appear before and after censorship in the matched Weibo analysis in chapter 4.

	Word related to censorship	English translation
1	代表们	representatives
2	以示	to show
3	国资委	State-owned Assets Supervision Commission
4	不作为	inaction; dereliction of duty
5	党外	outside of the party
6	反对党	opposition
7	喜马拉雅山	Himalayas
8	张牙舞爪	to bear fangs and brandish claw
9	纠纷	dispute
10	长成	grow up to be
11	受到	be subjected to
12	呼吁	advocate for
13	亮出	reveal
14	毕竟	after all
15	危害	harm
16	人大	National People's Congress
17	处罚	punishment
18	好不容易	with great difficulty
19	特首	Chief Executive of Hong Kong or Macao
20	请求	request
21	集团	(corporate) group
22	代言人	spokesperson
23	冤案	miscarriage of justice
24	惩罚	punishment
25	纠正	correct
26	老百姓	ordinary people
27	宣称	claim
28	白天	daytime
29	表叔	uncle who wears a watch
30	不去	don't go
31	伪劣	counterfeit or shoddy products

	Word related to censorship	English translation
32	何删删	deleted
33	作画	paint
34	使用者	user
35	借的	borrowed
36	值得一看	worth a look
37	农友	fellow peasant
38	出生入死	willing to risk life and limb
39	出车	dispatch a vehicle
40	利刀	sharp knife
41	嘿嘿嘿	heh heh heh (evil laughter)
42	学术界	academia
43	居所	residence
44	屈才	waste talent
45	屋前	in front of house
46	张思之	Zhang Sizhi (rights lawyer)
47	弹雨	hail of bullets
48	心弦	heartstrings
49	恩情	kindness
50	我校	our school
51	拨动	stir up
52	接轨	adapt to
53	敌杀	poison
54	新闻界	press
55	枪淋	hail of bullets
56	梭镖	spear
57	水流	water stream
58	海淀	Haidian
59	特殊性	particularity
60	监视	surveillance
61	相望	gaze at each other
62	知心话	Caring Talk (program on Radio Free Asia)

	Word related to censorship	English translation
63	裸身	naked body
64	隔山	separated by mountains
65	隔水	separated by waters
66	鼓噪	stir up chaos
67	控制	control
68	推翻	overthrow
69	贺卫方	He Weifang (professor and activist)
70	举报	report
71	重庆	Chongqing
72	最高	highest/supreme
73	无辜	innocent
74	泰坦尼克号	Titanic
75	rose	rose
76	二十多	over 20
77	借给	lend
78	公学	public school
79	军哥	military brother
80	出息	achievement
81	删减	censor/deduct
82	利剑	sharp sword
83	到瓜瓜	to Guagua (refers to B. Guagua)
84	十亿	billion
85	又是	also is
86	双规	detained and investigated
87	哈罗	Harrow school
88	围困	besiege
89	子孙们	offspring
90	忐忑	nervous
91	扩大化	escalation
92	新词	new words
93	朝阳区	Chaoyang district
94	永不忘	never forget

	Word related to censorship	English translation
95	派驻	dispatch
96	淹死	drown
97	珍重	treasure
98	看后	after viewing
99	答复	reply
100	行船	sailing

8.3 TIBET SELF-IMMOLATIONS NEGATIVE BINOMIAL MODEL

To supplement the analysis in chapter 5, I model the length of the social media bursts associated with self-immolation protests in Tibet using a negative binomial regression, where the length of the burst is the dependent variable and whether or not the self-immolation occurred on a weekend is the main independent variable of interest. Shown in table 8.1, controlling for characteristics of the self-immolator, I find that whether the event was on a weekend is still a significant predictor of the length of the burst.

Table 8.1: Negative binomial Model showing the impact of a self-immolation happening on a weekend on the length of the social media burst associated with that immolation event.

	Dependent variable: Length of social media burst	
	numafterdate	
	(1)	(2)
Weekend	0.692***	0.764***
	(0.187)	(0.189)
Age		−0.002
		(0.010)
Monk		0.290
		(0.192)

Table 8.1: Continued.

	Dependent variable: Length of social media burst	
	numafterdate	
	(1)	(2)
Died		0.321
		(0.396)
Constant	1.282***	0.865*
	(0.124)	(0.487)
Observations	120	111
Log likelihood	−320.273	−294.755
θ	1.228*** (0.194)	1.321*** (0.219)
Akaike inf. crit.	644.546	599.509

Note: *p<0.1; **p<0.05; ***p<0.01

WORKS CITED

Alexievich, Svetlana. 2006. *Voices from Chernobyl: The Oral History of a Nuclear Disaster*. New York: Picador.

Allcott, Hunt and Matthew Gentzkow. 2017. "Social Media and Fake News in the 2016 Election." *Journal of Economic Perspectives* 31(2):211–236.

Alston, Lee J, Gary D Libecap and Bernardo Mueller. 2010. "Interest Groups, Information Manipulation in the Media, and Public Policy: The Case of the Landless Peasants Movement in Brazil." National Bureau of Economic Research Working Paper.

Anderson, Lisa. 2006. "Searching Where the Light Shines: Studying Democratization in the Middle East." *Annual Review Political Science* 9:189–214.

Angus, Campbell, Philip Converse, Warren Miller and Donald Stokes. 1960. *The American Voter*. Ann Arbor: University of Michigan Press.

Aryan, Simurgh, Homa Aryan and J Alex Halderman. 2013. "Internet Censorship in Iran: A First Look." *Free and Open Communications on the Internet, Washington, DC, USA* .

Athey, Susan and Markus Mobius. 2012. "The Impact of News Aggregators on Internet News Consumption: The Case of Localization." Working Paper.

Avant, Deborah D. 2005. *The Market for Force: The Consequences of Privatizing Security*. Cambridge: Cambridge University Press.

Bahry, Donna and Brian D Silver. 1987. "Intimidation and the Symbolic Uses of Terror in the USSR." *American Political Science Review* 81(4):1065–1098.

Balkin, Jack M. 2004. "Digital Speech and Democratic Culture: A Theory of Freedom of Expression for the Information Society." *NYUL Rev.* 79:1.

Ball-Rokeach, Sandra J and Melvin L DeFleur. 1976. "A Dependency Model of Mass-Media Effects." *Communication Research* 3(1):3–21.

Bamman, David, Brendan O'Connor and Noah Smith. 2012. "Censorship and Deletion Practices in Chinese Social Media." *First Monday* 17(3).

Bandurski, David. 2008. "China's Guerrilla War for the Web." *Far Eastern Economic Review* 171(6):41.

Barberá, Pablo, Ning Wang, Richard Bonneau, John T Jost, Jonathan Nagler, Joshua Tucker and Sandra Gonžález Bailón. 2015. "The Critical Periphery in the Growth of Social Protests." *PLOS ONE* 10(11):e0143611.

Baum, Matthew A. 2002. "Sex, Lies, and War: How Soft News Brings Foreign Policy to the Inattentive Public." *American Political Science Review* 96(1):91–109.

Baum, Matthew A. 2003. *Soft News Goes to War: Public Opinion and American Foreign Policy in the New Media Age.* Princeton: Princeton University Press.

Baum, Matthew A and Tim Groeling. 2010. "Reality Asserts Itself: Public Opinion on Iraq and the Elasticity of Reality." *International Organization* 64(3):443–479.

Becker, Gary S. 1968. "Crime and Punishment: An Economic Approach." *Journal of Political Economy* 76(2):169–217.

Bellin, Eva. 2012. "Reconsidering the Robustness of Authoritarianism in the Middle East: Lessons from the Arab Spring." *Comparative Politics* 44(2):127–149.

Bernays, Edward L. 1923. *Crystallizing Public Opinion.* New York: Liveright Publishing Corporation.

Bertot, John C, Paul T Jaeger and Justin M Grimes. 2010. "Using ICTs to Create a Culture of Transparency: E-government and Social Media as Openness and Anti-Corruption Tools for Societies." *Government Information Quarterly* 27(3):264–271.

Besley, Timothy and Andrea Prat. 2006. "Handcuffs for the Grabbing Hand? The Role of the Media in Political Accountability." *American Economic Review* 96(3):720–736.

Boix, Carles and Milan W Svolik. 2013. "The Foundations of Limited Authoritarian Government: Institutions, Commitment, and Power-Sharing in Dictatorships." *The Journal of Politics* 75(2):300–316.

Bond, Robert M, Christopher J Fariss, Jason J Jones, Adam DI Kramer, Cameron Marlow, Jaime E Settle and James H Fowler. 2012. "A 61-Million-Person Experiment in Social Influence and Political Mobilization." *Nature* 489(7415):295–298.

Boydston, Michelle D. 1992. "Press Censorship and Access Restrictions During the Persian Gulf War: A First Amendment Analysis." *Loy. LAL Rev.* 25:1073.

Brady, Anne-Marie. 2008. *Marketing Dictatorship: Propaganda and Thought Work in Contemporary China.* Lanham: Rowman & Littlefield.

Brady, Anne-Marie. 2009. "Mass Persuasion as a Means of Legitimation and China's Popular Authoritarianism." *American Behavioral Scientist* 53(3):434–457.

Brodsgaard, Kjeld Erik. 1981. "The Democracy Movement in China, 1978–1979: Opposition Movements, Wall Poster Campaigns, and Underground Journals." *Asian Survey* 21(7):747–774.

Brownlee, Jason. 2007. *Authoritarianism in an Age of Democratization.* Cambridge: Cambridge University Press.

Brutlag, Jake. 2009. "Speed Matters for Google Web Search." *Google.* https://services.google.com/fh/files/blogs/ google_delayexp.pdf.

Bueno De Mesquita, Bruce, Alastair Smith, Randolph M Siverson and James D Morrow. 2003. *The Logic of Political Survival.* Cambridge: MIT Press.

Burnett, Sam and Nick Feamster. 2013. "Making Sense of Internet Censorship: A New Frontier for Internet Measurement." *ACM SIGCOMM Computer Communication Review* 43(3):84–89.

Cai, Yongshun. 2010. *Collective Resistance in China: Why Popular Protests Succeed or Fail.* Stanford: Stanford University Press.

Cairns, Christopher and Allen Carlson. 2016. "Real-World Islands in a Social Media Sea: Nationalism and Censorship on Weibo During the 2012 Diaoyu/Senkaku Crisis." *The China Quarterly* 225:23–49.

Calland, Richard. 2007. Prizing Open the Profit-Making World. In *The Right to Know: Transparency for an Open World*, ed. Ann Florini. New York: Columbia University Press.

Caplan, Bryan. 2007. *The Myth of the Rational Voter: Why Democracies Choose Bad Policies.* Princeton: Princeton University Press.

Carpenter, Serena. 2008. "How Online Citizen Journalism Publications and Online Newspapers Utilize the Objectivity Standard and Rely on External Sources." *Journalism & Mass Communication Quarterly* 85(3):531–548.

Charron, Nicholas and Victor Lapuente. 2011. "Which Dictators Produce Quality of Government?" *Studies in Comparative International Development* 46(4):397–423.

Chen, Jidong, Jennifer Pan and Yiqing Xu. 2015. "Sources of Authoritarian Responsiveness: A Field Experiment in China." *American Journal of Political Science* 60(2):383–400.

Chen, Jidong and Yiqing Xu. 2017*a*. "Information Manipulation and Reform in Authoritarian Regimes." *Political Science Research and Methods* 5(1):163–178.

Chen, Jidong and Yiqing Xu. 2017*b*. "Why Do Authoritarian Regimes Allow Citizens to Voice Opinions Publicly?" *The Journal of Politics* 79(3):792–803.

Chen, Xi. 2012. *Social Protest and Contentious Authoritarianism in China.* Cambridge: Cambridge University Press.

Chen, Yuyu and David Y. Yang. 2017. "1984 or the Brave New World? Evidence from a Field Experiment on Media Censorship in China." Working Paper.

Chenoweth, Erica and Maria J Stephan. 2011. *Why Civil Resistance Works: The Strategic Logic of Nonviolent Conflict.* New York: Columbia University Press.

Choi, Changkyu. 2003. "Does the Internet Stimulate Inward Foreign Direct Investment?" *Journal of Policy Modeling* 25(4):319–326.

Chwe, Michael Suk-Young. 2001. *Rational Ritual: Culture, Coordination, and Common Knowledge.* Princeton: Princeton University Press.

Cohen, J Elizabeth and Joseph J Amon. 2011. "Lead Poisoning in China." *The Lancet* 378(9803):e3.

Conover, Pamela Johnston and Stanley Feldman. 1984. "How People Organize the Political World: A Schematic Model." *American Journal of Political Science* 28(1):95–126.

Conrad, Courtenay Ryals and Will H Moore. 2010. "What Stops the Torture?" *American Journal of Political Science* 54(2):459–476.

Conroy, Meredith, Jessica T Feezell and Mario Guerrero. 2012. "Facebook and Political Engagement: A Study of Online Political Group Membership and Offline Political Engagement." *Computers in Human Behavior* 28(5):1535–1546.

Converse, Phillip. 1964. The Nature of Belief Systems in Mass Publics. In *Ideology and Its Discontents*, ed. David Apter. New York: The Free Press of Glencoe.

Cook, Timothy E. 1989. *Making Laws and Making News: Media Strategies in the US House of Representatives.* Washington, D.C.: Brookings Institution Press.

Crabtree, Charles, Christopher J Fariss and Holger L Kern. 2015. "Truth Replaced by Silence: A Field Experiment on Private Censorship in Russia." Working Paper.

Darby, Michael R and Edi Karni. 1973. "Free Competition and the Optimal Amount of Fraud." *The Journal of Law & Economics* 16(1):67–88.

Davenport, Christian. 2007. "State Repression and Political Order." *Annual Review Political Science* 10:1–23.

Deibert, Ronald, John Palfrey, Rafal Rohozinski and Jonathan Zittrain. 2011. *Access Contested: Security, Identity, and Resistance in Asian Cyberspace.* Cambridge: MIT Press.

Deibert, Ronald, John Palfrey, Rafal Rohozinski, Jonathan Zittrain and Janice Gross Stein. 2008. *Access Denied: The Practice and Policy of Global Internet Filtering.* Cambridge: MIT Press.

Deibert, Ronald, John Palfrey, Rafal Rohozinski, Jonathan Zittrain and Miklos Haraszti. 2010. *Access Controlled: The Shaping of Power, Rights, and Rule in Cyberspace.* Cambridge: MIT Press.

Del Vicario, Michela, Alessandro Bessi, Fabiana Zollo, Fabio Petroni, Antonio Scala, Guido Caldarelli, H Eugene Stanley and Walter Quattrociocchi. 2016. "The Spreading of Misinformation Online." *Proceedings of the National Academy of Sciences* 113(3):554–559.

Delli Carpini, Michael X and Scott Keeter. 1996. *What Americans Know About Politics and Why It Matters.* New Haven: Yale University Press.

Demick, Barbara. 2010. *Nothing to Envy: Ordinary Lives in North Korea.* New York: Spiegel & Grau.

Diamond, Larry. 2010. "Liberation Technology." *Journal of Democracy* 21(3):69–83.

Diamond, Larry. 2015. "Facing Up to the Democratic Recession." *Journal of Democracy* 26(1):141–155.

Dickson, Bruce. 2016. *The Dictator's Dilemma: The Chinese Communist Party's Strategy for Survival.* Oxford: Oxford University Press.

Ding, Yijiang. 2001. *Chinese Democracy After Tiananmen.* Vancouver: UBC Press.

Distelhorst, Greg and Yue Hou. 2017. "Constituency Service Under Nondemocratic Rule: Evidence from China." *The Journal of Politics* 79(3):1024–1040.

Downs, Anthony. 1957. *An Economic Theory of Democracy.* New York: Harper.

Edmond, Chris. 2013. "Information Manipulation, Coordination, and Regime Change." *The Review of Economic Studies* 80(4):1422–1458.

Edmonds, Rick, Emily Guskin, Tom Rosenstiel and Amy Mitchell. 2012. "Newspapers: By the Numbers." *The State of the News Media 2012.* http://www.stateofthemedia.org/2012/newspapers-building-digital-revenues-proves-painfully-slow/newspapers-by-the-numbers/.

Egorov, Georgy, Sergei Guriev and Konstantin Sonin. 2009. "Why Resource-Poor Dictators Allow Freer Media: A Theory and Evidence from Panel Data." *American Political Science Review* 103(4): 645–668.

Eisensee, Thomas and David Strömberg. 2007. "News Droughts, News Floods, and US Disaster Relief." *The Quarterly Journal of Economics* 122(2):693–728.

Eisenstein, Elizabeth L. 1983. *The Printing Revolution in Early Modern Europe.* Cambridge: Cambridge University Press.

Enikolopov, Ruben, Alexey Makarin and Maria Petrova. 2016. "Social Media and Protest Participation: Evidence from Russia." Working Paper.

Enikolopov, Ruben, Maria Petrova and Ekaterina Zhuravskaya. 2011. "Media and Political Persuasion: Evidence from Russia." *American Economic Review* 101(7):3253–3285.

Epstein, Robert and Ronald E Robertson. 2015. "The Search Engine Manipulation Effect (SEME) and its Possible Impact on the Outcomes of Elections." *Proceedings of the National Academy of Sciences* 112(33):E4512–E4521.

Esarey, Ashley and Qiang Xiao. 2011. "Digital Communication and Political Change in China." *International Journal of Communication* 5:298–319.

Ferdinand, Peter. 2000. "The Internet, Democracy and Democratization." *Democratization* 7(1):1–17.

Festinger, Leon. 1957. *A Theory of Cognitive Dissonance*. New York: Row, Peterson & Co.

Francisco, Ronald A. 2005. The Dictator's Dilemma. In *Repression and Mobilization*, ed. Christian Davenport, Hank Johnson and Carol Mueller. Minneapolis: University of Minnesota Press pp. 58–81.

Frey, Dieter. 1986. "Recent Research on Selective Exposure to Information." *Advances in Experimental Social Psychology* 19:41–80.

Friedman, Monroe. 1999. *Consumer Boycotts: Effecting Change Through the Marketplace and the Media*. New York: Routledge.

Friedrich, Carl J and Zbigniew K Brzezinski. 1965. *Totalitarian Dictatorship*. Cambridge: Harvard University Press.

Fu, King-wa, Chung-hong Chan and Marie Chau. 2013. "Assessing Censorship on Microblogs in China: Discriminatory Keyword Analysis and the Real-Name Registration Policy." *Internet Computing, IEEE* 17(3):42–50.

Gang, Qian and David Bandurski. 2011. China's Emerging Public Sphere: The Impact of Media Commercialization, Professionalism, and the Internet in an Era of Transition. In *Changing Media, Changing China*, ed. Susan L Shirk. Oxford: Oxford University Press pp. 38–76.

Gasiorowski, Mark. 1995. "Economic Crisis and Political Regime Change: An Event History Analysis." *The American Political Science Review* 89(4):882–897.

Geddes, Barbara and John Zaller. 1989. "Sources of Popular Support for Authoritarian Regimes." *American Journal of Political Science* 33(2):319–347.

Gehlbach, Scott and Konstantin Sonin. 2014. "Government Control of the Media." *Journal of Public Economics* 118:163–171.

Gentzkow, Matthew, Edward L Glaeser and Claudia Goldin. 2006. The Rise of the Fourth Estate. How Newspapers Became Informative and Why It Mattered. In *Corruption and Reform: Lessons from America's Economic History*. Chicago: University of Chicago Press pp. 187–230.

Gentzkow, Matthew and Jesse M Shapiro. 2006. "Media Bias and Reputation." *Journal of Political Economy* 114(2):280–316.

Ghanem, Dalia and Junjie Zhang. 2014. "Effortless Perfection: Do Chinese Cities Manipulate Air Pollution Data?" *Journal of Environmental Economics and Management* 68(2):203–225.

Gilley, Bruce. 2003. "The Limits of Authoritarian Resilience." *Journal of Democracy* 14(1):18–26.

Gohdes, Anita R. 2015. "Pulling the Plug: Network Disruptions and Violence in Civil Conflict." *Journal of Peace Research* 52(3):352–367.

Gold, Thomas B. 1985. "After Comradeship: Personal Relations in China Since the Cultural Revolution." *The China Quarterly* 104:657–675.

González-Bailón, Sandra, Javier Borge-Holthoefer, Alejandro Rivero and Yamir Moreno. 2011. "The Dynamics of Protest Recruitment Through an Online Network." *Scientific Reports* 1(197).

Gormley, William T and Steven J Balla. 2013. *Bureaucracy and Democracy: Accountability and Performance.* Third ed. Thousand Oaks: SAGE CQ Press.

Graber, Doris Appel. 1988. *Processing the News: How People Tame the Information Tide.* New York: Longman.

Greve, Louisa. 2013. "The Troubled Periphery." *Journal of Democracy* 24(1):73–78.

Grimmer, Justin. 2013. *Representational Style in Congress: What Legislators Say and Why It Matters.* Cambridge: Cambridge University Press.

Gunitsky, Seva. 2015. "Corrupting the Cyber-Commons: Social Media as a Tool of Autocratic Stability." *Perspectives on Politics* 13(1): 42–54.

Gup, Ted. 2008. *Nation of Secrets: The Threat to Democracy and the American Way of Life.* New York: Anchor Books.

Guriev, Sergei M and Daniel Treisman. 2015. "How Modern Dictators Survive: Cooptation, Censorship, Propaganda, and Repression." Working Paper.

Haggard, Stephan and Jong-sung You. 2015. "Freedom of Expression in South Korea." *Journal of Contemporary Asia* 45(1):167–179.

Hamilton, James. 2004. *All the News That's Fit to Sell: How the Market Transforms Information into News.* Princeton: Princeton University Press.

Hamilton, James. 2005. *Regulation through Revelation: The Origin, Politics, and Impacts of the Toxics Release Inventory Program.* Cambridge: Cambridge University Press.

Hamilton, James. 2011. What's the Incentive to Save Journalism? In *Will the Last Reporter Please Turn Out the Lights: The Collapse of Journalism and What Can Be Done to Fix It,* ed. Robert W McChesney and Victor Pickard. New York: New Press.

Han, Rongbin. 2015. "Manufacturing Consent in Cyberspace: China's 'Fifty-Cent Army'." *Journal of Current Chinese Affairs* 44(2): 105–134.

He, Baogang and Mark E Warren. 2011. "Authoritarian Deliberation: The Deliberative Turn in Chinese Political Development." *Perspectives on Politics* 9(2):269–289.

Hiruncharoenvate, Chaya, Zhiyuan Lin and Eric Gilbert. 2015. Algorithmically Bypassing Censorship on Sina Weibo with Nondeterministic Homophone Substitutions. In *Ninth International AAAI Conference on Web and Social Media.*

Hobbs, William and Margaret E Roberts. 2016. "How Sudden Censorship Can Increase Access to Information." Working Paper.

Hoelzle, Urs. January 2012. "The Google Gospel of Speed." *Google Think Insights.* http://www.thinkwithgoogle.com/articles/the-google-gospel-of-speed-urs-hoelzle.html.

Hong, Yu. 2014. The Internet and Economic Development. In *The Internet in China: Cultural, Political, and Social Dimensions*, ed. Ashley Esarey and Randolph Kluver. Great Barrington: Berkshire Publishing Group, LLC.

Huang, Haifeng. 2015. "Propaganda as Signaling." *Comparative Politics* 47(4):419–444.

Huang, Yasheng. 1994. "Information, Bureaucracy, and Economic Reforms in China and the Soviet Union." *World Politics* 47(1):102–134.

Iacus, Stefano M., Gary King and Giuseppe Porro. 2009. "CEM: Software for Coarsened Exact Matching." *Journal of Statistical Software* 30(9). http://gking.harvard.edu/cem.

Ingram, Peter G. 2000. *Censorship and Free Speech: Some Philosophical Bearings*. Brookfield: Ashgate Publishing.

Iyengar, Shanto. 1990. "The Accessibility Bias in Politics: Television News and Public Opinion." *International Journal of Public Opinion Research* 2(1):1–15.

Jansen, Sue Curry and Brian Martin. 2003. "Making Censorship Backfire." *Counterpoise* 7(3):5–15.

Jansen, Sue Curry and Brian Martin. 2015. "The Streisand Effect and Censorship Backfire." *International Journal of Communication* 9:656–671.

Johnson, Ian. 2016. The Presence of the Past: A Coda. In *The Oxford Illustrated History of Modern China*, ed. Jeffrey N Wasserstrom. Oxford: Oxford University Press.

Kain, Daniel J. 2009. "It's Just a Concussion: The National Football League's Denial of a Casual Link between Multiple Concussions and Later-Life Cognitive Decline." *Rutgers LJ* 40:697–736.

Kalathil, Shanthi and Taylor C Boas. 2010. *Open Networks, Closed Regimes: The Impact of the Internet on Authoritarian Rule*. Washington, D.C.: Carnegie Endowment for International Peace.

Kern, Holger Lutz and Jens Hainmueller. 2009. "Opium for the Masses: How Foreign Media Can Stabilize Authoritarian Regimes." *Political Analysis* 17(4):377–399.

King, Gary, Jennifer Pan and Margaret E Roberts. 2013. "How Censorship in China Allows Government Criticism but Silences Collective Expression." *American Political Science Review* 107(2):1–18.

King, Gary, Jennifer Pan and Margaret E Roberts. 2014. "Reverse-Engineering Censorship in China: Randomized Experimentation and Participant Observation." *Science* 345(6199):1251722–1251722.

King, Gary, Jennifer Pan and Margaret E Roberts. 2017. "How the Chinese Government Fabricates Social Media Posts for Strategic Distraction, not Engaged Argument." *American Political Science Review* 111(3): 484–501.

King, Gary, Patrick Lam and Margaret E Roberts. 2017. "Computer-Assisted Keyword and Document Set Discovery from Unstructured Text." *American Journal of Political Science* 61(4):971–988.

Knockel, Jeffrey, Lotus Ruan and Masashi Crete-Nishihata. 2017. "We (Can't) Chat: "709 Crackdown" Discussions Blocked on Weibo and WeChat." *Citizen Lab Report.*

Knockel, Jeffrey, Masashi Crete-Nishihata, Jason Q Ng, Adam Senft and Jedidiah R Crandall. 2015. Every Rose Has Its Thorn: Censorship and Surveillance on Social Video Platforms in China. In *5th USENIX Workshop on Free and Open Communications on the Internet (FOCI 15).*

Krishnan, S Shunmuga and Ramesh K Sitaraman. 2013. "Video Stream Quality Impacts Viewer Behavior: Inferring Causality Using Quasi-Experimental Designs." *IEEE/ACM Transactions on Networking,* 21(6):2001–2014.

Krosnick, Jon A. 1990. "Government Policy and Citizen Passion: A Study of Issue Publics in Contemporary America." *Political Behavior* 12(1):59–92.

Kuran, Timur. 1989. "Sparks and Prairie Fires: A Theory of Unanticipated Political Revolution." *Public Choice* 61(1):41–74.

Kuran, Timur. 1997. *Private Truths, Public Lies: The Social Consequences of Preference Falsification.* Cambridge: Harvard University Press.

Kuran, Timur. 1998. Social Mechanisms of Dissonance Reduction. In *Social Mechanisms: An Analytical Approach To Social Theory,* ed. Peter Hedström and Richard Swedberg. Cambridge: Cambridge University Press pp. 147–171.

Lam, Onyi. 2017. "Advertisers Capture: Evidences from Hong Kong." Working Paper.

Lam, Willy Wo-Lap. 2015. *Chinese Politics in the Era of Xi Jinping: Renaissance, Reform, or Retrogression?* New York: Routledge.

Landry, Pierre F and Mingming Shen. 2005. "Reaching Migrants in Survey Research: The Use of the Global Positioning System to Reduce Coverage Bias in China." *Political Analysis* 13(1):1–22.

Lasswell, Harold D. 1930. "Censorship." *Encyclopedia of the Social Sciences* 3:290–294.

Lee, Francis LF and Angel MY Lin. 2006. "Newspaper Editorial Discourse and the Politics of Self-Censorship in Hong Kong." *Discourse & Society* 17(3):331–358.

Leetaru, Kalev, Shaowen Wang, Guofeng Cao, Anand Padmanabhan and Eric Shook. 2013. "Mapping the Global Twitter Heartbeat: The Geography of Twitter." *First Monday* 18(5).

Lessig, Lawrence. 1999. *Code: And Other Laws of Cyberspace.* New York: Basic Books.

Lewis-Beck, Michael S. 2008. *The American Voter Revisited.* Ann Arbor: University of Michigan Press.

Lewis, David. 2008. *Convention: A Philosophical Study.* Chichester: John Wiley & Sons.

Li, Wei and Dennis Tao Yang. 2005. "The Great Leap Forward: Anatomy of a Central Planning Disaster." *Journal of Political Economy* 113(4): 840–877.

Lichbach, Mark Irving. 1987. "Deterrence or Escalation? The Puzzle of Aggregate Studies of Repression and Dissent." *Journal of Conflict Resolution* 31(2):266–297.

Lieberthal, Kenneth. 1995. *Governing China: From Revolution Through Reform.* New York: WW Norton.

Liebman, Benjamin L. 2005. "Watchdog or Demagogue? The Media in the Chinese Legal System." *Columbia Law Review* 105(1): 1–157.

Liebman, Benjamin L. 2011. "The Media and the Courts: Towards Competitive Supervision?" *The China Quarterly* 208:833–850.

Link, Perry. 2002. "The Anaconda in the Chandelier: Censorship in China Today." *New York Review of Books.*

Little, Andrew T. 2016. "Communication Technology and Protest." *The Journal of Politics* 78(1):152–166.

Loftin, Colin, Brian Wiersema, David McDowall and Adam Dobrin. 2003. "Underreporting of Justifiable Homicides Committed by Police Officers in the United States, 1976–1998." *American Journal of Public Health* 93(7):1117–1121.

Lohmann, Susanne. 1994. "The Dynamics of Informational Cascades: The Monday Demonstrations in Leipzig, East Germany, 1989–1991." *World Politics* 47(1):42–101.

Lorentzen, Peter. 2014. "China's Strategic Censorship." *American Journal of Political Science* 58(2):402–414.

Lorentzen, Peter. 2015. "China's Controlled Burn: Information Management and State-Society Relations under Authoritarianism." *Book Manuscript.*

Lorentzen, Peter L. 2013. "Regularizing Rioting: Permitting Public Protest in an Authoritarian Regime." *Quarterly Journal of Political Science* 8(2):127–158.

Lotan, Gilad, Erhardt Graeff, Mike Ananny, Devin Gaffney, Ian Pearce and Danah Boyd. 2011. "The Revolutions Were Tweeted: Information

Flows During the 2011 Tunisian and Egyptian Revolutions." *International Journal of Communication* 5:1375–1405.

Loveless, Matthew. 2008. "Media Dependency: Mass Media as Sources of Information in the Democratizing Countries of Central and Eastern Europe." *Democratization* 15(1):162–183.

Lupia, Arthur and Mathew D McCubbins. 1998. *The Democratic Dilemma: Can Citizens Learn What They Need to Know?* Cambridge: Cambridge University Press.

Lynch, Daniel C. 1999. *After the Propaganda State: Media, Politics, and "Thought Work" in Reformed China.* Stanford: Stanford University Press.

Lynch, Marc. 2011. "After Egypt: The Limits and Promise of Online Challenges to the Authoritarian Arab State." *Perspectives on Politics* 9(2):301–310.

MacKinnon, Rebecca. 2008. "Flatter World and Thicker Walls? Blogs, Censorship and Civic Discourse in China." *Public Choice* 134(1–2): 31–46.

MacKinnon, Rebecca. 2009. "China's Censorship 2.0: How Companies Censor Bloggers." *First Monday* 14(2).

MacKinnon, Rebecca. 2012. *Consent of the Networked: The Worldwide Struggle For Internet Freedom.* New York: Basic Books.

Magaloni, Beatriz. 2008. "Credible Power-Sharing and the Longevity of Authoritarian Rule." *Comparative Political Studies* 41(4–5):715–741.

Manning, Christopher D, Prabhakar Raghavan and Hinrich Schütze. 2008. *Introduction to Information Retrieval.* Cambridge: Cambridge University Press.

Marcus, George E, W Russell Neuman and Michael MacKuen. 2000. *Affective Intelligence and Political Judgment.* Chicago: University of Chicago Press.

Mark, Gloria, Stephen Voida and Armand Cardello. 2012. A Pace Not Dictated by Electrons: An Empirical Study of Work Without Email. In *Proceedings of the SIGCHI Conference on Human Factors in Computing Systems.* ACM pp. 555–564.

Mayhew, David. 1974. *The Electoral Connection.* New Haven: Yale University Press.

McCombs, Maxwell E and Donald L Shaw. 1972. "The Agenda-Setting Function of Mass Media." *Public Opinion Quarterly* 36(2): 176–187.

Meng, Tianguang, Jennifer Pan and Ping Yang. 2014. "Conditional Receptivity to Citizen Participation: Evidence from a Survey Experiment in China." *Comparative Political Studies* 50(4):399–433.

Miller, Blake. 2016. "Automated Detection of Chinese Government Astroturfers Using Network and Social Metadata." Working Paper.

Miller, Blake. 2017. "The Limits of Commercialized Censorship in China." Working Paper.

Milner, Helen V. 2006. "The Digital Divide: The Role of Political Institutions in Technology Diffusion." *Comparative Political Studies* 39(2):176–199.

Mitchell, Neil J, Sabine C Carey and Christopher K Butler. 2014. "The Impact of Pro-Government Militias on Human Rights Violations." *International Interactions* 40(5):812–836.

Mollenhoff, Clark R. 1981. *Investigative Reporting.* New York: Macmillian.

Morozov, Evgeny. 2011. *The Net Delusion: The Dark Side of Internet Freedom.* New York: PublicAffairs.

Mossberger, Karen, Caroline J Tolbert and Ramona S McNeal. 2007. *Digital Citizenship: The Internet, Society, and Participation.* Cambridge: MIT Press.

Muggli, Monique E, Jean L Forster, Richard D Hurt and James L Repace. 2001. "The Smoke You Don't See: Uncovering Tobacco Industry Scientific Strategies Aimed Against Environmental Tobacco Smoke Policies." *American Journal of Public Health* 91(9):1419–1423.

Mullainathan, Sendhil and Andrei Shleifer. 2005. "The Market for News." *American Economic Review* 95(4):1031–1053.

Nathan, Andrew. 2003. "Authoritarian Resilience." *Journal of Democracy* 14(1):6–17.

National Academy for Propaganda Cadres, ed. 2011. *Xuanchuan sixiang wenhua gongzuo: anli xuanbian [Propaganda, thought and cultural work: selected cases].* Beijing: Study Press.

National Committee for Cadre Training Materials, ed. 2011. *Gonggong shijian zhong meiti yunyong he yulun yingdui [Media use and public opinion response during public events].* Beijing: The People's Press.

Naughton, Barry. 1996. *Growing Out of the Plan: Chinese Economic Reform, 1978–1993.* Cambridge: Cambridge University Press.

Ng, Jason. 2013. *Blocked on Weibo: What Gets Suppressed on China's Version of Twitter (And Why).* New York: New Press.

Nichols, John and Robert W McChesney. 2009. "The Death and Life of Great American Newspapers." *The Nation.*

Norris, Pippa. 2001. *Digital Divide: Civic Engagement, Information Poverty, and the Internet Worldwide.* Cambridge: Cambridge University Press.

Nyhan, Brendan and Jason Reifler. 2010. "When Corrections Fail: The Persistence of Political Misperceptions." *Political Behavior* 32(2):303–330.

O'Brien, Kevin J and Yanhua Deng. 2015. "Repression Backfires: Tactical Radicalization and Protest Spectacle in Rural China." *Journal of Contemporary China* 24(93):457–470.

O'Brien, Kevin and Lianjiang Li. 2006. *Rightful Resistance in Rural China.* Cambridge: Cambridge University Press.

O'Donnell, Guillermo A. 1973. *Modernization and Bureaucratic-Authoritarianism: Studies in South American Politics.* Berkeley: Institute of International Studies, University of California.

Olson, Mancur. 2009. *The Logic of Collective Action.* Cambridge: Harvard University Press.

Pan, Jennifer. 2016. "How Market Dynamics of Domestic and Foreign Social Media Firms Shape Strategies of Internet Censorship." *Problems of Post-Communism* 64(3–4):167–188.

Pan, Jennifer and Yiqing Xu. Forthcoming. "China's Ideological Spectrum." *The Journal of Politics.*

Patell, James M and Mark A Wolfson. 1982. "Good News, Bad News, and the Intraday Timing of Corporate Disclosures." *The Accounting Review* 57(3):509–527.

Pearce, Katy E and Sarah Kendzior. 2012. "Networked Authoritarianism and Social Media in Azerbaijan." *Journal of Communication* 62(2): 283–298.

Perry, Elizabeth J. 2013. "Cultural Governance in Contemporary China: Re-orienting Party Propaganda." Working Paper.

Petrova, Maria. 2011. "Newspapers and Parties: How Advertising Revenues Created an Independent Press." *American Political Science Review* 105(04):790–808.

Petrova, Maria. 2012. "Mass Media and Special Interest Groups." *Journal of Economic Behavior & Organization* 84(1):17–38.

Pomerantsev, P. 2014. *Nothing Is True and Everything Is Possible: The Surreal Heart of the New Russia.* New York: PublicAffairs.

Popkin, Samuel. 1994. *The Reasoning Voter: Communication and Persuasion in Presidential Campaigns.* Chicago: University of Chicago Press.

Prior, Markus. 2005. "News vs. Entertainment: How Increasing Media Choice Widens Gaps in Political Knowledge and Turnout." *American Journal of Political Science* 49(3):577–592.

Qin, Bei, David Strömberg and Yanhui Wu. 2017. "Why Does China Allow Freer Social Media? Protests versus Surveillance and Propaganda." *The Journal of Economic Perspectives* 31(1):117–140.

Ratkiewicz, Jacob, Filippo Menczer, Santo Fortunato, Alessandro Flammini and Alessandro Vespignani. 2010. Traffic in Social Media II: Modeling Bursty Popularity. In *Social Computing, 2010 IEEE Second International Conference.* IEEE pp. 393–400.

Ratkiewicz, Jacob, Michael Conover, Mark R Meiss, Bruno Gonçalves, Alessandro Flammini and Filippo Menczer. 2011. Detecting and Tracking Political Abuse in Social Media. In *Proceedings of the Fifth*

International AAAI Conference on Weblogs and Social Media. Vol. 11 pp. 297–304.

RePass, David E. 1971. "Issue Salience and Party Choice." *American Political Science Review* 65(02):389–400.

Reynolds, Matthew. 2014. Semi-Censorship in Dryden and Browning. In *Modes of Censorship: National Contexts and Diverse Media,* ed. Francesca Billani. New York: Routledge pp. 187–204.

Ritter, Emily Hencken and Courtenay R Conrad. 2016. "Preventing and Responding to Dissent: The Observational Challenges of Explaining Strategic Repression." *American Political Science Review* 110:85–99.

Roberts, Margaret E and Brandon M Stewart. 2016. "Localization and Coordination: How Propaganda and Censorship Converge in Chinese Newspapers." Working Paper.

Roberts, Margaret E, Brandon M Stewart and Edoardo M Airoldi. 2016. "A Model of Text for Experimentation in the Social Sciences." *Journal of the American Statistical Association* 111(515):988–1003.

Rød, Espen Geelmuyden and Nils B Weidmann. 2015. "Empowering Activists or Autocrats? The Internet in Authoritarian Regimes." *Journal of Peace Research* 52(3):338–351.

Rose-Ackerman, Susan. 1978. *Corruption: A Study in Political Economy.* New York: Academic Press.

Scanlon, Thomas. 1972. "A Theory of Freedom of Expression." *Philosophy & Public Affairs* 1(2):204–226.

Schlozman, Kay Lehman, Sidney Verba and Henry E Brady. 2010. "Weapon of the Strong? Participatory Inequality and the Internet." *Perspectives on Politics* 8(2):487–509.

Shambaugh, David. 2007. "China's Propaganda System: Institutions, Processes and Efficacy." *The China Journal* (57):25–58.

Shambaugh, David. 2013. *China Goes Global: The Partial Power.* Oxford: Oxford University Press.

Shapiro, Jesse M. 2016. "Special Interests and the Media: Theory and an Application to Climate Change." *Journal of Public Economics* 144:91–108.

Shirk, Susan L. 1982. *Competitive Comrades: Career Incentives and Student Strategies in China.* Berkeley: University of California Press.

Shirk, Susan L. 1993. *The Political Logic of Economic Reform in China.* Berkeley: University of California Press.

Shirk, Susan L. 2011. *Changing Media, Changing China.* Oxford: Oxford University Press.

Shirky, Clay. 2008. *Here Comes Everybody: The Power of Organizing Without Organizations.* New York: Penguin Press.

Shorey, Samantha and Philip N Howard. 2016. "Automation, Big Data, and Politics: A Research Review." *International Journal of Communication* 10:5032–5055.

Sniderman, Paul M, Phillip E Tetlock and Richard A Brody. 1991. *Reasoning and Choice: Explorations in Political Psychology*. Cambridge: Cambridge University Press.

Sobbrio, Francesco. 2011. "Indirect Lobbying and Media Bias." *Quarterly Journal of Political Science* 6(3–4):235–274.

Soley, Lawrence. 2002. *Censorship Inc: The Corporate Threat to Free Speech in the United States*. New York: Monthly Review Press.

Steele, Cherie and Arthur Stein. 2002. Communications Revolutions and International Relations. In *Technology, Development, and Democracy: International Conflict and Cooperation in the Information Age*, ed. Juliann Emmons Allison. Albany: SUNY Press pp. 25–54.

Steinert-Threlkeld, Zachary C. 2017. "Spontaneous Collective Action: Peripheral Mobilization During the Arab Spring." *American Political Science Review* 111(2):379–403.

Stern, Rachel E and Jonathan Hassid. 2012. "Amplifying Silence: Uncertainty and Control Parables in Contemporary China." *Comparative Political Studies* 45(10):1230–1254.

Stiglitz, Joseph E. 2002. "Information and the Change in the Paradigm in Economics." *The American Economic Review* 92(3):460–501.

Stockmann, Daniela. 2012. *Media Commercialization and Authoritarian Rule in China*. Cambridge: Cambridge University Press.

Stockmann, Daniela and Mary E Gallagher. 2011. "Remote Control: How the Media Sustain Authoritarian Rule in China." *Comparative Political Studies* 44(4):436–467.

Stockmann, Daniela and Ting Luo. 2017. "Which Social Media Facilitate Online Public Opinion in China?" *Problems of Post-Communism* 64(3–4):189–202.

Stone, Daniel F. 2011. "A Signal-Jamming Model of Persuasion: Interest Group Funded Policy Research." *Social Choice and Welfare* 37(3): 397–424.

Suárez-Serrato, Pablo, Margaret E Roberts, Clayton Davis and Filippo Menczer. 2016. On the Influence of Social Bots in Online Protests. In *International Conference on Social Informatics*. Springer pp. 269–278.

Tai, Zixue. 2014. The Great Firewall. In *The Internet in China: Cultural, Political, and Social Dimensions*, ed. Ashley Esarey and Randolph Kluver. Great Barrington: Berkshire Publishing Group.

Taubman, Geoffry. 1998. "A Not-So World Wide Web: The Internet, China, and the Challenges to Nondemocratic Rule." *Political Communication* 15(2):255–272.

Teiwes, Frederick C and Warren Sun. 2004. "The First Tiananmen Incident Revisited: Elite Politics and Crisis Management at the End of the Maoist Era." *Pacific Affairs* 77(2):211–235.

Thaler, Richard H. and Cass R. Sunstein. 2009. *Nudge: Improving Decisions About Health, Wealth, and Happiness*. New York: Penguin Books.

Tilly, Charles. 1978. *From Mobilization to Revolution*. New York: McGraw-Hill.

Tong, Jingrong. 2011. *Investigative Journalism in China: Journalism, Power, and Society*. New York: Continuum.

Tong, Jingrong and Colin Sparks. 2009. "Investigative Journalism in China Today." *Journalism Studies* 10(3):337–352.

Truex, Rory. 2016. "Focal Points, Dissident Calendars, and Preemptive Repression." Working Paper.

Tufekci, Zeynep. 2014. "Engineering the Public: Big Data, Surveillance and Computational Politics." *First Monday* 19(7).

Tufekci, Zeynep and Christopher Wilson. 2012. "Social Media and the Decision to Participate in Political Protest: Observations from Tahrir Square." *Journal of Communication* 62(2):363–379.

Unger, Jonathan. 1982. *Education Under Mao: Class and Competition in Canton Schools, 1960–1980*. New York: Columbia University Press.

Vogel, Ezra F. 1965. "From Friendship to Comradeship: The Change in Personal Relations in Communist China." *The China Quarterly* 21(1):46–60.

Wacker, Gudrun. 2003. The Internet and Censorship in China. In *China and the Internet: Politics of the Digital Leap Forward*, ed. Christopher R Hughes and Gudrun Wacker. New York: Routledge.

Walder, Andrew G. 1988. *Communist Neo-Traditionalism: Work and Authority in Chinese Industry*. Berkeley: University of California Press.

Wallace, Jeremy L. 2016. "Juking the Stats? Authoritarian Information Problems in China." *British Journal of Political Science* 46(01):11–29.

Wang, Stephanie and Robert Faris. 2008. "Welcome to the Machine." *Index on Censorship* 37(2):106–113.

Wang, Yuhua and Carl Minzner. 2015. "The Rise of the Chinese Security State." *The China Quarterly* 222:339–359.

Wedeen, Lisa. 1999. *Ambiguities of Domination: Politics, Rhetoric, and Symbols in Contemporary Syria*. Chicago: University of Chicago Press.

Weidmann, Nils B, Suso Benitez-Baleato, Philipp Hunziker, Eduard Glatz and Xenofontas Dimitropoulos. 2016. "Digital Discrimination: Political Bias in Internet Service Provision Across Ethnic Groups." *Science* 353(6304):1151–1155.

Weiss, Jessica Chen. 2014. *Powerful Patriots: Nationalist Protest in China's Foreign Relations*. Oxford: Oxford University Press.

Wintrobe, Ronald. 1990. "The Tinpot and the Totalitarian: An Economic Theory of Dictatorship." *American Political Science Review* 84(3):849–872.

Wintrobe, Ronald. 1998. *The Political Economy of Dictatorship*. Cambridge: Cambridge University Press.

Wolfsfeld, Gadi. 2011. *Making Sense of Media and Politics: Five Principles in Political Communication*. New York: Routledge.

Wu, Jason and Tianguang Meng. 2016. "The Nature of Ideology in Urban China.". Working Paper.

Xiao, Qiang. 2011. The Rise of Online Public Opinion and Its Political Impact. In *Changing Media, Changing China*, ed. Susan L Shirk. Oxford: Oxford University Press pp. 202–224.

Yang, Guobin. 2009a. "Online Activism." *Journal of Democracy* 20(3): 33–36.

Yang, Guobin. 2009b. *The Power of the Internet in China: Citizen Activism Online*. New York: Columbia University Press.

Yang, Guobin. 2013. Social Dynamics in the Evolution of China's Internet Content Control Regime. In *Routledge Handbook of Media Law*, ed. Monroe E Price, Stefaan Verhulst and Libby Morgan. New York: Routledge pp. 285–302.

Yeykelis, Leo, James J Cummings and Byron Reeves. 2014. "Multitasking on a Single Device: Arousal and the Frequency, Anticipation, and Prediction of Switching Between Media Content on a Computer." *Journal of Communication* 64(1):167–192.

Young, Lauren E. 2016. "The Psychology of Political Risk in Autocracy." Working Paper.

Yu, Frederick Teh-Chi. 1964. *Mass Persuasion in Communist China*. New York: Praeger.

Zaller, John. 1999. "A Theory of Media Politics." Book Manuscript.

Zaller, John R. 1992. *The Nature and Origins of Mass Opinion*. Cambridge: Cambridge University Press.

Zeitzoff, Thomas. 2017. "How Social Media is Changing Conflict." *Journal of Conflict Resolution* 61(9):1970–1991.

Zhao, Suisheng. 1998a. "A State-Led Nationalism: The Patriotic Education Campaign in Post-Tiananmen China." *Communist and Post-Communist Studies* 31(3):287–302.

Zhao, Yuezhi. 1998b. *Media, Market, and Democracy in China: Between the Party Line and the Bottom Line*. Urbana: University of Illinois Press.

Zhou, Yuezhi. 2000. "Watchdogs on Party Leashes? Contexts and Implications of Investigative Journalism in Post-Deng China." *Journalism Studies* 1(4):577–597.

Zhu, Tao, David Phipps, Adam Pridgen, Jedidiah R Crandall and Dan S Wallach. 2013. "The Velocity of Censorship: High-Fidelity Detection of Microblog Post Deletions." *USENIX Security Symposium* pp. 227–240.

Zuckerman, Ethan. 2015. Cute Cats to the Rescue? Participatory Media and Political Expression. In *From Voice to Influence: Understanding Citizenship in a Digital Age*, ed. Danielle Allen and Jennifer S. Light. Chicago: University of Chicago Press.

INDEX

Page numbers in *italics* indicate graphs and charts.